# Crowdfunding and Entrepreneurial Finance

An increase in the restrictions on the availability of funding for new and growing businesses in the aftermath of the global financial crisis has been accompanied by the emergence and growth of crowdfunding as an alternative method of raising capital. Crowdfunding contributes towards the disintermediation of the finance market as funders and promoters are brought together directly, democratising both fundraising by businesses and investment by individuals.

This book extends entrepreneurial finance research to the study of crowdfunding. Contributions review the history, status and future of crowdfunding, analyse the patterns of fundraising, assess the potential of crowdfunding for the financing of social ventures in particular, and discuss the regulatory implications of recent developments. What is clear from this collection is that the crowdfunding space is still evolving, institutional forms are still developing as models are refined, new institutional collaborations (e.g. between equity platforms and business angel networks) are emerging, and new challenges, particularly regulatory challenges, are being encountered. While crowdfunding is not a universal solution for SME finance in a post-crisis financial landscape, it remains too early to determine whether crowdfunding represents a large-scale transformation of the early stage risk capital market or a minor addition to it.

This book was originally published as a special issue of *Venture Capital: An International Journal of Entrepreneurial Finance*.

**Richard Harrison** is Professor of Entrepreneurship and Innovation, and Co-Director of the Centre for Strategic Leadership, at the University of Edinburgh Business School, UK. He is the founding co-editor of *Venture Capital: An International Journal of Entrepreneurial Finance*, and the author of 5 books and over 100 academic papers.

# Crowdfunding and Entrepreneurial Finance

*Edited by*
**Richard Harrison**

LONDON AND NEW YORK

First published 2016
by Routledge
2 Park Square, Milton Park, Abingdon, Oxon, OX14 4RN, UK

and by Routledge
711 Third Avenue, New York, NY 10017, USA

*Routledge is an imprint of the Taylor & Francis Group, an informa business*

© 2016 Taylor & Francis

*British Library Cataloguing in Publication Data*
A catalogue record for this book is available from the British Library

ISBN 13: 978-1-138-92756-8

Typeset in Times New Roman
by RefineCatch Limited, Bungay, Suffolk

**Publisher's Note**
The publisher accepts responsibility for any inconsistencies that may have
arisen during the conversion of this book from journal articles to book chapters,
namely the possible inclusion of journal terminology.

**Disclaimer**
Every effort has been made to contact copyright holders for their permission to
reprint material in this book. The publishers would be grateful to hear from any
copyright holder who is not here acknowledged and will undertake to rectify
any errors or omissions in future editions of this book.

# Contents

# Citation Information

The following chapters were originally published in *Venture Capital: An International Journal of Entrepreneurial Finance*, volume 15, issue 4 (October 2013). When citing this material, please use the original page numbering for each article, as follows:

**Chapter 1**
*Editorial: Crowdfunding and the revitalisation of the early stage risk capital market: catalyst or chimera?*
Richard Harrison
*Venture Capital: An International Journal of Entrepreneurial Finance*, volume 15, issue 4 (October 2013) pp. 283–287

**Chapter 2**
*Crowdfunding social ventures: a model and research agenda*
Othmar M. Lehner
*Venture Capital: An International Journal of Entrepreneurial Finance*, volume 15, issue 4 (October 2013) pp. 289–311

**Chapter 3**
*Individual crowdfunding practices*
Paul Belleflamme, Thomas Lambert and Armin Schwienbacher
*Venture Capital: An International Journal of Entrepreneurial Finance*, volume 15, issue 4 (October 2013) pp. 313–333

**Chapter 4**
*A conceptualized investment model of crowdfunding*
Alan Tomczak and Alexander Brem
*Venture Capital: An International Journal of Entrepreneurial Finance*, volume 15, issue 4 (October 2013) pp. 335–359

**Chapter 7**
*Demand-driven securities regulation: evidence from crowdfunding*
Douglas Cumming and Sofia Johan
*Venture Capital: An International Journal of Entrepreneurial Finance*, volume 15, issue 4 (October 2013) pp. 361–379

CITATION INFORMATION

The following chapters were originally published in *Venture Capital: An International Journal of Entrepreneurial Finance*, volume 16, issue 3 (July 2014). When citing this material, please use the original page numbering for each article, as follows:

**Chapter 5**
*Exploring entrepreneurial legitimacy in reward-based crowdfunding*
Denis Frydrych, Adam J. Bock, Tony Kinder and Benjamin Koeck
*Venture Capital: An International Journal of Entrepreneurial Finance*, volume 16, issue 3 (July 2014) pp. 247–269

**Chapter 6**
*Social finance and crowdfunding for social enterprises: a public–private case study providing legitimacy and leverage*
Othmar M. Lehner and Alex Nicholls
*Venture Capital: An International Journal of Entrepreneurial Finance*, volume 16, issue 3 (July 2014) pp. 271–286

For any permission-related enquiries please visit:
http://www.tandfonline.com/page/help/permissions

# Notes on Contributors

**Paul Belleflamme** is Professor at the Center for Operations Research and Econometrics at the Université catholique de Louvain, Belgium.

**Adam J. Bock** is Senior Lecturer in Entrepreneurship at the Business School, University of Edinburgh, UK.

**Alexander Brem** is based in the Department of Idea and Innovation Management at Friedrich Alexander Universität Erlangen-Nürnberg, Germany.

**Douglas Cumming** is Professor in Finance and Entrepreneurship at York University, Toronto, Canada. His research areas span topics that include law and finance, public policy, entrepreneurial finance, venture capital, private equity, IPOs, hedge funds, and exchange regulation and surveillance.

**Denis Frydrych** is a PhD candidate in the Business School at the University of Edinburgh, UK.

**Richard Harrison** is Professor of Entrepreneurship and Innovation, and Co-Director of the Centre for Strategic Leadership at the University of Edinburgh Business School, UK. He is the founding co-editor of *Venture Capital: An International Journal of Entrepreneurial Finance,* and the author of 5 books and over 100 academic papers.

**Sofia Johan** is an Adjunct Professor in the Schulich School of Business, York University, Toronto, Canada.

**Tony Kinder** is Senior Lecturer in Entrepreneurship at the Business School, University of Edinburgh, UK.

**Benjamin Koeck** is a PhD candidate in the Business School at the University of Edinburgh, UK.

**Thomas Lambert** holds a PhD in Finance jointly from the Université catholique de Louvain, Belgium, and Université Lille 2, France. From September 2015, he will be Assistant Professor in the Rotterdam School of Management, Erasmus University, The Netherlands.

**Othmar M. Lehner** is Director of the ACRN Oxford Research Centre, University of Oxford, UK, and Professor of Finance and Risk at the University of Applied Sciences Upper Austria.

**Alex Nicholls** is Professor of Social Entrepreneurship within the Skoll Centre for Social Entrepreneurship at Saïd Business School, University of Oxford, UK. His research interests range across several key areas within social entrepreneurship and social innovation.

**Armin Schwienbacher** is Professor of Accounting and Finance at the SKEMA Business School, Lille, France.

**Alan Tomczak** is based in the Department of Idea and Innovation Management at Friedrich Alexander Universität Erlangen-Nürnberg, Germany.

# Crowdfunding and the revitalisation of the early stage risk capital market: catalyst or chimera?

One of the features of the entrepreneurial landscape of recent years has been the transformation of the early stage risk capital market. This is reflected in a number of developments. First, following the post-2008 global financial crisis (GFC), there has been a sharp fall in the availability of bank lending to new and small businesses, to the extent that in the UK there is an estimated gap between the demand for and supply of SME lending of between £26 billion and £53 billion over a five-year period (Breedon Report 2012). Second, there has been a change in the supply of early stage equity finance, reflected in the collapse of the so-called funding escalator (Gill 2010).

Pre-2008, initial funding for the highest risk stages of the business start-up and development process came from a combination of 'love money' in the form of the 5Fs – founders, family, friends, fans and fools – and state grant-based funding (Figure 1(a)). In some cases, notably but not exclusively social enterprises, it is also possible to see early stage funding coming from philanthropic and altruistic sources and from supporters characterised as idealists and followers of the goals of the project, sources also described by Hemer et al. (2011) as love money. As the business moves from early stage into prototyping and towards commercialisation, more formal sources of capital become available, initially drawn from business angels and then from venture capital and private equity investors. Throughout the process, particularly in technology-based ventures, the entrepreneurs may undertake consultancy or project work to provide initial cash flow for the business, and this, as Hemer et al. (2011) point out, may also include the development of commercial and quasi-commercial arrangements leading to donations of cash and assets from sponsors, as in collaborative R&D support. This funding escalator model matches funders with the venture at different stages of the business development process; it also brings funders in with different appetites for risk, from the providers of love and grant money at the highest risk stages, business angel investors at medium risk stages (where risk is being interpreted in relative not absolute terms) to VC and private equity investors with lower appetites for risk.

Post-2008, the picture looks very different (Figure 1(b)). Funding from the 5Fs has attenuated, as household budgets have tightened and the collapse in house prices has reduced the possibility of securing business finance against personal assets. With the restructuring of government support programmes as part of the post-GFC austerity economics, grant funding has been significantly reduced or eliminated. Business angel funding continues to be available. However, reflecting the further withdrawal of venture capital and private equity from this segment of the market, it is increasingly being deployed as follow-on investment in existing portfolio companies rather than into new ventures (Mason, Botelho, and Harrison 2013). Bank finance is less available, notwithstanding government-led programmes to stimulate it, both because of a restriction in supply as banks seek to restructure their balance sheets and adjust their risk exposure profiles and because of a shortfall in demand as firms delay or defer their applications for lending in the face of

(a)

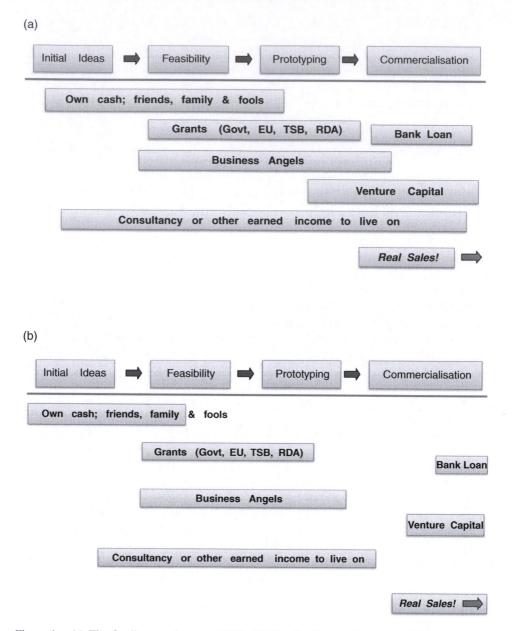

(b)

Figure 1. (a) The funding escalator pre-2008. (b) The funding escalator post-2010.

continuing economic uncertainty. Finally, soft financing options, such as consultancy earnings and sponsorship funding, along with much philanthropic, altruistic and patron funding, have also reduced in the face of the post-2008 economic recessions.

This shift in the availability of funding for new and growing businesses represents one of the most severe tightenings in the market in recent times. However, it has been accompanied by the emergence and growth of crowdfunding as an alternative way of raising capital. Although not a recent phenomenon – the Statue of Liberty was crowdfunded, for example – the Internet has made possible the expansion of this activity, initially as an efficient and effective way to raise charitable donations and more recently as a source of project and business funding. Crowdfunding, to its advocates, represents the use of the Internet to democratise both fund raising by businesses (anyone with an idea and access to the Internet can raise funds for a project from a large number of people) and investment by individuals (who have access and can commit funding to new projects on a scale of their choosing and at a level very much lower than that typically associated with 5Fs or business angel investing). The scale of this funding is not trivial: industry estimates suggest that across some 800 crowdfunding platforms of various types globally, some US$2.7 billion was raised across 1 million individual campaigns (up 81% on the preceding year), with estimates that the industry will grow to UD$5.1 billion in 2013 (Massolution 2013). In the UK, NESTA estimates that the crowdfunding market in 2012 was worth £200 million, with an estimated increase to £300 million in 2013 (Davis 2012). In a European context, the potential of crowdfunding has been explored at the EU level (European Commission 2013; EURADA 2011), and in the USA the JOBS Act (Jumpstart Our Business Startups) has sought, though without success commensurate with the rhetoric, to introduce a crowdfunding exemption to enable capital raising from the public under certain conditions without securities and exchange commission (SEC) regulation (Cunningham 2012).

Although the term crowdfunding itself first appeared in 2006 (Lawton and Marom 2010), the phenomenon itself has been described as the coming together of two existing concepts (Vitale 2013): crowdsourcing, as the collection of contributions (services, ideas and content) from a large group of people to achieve a task, dividing an otherwise overwhelming task into small enough pieces so as to make it achievable (Howe 2008); and microfinance, the lending of very small amounts to socially or economically disadvantaged borrowers typically unable to access finance from more conventional channels (Armendariz and Morduch 2010). Despite the growing prominence and discussion of crowdfunding, it is not an undifferentiated phenomenon, and assessment of its potential as a counter to the SME funding constraints of a post-GFC environment need to take into account these differences. Five distinct crowdfunding business models can be identified. First, donation models provide contributors with nothing, not even a return on their original investment. These platforms are concentrated, but not exclusively, on the not-for-profit and charitable sectors. Second, the reward model offers the contributor a nominal token in return for their funding, but does not offer an interest in the earnings flow from the project nor does it provide contributors with a share of the project or business. Third, the pre-purchase model is similar to the reward model, but rather than a nominal return (a tee shirt, a name check credit on a CD sleeve), the contributor receives the product that the entrepreneur is making. Not only does this provide the supplier with access to capital, it also provides market validation in the form of demonstrable demand for the product, which may help in accessing additional funding from more traditional sources, and substantially de-risks the product development process, overcoming the liability of newness. Fourth, and moving from project (creative, artistic or product development) to business development, the lending or peer-to-peer (P-2-P) model has attracted increased interest as a way of introducing increased liquidity into the market. As such, this is an area where direct support from government is seen, as in the commitment of £30 million from the Business Finance partnership through the Department of Business, Innovation and Skills in the UK to two P-2-P platforms. In this model, contributors expect return of their capital, and there are variants of the model in which the principal is interest-bearing and in which it is not. By comparison with the donation, reward and pre-purchase models, which raise relatively few regulatory issues and offer demonstrable benefits (market testing and de-risking), P-2-P models raise more issues of borrower and lender protection in the process of facilitating the reduction of barriers to finance for SMEs. Finally, and of most interest recently, the equity model of crowdfunding offers investors a stake in a business or a share of the profit stream resulting from the supported project. As such, this involves the sale of a security, a financial product or an interest in a managed investment scheme and falls under the regulatory regime governing such products. Accordingly, while effective models for equity crowdfunding have developed in the UK with appropriate regulation, this is not the case elsewhere, and as the case of the SEC's attempts to implement a crowdfunding exemption under the JOBS Act in the US demonstrate, progress may be slow in extending this model.

What is clear is that there is considerable diversity in the business models in the crowdfunding space. However, regardless of the crowdfunding model and the focus on project or business funding, crowdfunding represents the disintermediation of the finance market as funders and promoters are brought together directly. It has also seen the emergence of new institutional forms, as the crowdfunding platforms themselves play an increased role as actors in the market, notably in the equity model. It is, therefore, appropriate to begin to extend entrepreneurial finance research to the study of crowdfunding. In this Special Issue, we collect together papers that review the history, status and future of crowdfunding, analyse the patterns of fund raising, assess the potential of crowdfunding for the financing of social ventures in particular and discuss the regulatory implications of recent developments. What is clear from these papers is that the crowdfunding space is still evolving, institutional forms are developing and changing as models are refined, new institutional collaborations (e.g. between equity platforms and business angel networks) are emerging and new challenges, particularly regulatory challenges, are being encountered. While early expectations that P-2-P and equity models would expand in the manner of other crowdfunding platform models have proved optimistic to date, confirming that this is not a panacea for SME finance in a post-GFC world, it remains too early to determine whether crowdfunding represents a transformation of the early stage risk capital market or a minor addition to it.

## References

Armendariz, B., and J. Morduch. 2010. *The Economics of Microfinance*. Cambridge, MA: MIT Press.

Breedon Report. 2012. *Boosting Finance Options for Business*. London: Department for Business, Innovation and Skills.

Cunningham, W. M. 2012. *The JOBS Act: Crowdfunding for Small Businesses and Startups*. New York: APRESS.

Davis, A. 2012. *Beyond the Banks. Innovative Ways to Finance Britain's Small Businesses*. London: NESTA.

EURADA. 2011. "Realising the Full Potential of Crowdfunding Initiatives." Accessed August 27, 2013. http://www.eurada.org/files/Bielsko-Biala%20Declaration(1).pdf

European Commission. 2013. *Crowdfunding: Untapping Its Potential, Reducing the Risks*. Brussels: European Commission.

Gill, D. 2010. "The Collapse of the Funding Escalator: How It Happened About What to Do About It." Paper presented at IfM, June 24, University of Cambridge.

Hemer, J., U. Schneider, F. Dornbusch, and S. Frey. 2011. *Crowdfunding und Andere Formen Informetter Microfinanzierung in der Projekt- und Innovations Finanzierung*. Stuttgart: Fraunhofer Verlag.

Howe, J. 2008. *Crowdsourcing: Why the Power of the Crowd is Driving the Future of Business*. New York: Random House.

Lawton, K., and D. Marom. 2010. *The Crowdfunding Revolution: Social Networking Meets Venture Financing*. New York: McGraw Hill.

Mason, C. M., T. Botelho, and R. T. Harrison. 2013. "The Transformation of the Business Angel Market: Evidence from Scotland." Working Paper, Adam Smith Business School, University of Glasgow and University of Edinburgh Business School.

Massolution. 2013. "The Crowdfunding Industry Report." Accessed August 27, 2013. http/research. crowdsourcing.org/2013cf-crowdfunding-industry-report

Vitale, M. 2013. "Crowdfunding: Recent International Developments and Analysis of Its Compatibility with Australia's Existing Regulatory Framework." Mimeo. Accessed October 25, 2013. http://ssrn.com/abstract=2324573

Richard Harrison
*University of Edinburgh Business School*

# Crowdfunding social ventures: a model and research agenda

Othmar M. Lehner

*ACRN U. Centre for Research Methodology Austria, Cambridge, UK*

Crowdfunding (CF) in a social entrepreneurship (SE) context is praised in media narrations for its multifaceted potential. From an academic point of view, little has been written about CF as a whole, and enquiries from the SE sphere are mostly concerned with donation-based CF. This paper first reviews extant literature on financing social ventures and CF. Based upon the findings, the author draws up a schema of CF's inner workings and subsequently discusses it in an SE context. From this model, a research agenda consisting of eight themes is derived: types and utility functions; corporate governance; investor relations, reporting and risk; opportunity recognition; networking; legitimacy; financial metrics and legal and regulatory hurdles.

## Introduction

Media and public alike recognize the promise of crowdfunding (CF) for social entrepreneurs in the news; however, few to none scholarly articles exist that address the inner workings and implications of CF in such a context. The author therefore set out to thematically analyse existing nascent enquiries by reviewing extant literature, draws up a schema as a model and derives an agenda of eight-related research themes from it.

On the very basis, CF means tapping a large dispersed audience, dubbed as 'the crowd', for small sums of money to fund a project or a venture. CF is typically empowered by the social media communication over the Internet, through for example embracing user-generated content as guides for investors. CF has been addressed in the literature so far mostly in the context of creative industries, such as producing Indie music records or retro software games (Belleflamme et al. 2010a; Ward and Ramachandran 2010). The context of social ventures has remained largely unexplored so far.

Improving our knowledge of CF seems especially important for social entrepreneurship (SE) as traditional means of finance have proven as subpar or sometimes even inadequate in starting and sustaining growth of the many forms of SE (Agrawal et al. 2010; Brown and Murphy 2003; Fedele and Miniaci 2010; Ridley-Duff 2008).

Differences of SEs to traditional for-profits are shown in the literature to stem from

- ambiguous and sometimes dichotomous aims of SEs (Dacin et al. 2010), torn between the social and commercial (Lehner 2011b; Moss et al. 2011),
- alien corporate governance and legal and organizational structures in SEs that are

difficult to accept for traditional investors and lenders (Agrawal et al. 2011; Gundry et al. 2011),

- cultural and cognitive distance-related barriers between for-profit investors and SEs that hinder communication (Bauer-Leeb and Lundqvist 2012),
- social entrepreneurs' narrations that are being hooked in the 'social' sphere (Brown and Murphy 2003) and are lacking the managerial terminology, which leads to severe scepticism in their managerial capabilities.

Such peculiarities of social ventures additionally aggravate the already difficult financing situation that many start-ups find themselves in Cosh et al. (2009). Recent developments such as the financial crisis also contribute to the situation and increase pressure to find alternative access to funding and financing new social ventures, as the public sector has to reduce spending to cope with the high-accumulated governmental debts (Bielefeld 2009; Ferrera et al. 2004; Lehner 2011b).

Finding alternative, tailored methods of funding and financing by innovatively combining existing factors, such as everyday people's values and opinions, social media platforms and alternative reward systems, seems a consistent step for social entrepreneurs and fits well to the new emancipation of the crowd (Drury and Stott 2011; Reyes and Finken 2012; Valenzuela et al. 2012).

CF may offer one especially suited answer to the financing needs of social ventures, as crowd investors typically do not look much at collaterals or business plans, but at the ideas and core values of the firm (Ekedahl and Wengström 2010) and thus at its legitimacy. Aspects that are typically regarded very positive in social entrepreneurial initiatives, and thus in theory CF and SE should match well (Dart 2004).

Such crowd-based processes may bring the additional benefit of being perceived by the public as *per se* democratic (Drury and Stott 2011), thus addressing critics of SEs' capitalist steering (Meyer 2009). In addition, the recent passing of the Jumpstart our business start-ups (JOBS) act in the USA (Martin 2012; Parrino and Romeo 2012), which legalizes certain forms of equity CF for small businesses and start-ups based on volume criteria, shows that governments are becoming aware of the untapped potential and are trying to reduce legal barriers for entrepreneurs (Parrino and Romeo 2012).

Despite this potential for social entrepreneurs, few academic articles exist so far that address CF in this context – apart for a small stream focusing solely on donations (Firth 2012; Muller and Kräussl 2011). Even in the business-venturing domain as a whole, research on CF is only starting to emerge and is often based on anecdotal evidence with a focus on finite projects and the creative industry (Agrawal et al. 2010).

As for a definition of SE, the author addresses all kinds of ventures that have a social or environmental mission as their primal goal, which aim to be financially and legally independent and strive to become self-sustainable by means of the market. Such a broad characterization acknowledges the ongoing discussion on definitions, for example from the EMES or the Social Enterprise London (SEL; Defourny and Nyssens 2009a; Lehner 2011b; SEL 2001; Zahra et al. 2009), while it is open and wide-ranging enough not to exclude needlessly and perhaps even too early in this pre-paradigmatical field (Nicholls 2010c).

Addressing this void in literature, this paper thus set out to propose future research themes of CF in a social entrepreneurial context. It first debates current findings on financing and funding of social ventures. Subsequently, the small existing research canon on CF is explored in the literature and the author draws up a schema of CF.

Examining the perspectives of this schema in an SE context, eight themes are derived and proposed as a future research agenda.

## Funding SE

As stated earlier, funding and financing in the SE domain have to deal with idiosyncrasies of social ventures (Shaw and Carter 2007). Some of these may arise from the entrepreneurs or founders themselves, as they often origin from traditional non-profit organizations and have a non-business-related educational background. The terminology thus used and the values implied in their narrations make it difficult to communicate with traditional investors and financial intermediaries (Bauer-Leeb and Lundqvist 2012). Social entrepreneurs' presentations often primarily deal with the social vision, impact and outcome and at the same time neglect aspects of cash-flow liquidity, long-term financial returns and planning and forecasting (Brown and Murphy 2003; Ridley-Duff 2009). A 2003 study of the Bank of England consequently finds that social entrepreneurs indeed have a hard time accessing traditional debt finance.

In addition to these idiosyncratic hurdles for social entrepreneurs, many of the known problems for start-ups also hold true in SE (Berger and Udell 2006; Dushnitsky and Shapira 2010; Irwin and Scott 2010; Lam 2010) – for example the effectuation principles used by entrepreneurs are barely compatible with the traditional rationales of banks, basing their financing decisions in project finance upon the long-term planning of stable cash flows (Chandler et al. 2011; Perry et al. 2011).

Centred upon these specifics, a specialized financial market has started to emerge for social entrepreneurs (Bull and Crompton 2006; Fedele and Miniaci 2010; Ridley-Duff 2009; SEC 2004). It includes very different forms of rewards, narrations and discourses as a whole, compared to traditional financial markets. Instead of focusing on financial returns on investments, for example entrepreneurs have to participate with their social ideas in competitions organized by foundations such as Skoll or Ashoka, or increasingly by traditional for-profit companies as part of their CSR activities (Baron 2007; Cornelius et al. 2008; Gallego-Álvarez et al. 2011; Janney and Gove 2011). Specialized investment and performance metrics such as the social return on investment (SROI) have been proposed as instruments in decision-making and legitimization of investments (Flockhart 2005).

Many social ventures, however, still rely at least partially on donations and public grants (Bull and Crompton 2006; Fedele and Miniaci 2010; Ridley-Duff 2009) despite their aim of financial independence. This is especially true for developed countries with a corporate-statist welfare regime (Esping-Andersen 2006), where social enterprises often act as intermediaries between the public and private sectors in the provision of social welfare support (Lehner 2011a). However, recent cut-downs on welfare spending make it increasingly difficult for SEs to access public money, and on the other hand, donations are already highly competed for.

On the progressive side, several special banks, such as Kiva (Larralde and Schwienbacher 2012; Pope 2011; Rubinton 2011) or the Grameen Bank (Yunus and Weber 2007), have emerged, dealing with micro-financing of socially desirable and sustainable investments, especially in the realm of local micro-loans. In addition, several philanthropic venture capital funds and related investors/donors have surfaced, delivering funds, and also other resources such as networks and advice to social ventures (Scarlata and Alemany 2012). Investors' rewards often lie in a certain social impact, and amongst the tailored management performance measurement instruments, the SROI plays an important role, in which cascading social effects of the (social) venture are computed as monetary impact on public spending and income (Flockhart 2005).

Reporting practises of social entrepreneurs have been examined by Nicholls (2009, 2010b) in the context of the community interest company (CIC) in the UK. He found that the reporting practises not only account for financial performance but also include discussions on the social and environmental impacts, a logic that seems necessary when dealing with a multitude of stakeholders with differing aims, some driven by the social mission, others by financial sustainability.

One important aspect for financing social ventures has been almost neglected so far in literature; the trustworthiness of social entrepreneurs is regarded to be much higher due to the primacy of the social aim, and thus the costs of fraudulent risk should be reduced in theory (Lambert et al. 2012). We see early empirical claims for this based on the traditional non-profit literature (Frumkin and Kim 2001; Hansmann 1987; Haugh 2006; Herman and Renz 2008; Kerlin 2006; Laratta 2010), but so far it has not improved social entrepreneurs' situation when seeking money from traditional sources.

Nicholls (2010a) examines types of social investors and their respective investment logics based upon a Weberian analytic lens between value and purpose. He creates a matrix of nine distinct models and captures early evidence of the actual flow of capital within the social investment landscape in the UK. His conclusion, based upon the dominance of a singular investor reality, will provide an interesting counterproposition to the rationale of the crowd, consisting of equal investors with various logics.

In Tables 1 and 2, the author presents a list of investor types, clustered by debt and equity claims, based on the literature as examined earlier and adapting and enhancing previous work by Larralde and Schwienbacher (2012). These tables specifically address the stage in which the various means are most applicable. Although previous literature hints that CF may be especially suitable in the start-up phase (Firth 2012; Lambert and Schwienbacher 2010; Ward and Ramachandran 2010), its potential for funding growth and expansion (Hynes 2009) has yet to be empirically examined.

## CF literature in an SE context

Widespread Internet access and functioning social networking platforms together with the emancipation of the crowd (Drury and Stott 2011) propose interesting opportunities (Reyes and Finken 2012). Leveraging these phenomena in a process called CF can help entrepreneurs gain necessary start-up capital. Such a quest for alternative start-up capital is relevant as new ventures do not easily gain access to the necessary external finance at their early stages (Cosh et al. 2009). In later periods, business angels and venture capital funds may fill gaps for larger amounts; however, costs for proof-of-concepts and the first entrepreneurial steps are often only financed by the entrepreneur, family and friends (Cumming 2012; Dushnitsky and Shapira 2010; Irwin and Scott 2010). Early debt finance in such ventures is often brought up through a process identified in the literature as Bootstrapping (Lam 2010).

So, instead of relying on decisions made by a small group of relatively high-sophisticated investors and bank managers, the idea of CF is to tap and motivate a large audience, with each individual member of the crowd contributing only little (Belleflamme et al. 2010b) but with a high combined impact.

CF may thus provide a much-needed alternative for raising start-up capital for ventures seeking donations, debt or equity finance. CF as a constructed term is often

Table 1.   Equity investor types, SE accessibility and stages, source: author, adapted from Larralde (2012).

| | Equity claims | | |
| --- | --- | --- | --- |
| Type | Description | Accessible for SE | Stage |
| Entrepreneur and family | Investing his/her own money into the social venture, or money borrowed privately from friends and family. | +++ | Early start-up |
| Social target group | A form of crowdsourcing by tapping the beneficiaries. Successful when the entrepreneurial innovation is understood and the leverage is perceived high enough. Suitable when many people are involved with small contributions from each individual. Complex forms of governance. | +++ | Innovating, perhaps after some initial proof. Great impact on CG. |
| Business angels | Wealthy individuals, willing to invest in small social projects that fit to their intrinsic values and agenda. | ++ | Early stages, difficult to tap and scarce |
| Venture capitalists | Specialized investors, placing their fund-investors' money into larger projects for a longer period of time, however with a clear exit strategy. Fiduciary duties, lots of reporting necessary. | + | Growth. More specialized VC firms for SE emerge, not suitable for early start-ups. |
| Other companies | Decide to invest in projects that have a strategic value for them. Perhaps from a real-options logic to secure certain environmental patents, or as part of their CSR activities. Strategic entrepreneurship. | − | All stages, but only as addition. Often highly selective, and with a negative impact on ventures' reputation. |
| Stock markets | Public offering to invest in the company. Often problematic in social ventures due to the expected risk-adjusted return on investment. Some specialized funds targeting 'ethical' investments exist however. Possible negative consequences due to loss of control and high regulative efforts. | − | Globalization and tremendous scaling up of established and recognized social solutions. |

considered in the literature as project-based funding only and so the term in its current usage does not fully comprise its full potential, which would also include more long-term commitments such as debt or equity shares (Crowdsourcing 2012). Also a distinct focus on donation-based CF for social entrepreneurs leaves out important market alternatives, where crowd members actually become shareholders. Especially equity-based CF will thus inevitably cross the border of simple project financing (Larralde and Schwienbacher 2012).

Scholars see the roots of CF in a movement that has been labelled as crowdsourcing, which comprises using the crowd to obtain ideas, feedback and solutions in order to develop corporate activities (Brabham 2008; Howe 2006; Kleemann et al. 2008). A distinct feature of the 'crowd' is seen in the literature as consisting of a large number of people, each contributing little, but with a possible high combined impact (Belleflamme et al. 2010b). However, such a crowd is supposed to behave in unforeseen,

Table 2.  Debt investor types, SE accessibility and stages, source: author, adapted from Larralde (2012).

| | Debt claims | | |
|---|---|---|---|
| Type | Description | Accessible for SE | Stage |
| Banks | Loans. Special banks for social ventures exist. Often project finance with little mutual understanding between (social aim) seeker and provider. Problems in terminology and cultural distance. | ++ | All stages, depending on the entrepreneurs' preferences for control and risk-taking. Increasing importance due to specialized banks. |
| Leasing companies | Providing machinery and equipment to entrepreneurs against lease payments. Suitable for all types of ventures, when cash flows are stable and investment is relatively standardized. | + | Start-up and expansion, for certain types of investment only. Often investment as collateral. |
| Government, agencies | Subsidies, grants and credit to improve rating. Perhaps forms of public private partnerships. Also service-based public funding. Highly competed for, problematic in times of government austerity. | ++ | High importance for socially desirable projects that can be run sustainably with a managerial attitude, but would not be attractive for traditional investors and entrepreneurs. |
| Customers/ suppliers | Trade credit and upfront payments for future goods and services. Sometimes used in CF for special niche products. | ++ | Operational expenses, depending on industry. |
| Bootstrapping | Clever use of working capital management and Bricolage to start a business, together with a strict eye on expenses. Often used by small social entrepreneurial initiatives. | +++ | Early stages, when motivation of stakeholders and entrepreneurs are high. Perhaps based upon personal traits. |
| Donations | While given for free, donors expect a certain type of reward, for example through achieving a certain social impact. This reward can also be personal for example through creating a noble feeling or a better standing in society. | ++ | Still many social ventures rely partly on donations. Will become scarce with more competitors. Often used in CF initiatives with a honorary element. |

chaotic and complex manners (Drury and Reicher 1999; Drury and Stott 2011; Ivancevic et al. 2010; Massink et al. 2010), and therefore, a careful examination of the influential factors and functions is necessary.

CF in an SE perspective can provide additional legitimacy to the venture, as the selection process by the crowd is perceived as *per se* democratic, and the crowd will thus select the social ideas it deems worthy and needed (Belleflamme et al. 2010b; Drury and Stott 2011; Rubinton 2011).

The concept of CF has been demonstrated in cases to work miraculously well. The amounts of money obtained even reach GBP 1 million, as in the case of Trampoline Systems UK, a high-tech start-up (Belleflamme et al. 2010b). The involved processes, from communication, utility functions to legal aspects, however, are far from being clear. Much need for experimentation, last minute changes and unforeseen legal hurdles have put the effort of Trampoline almost in jeopardy.

Belleflamme et al. (2010a) examine CF from an industrial organization perspective and associate CF with pre-ordering and the resulting price discrimination. Such a model may not hold well in an SE context as the investors' motives for investment may differ in that they are less concerned about costs but the outcome (Delanoë 2011; Fayolle et al. 2005; Shaw and Carter 2007). Belleflamme et al. also provide some theoretical underpinnings why non-profit organizations tend to be more successful in using CF by examining the literature on contract failure theory. This theory is based on the view that limiting monetary motivations of owners, such as prohibiting or limiting dividend pay-outs in some forms of SE (Lehner 2011b), attracts donations more easily and invites other forms of participation, such as voluntary work. Such a limit on monetary motivation for owners can also be seen as a strong *signal* that the owners put a significant weight on the quality of the outcome and less on monetary gains (Chillemi and Gui 1991; Van Slyke 2006). This invites perspectives from information economics and signalling on CF (Akerlof 1970; Balakrishnan and Koza 1993; Lambert et al. 2012).

Pope (2011) identifies legal hurdles for equity-based CF in the USA, asserted by the Security Exchange Commission, which can be transferred to some extent also to Europe and many other countries with a regulated capital market. He scrutinizes difficulties for micro-start-ups in gaining necessary equity capital and their willingness to bootstrap, using their own available resources. As the public offering of equity is highly regulated, it brings tremendous costs for auditing, creating prospectuses and consulting law firms and financial intermediaries. Pope thus observes equity-based CF in start-up ventures as being severely limited in the current legal situation. It is therefore logical that many forms of CF so far do not offer equity shares but other forms of rewards, for example early access to products, honorary recognition or some interest payments. However, to reflect on CF origins in crowdsourcing, equity stakes may on the one hand provide a pronounced democratic corporate governance (CG) model for social ventures, and on the other hand be the one missing opportunity for small investors in the crowd, seeking for ethical investments and rewards on alternative financial markets (Fox 2012). As reported eralier, legal and regulatory hurdles for equity CF are addressed in a perhaps ground-breaking manner by the recently passed JOBS act by the US President Obama. It lowers restrictions on Rule 506 offerings and frees seekers for small CF volumes < 100k USD, and to a lesser extent < 500k USD from several costly regulations (Heminway and Hoffman 2011; Pope 2011; Rubinton 2011).

Larralde and Schwienbacher (2012) identify business models for CF, namely donations, passive and active investments by the crowd. Donation-based CF has been a long-established means of finance for NPOs and NGOs (Hansmann 1987; Nyssens et al. 2006). However, as the number of CF initiatives and platforms rises, the resource 'crowd' for donations becomes highly competed for and thus scarce. Larralde and Schwienbacher distinguish between active and passive CF. Passive CF sees some reward for its investors, for example tailored products, honorary recognition or other forms of revenue sharing. However, the interaction between the company and its crowd investors is limited to the rewarding function. Active CF differs in that aspect, as its investors are not only supplying money but are also in the best manner of crowdsourcing included in a constant dialogue with the company, helping for example in designing new features, testing products, suggesting paths for the company and supplying their network scope and individual expertise. This active form of CF is also very fruitful in providing a means for corporate communication and public relations and through the dispersed positive discourse, dubbed 'buzz', it ultimately improves a company's legitimacy.

Such a quest for legitimacy is of high value especially for social ventures because of their dealing between the market, civil society and public sphere (Kerlin 2006). Social entrepreneurs on one hand address social voids by market activities but on the other hand also work as social *change makers* by influencing systems and policies (Cho 2006; Drayton 2006; Gunn et al. 2008). Such attempted policy change, however, may inevitably see resistance from incumbent powers and institutions (Ahlstrom and Bruton 2010; Bonoli and Palier 2009; Levander 2010; Lim et al. 2010; Mair and Marti 2009; Meyer et al. 2009), and therefore, needs to be backed by the power of the people in what they perceive a legit case.

CF activities are also demonstrated to have a true global outreach through the means of the Internet and specialized social media platforms, Agrawal et al. (2011) examine this on the case of the record industry, and find that CF indeed shows a broad geographic dispersion of investors and that the negative impact of distance-sensitive costs is mitigated; a finding standing in contrast to traditional finance theory, which would hold a perspective of a rising distrust with distance. This broad geographic dispersion, however, also reflects well on SE, which is also designated as a truly global phenomenon (Zahra et al. 2009, 2008), and in which many initiatives work on a very international level even from the beginning (Korsgaard 2011; Meyskens et al. 2010; Zahra et al. 2008).

## A proposed schema of CF

Based on the previously examined literature and some early empirical evidence as discussed in the previous sections, the author presents an early schema of the inner workings of CF, which is then applied and discussed in an SE context (Figure 1).

### *Overview of the schema*

This schema displays the matchmaking process between the venture, offering debt or equity investments, and the crowd. Opportunity recognition (OR) in this schema is essential, not only the entrepreneur but also the crowd has to recognize it, informed through communication channels and the user-generated content on the Web platforms. Matchmaking takes place when members of the crowd decide to participate in the exploitation of this opportunity based upon its perceived legitimacy. This participation in the venture can take place within one of the four quadrants, spanning business models (active–passive) as well as type of capital (debt–equity). Communication and business strategies of the Web-based CF platforms as intermediaries; networks of crowd members pointing to these and aspects of information economics (reducing the asymmetry) together with the crowd members' individual risk equivalents will form the so-called motivational block (based upon utility functions). The outcome will be moderated by reward, levels of control and participation offered, but more so by the intermediary platform's business model. Laws and regulations (including related costs) finally will form a strong mediator block between the crowd, the CF platform and the desired participation in the venture.

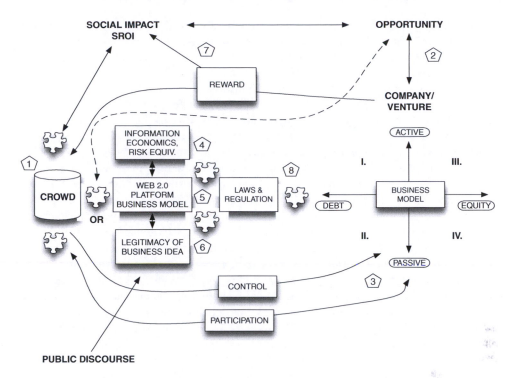

Figure 1.   Schema of CF, Source: Lehner 2012, numbers relate to the proposed research themes.

The four quadrants describe the actual nature of the investment offering, between debt and equity, active or passive participation. Debt or equity financing, however, is not a purely deliberate choice of investors and entrepreneurs likewise. Rather the stage and phase of the venture, aspects of risk dispersion, legal regulations, as well as non-monetary goals such as CG and reputation have a big influence on capital formation (Berger and Udell 1998; Kreiser et al. 2010).

The enthusiasm of the investing group regarding the desired outcome (Duckett and Swerissen 1996; Qiongzhi 2007; Ruebottom 2011) of the crowd-funded venture seems to be a much higher motivation for an active participation than to ensure monetary, interest-like incentives and influence risk taking. As has been seen in cases of Kittur (2010), Kleemann et al. (2008) and Whitla (2009), such active participation can take many forms of crowdsourcing (Brabham 2008), from testing early prototypes to advertising and viral marketing and from volunteering work such as translating texts to serving at events. It seems beneficial even to the funding process itself to offer and invite some form of investors' partaking. Participation of the crowd will typically create 'buzz' in the social media that may draw even more future potential investors to the CF platform site (Belleflamme et al. 2010b). However, previous literature by Larralde and Schwienbacher suggests there will be a recurring shift between active and passive involvements, depending on the individuals' circumstances as well as on the stage of the venture.

Capital formation is essential to economic developments, as it enables entrepreneurs to create new solutions to opportunities (Cumming 2012; Seghers et al. 2012). This also holds true for social entrepreneurs in their opportunity seeking and exploitation strategies (Cha and Bae 2010; Korsgaard 2011; Lehner and Kaniskas 2012).

Due to legal restrictions, so far few long-term maturing, crowd-funded bonds have been issued outside of the traditional regulated market, so we can only guess on required interest rates or the level of control and reporting expected from long-term lenders in CF (Larralde and Schwienbacher 2012; Pope 2011; Rubinton 2011). Most cases of debt financing so far have been of the type of advance payments (Agrawal et al. 2010; Firth 2012; Larralde and Schwienbacher 2012; Ward and Ramachandran 2010) for future goods or services; however, another interesting aspect of debt may be crowd-funded donations and grants.

Equity financing may provide the greatest challenges but also the greatest opportunities for crowd-funded social ventures (Artiach and Clarkson 2011). Typically, equity investments are legally linked with several rights, among the rights of information and control, and the right to participate in the earnings or added value of the company (Berger and Udell 1998). Selling shares of equity is ultimately a means of distributing risk onto the shoulders of many investors, compared to debt finance, in which the entrepreneur shoulders all risk himself/herself (Amit et al. 1990; Sharfman and Fernando 2008). Equity-based CF does therefore come at a much higher cost for the ventures, but perhaps contrary to the traditional theories less in a monetary sense but more so in terms of control, governance and stewardship (Meuleman et al. 2009; Williamson 1988).

Dispersing control is counted as a detrimental aspect in traditional for-profit financing; however, this impact on CG may hold positive merits in social ventures, as increased shareholder participation will improve legitimacy in the eyes of the public and may also refine the actual approach to the social needs towards higher effectiveness (Beckmann 2011; Bull et al. 2010; Ridley-Duff 2009, 2010). However, besides the positive, an increased dispersion of control may well hinder thoughtful experimentation and necessary changes of strategy by the founders, lessening the chances of entrepreneurial innovation (Huarng and Yu 2011; Ruvinsky 2012; Vaccaro et al. 2012).

The challenges for equity-based CF are thus multi-faceted; they comprise legal and regulatory hurdles (Heminway and Hoffman 2011; Larralde and Schwienbacher 2012; Pope 2011; Rubinton 2011; Schwienbacher and Larralde 2010), as well as considerations about governance and control. Public offering (exceeding to a certain amount of people) of a company's equity is highly regulated in most developed countries – the main reasons given to prevent fraud (Altman and Sabato 2007; Hmieleski and Baron 2008) and to enable an efficient market through reducing information asymmetry (Deakins and Hussain 1994; Lambert et al. 2012; Schnatterly et al. 2008). Even the sharing of net revenues to investors is seen as a security offering and thus highly regulated. Therefore, CF platforms in various countries such as the UK or the Netherlands, which allow CF for equity, need to use complex schemes of partaking and control in the entity to avoid legal pitfalls.

Concerning the traditional reward systems of shareholder value and dividends, possible utility functions of equity investors in crowd-funded social ventures may differ from those of traditional for-profit investors, such as business angels or venture capital funds. Several legal forms, tailored for social enterprises, such as the CIC in the UK or L3C in the USA, have some kind of dividend pay-out prohibition (Nicholls 2009, 2010b; Ridley-Duff 2008, 2009) and any accumulated wealth cannot be paid out to shareholders, even after closure of such a firm. These rules may thus prevent interest from many investors and the ongoing discussion on the usefulness of distinct SE legal forms has a new facet (Galera and Borzaga 2009).

There are also the more strategic and for-profit considerations based upon real-options logic (Levitas and Chi 2010; Scherpereel 2008; Tong and Reuer 2007) that may bring crowd-investors to fund social ventures with equity finance. Some relatively small financing early at the beginning may provide access and control over the investment if it turns out to be successful later (Husted 2005; Levitas and Chi 2010; Scherpereel 2008; Tong and Reuer 2007; Wang and Lim 2008). In an SE context, this option may well be embedded in the CSR strategy of larger companies and can also provide a very tangible competitive advantage later for example through access to patents that may come in handy in ever changing energy and other environmental regulations (Block 2012; Brettel et al. 2012; Cuervo Cazurra and Annique Un 2010; Husted 2005; Mcwilliams and Siegel 2010).

## Proposing a research agenda

Derived from the proposed schema, eight themes are identified (see related numbers in Figure 1) to further the field by using a stepwise refinement research methodology based upon the maturity of the theory (Edmondson and Mcmanus 2007). The first steps need to be descriptive in nature, to assess the relevance of the individual blocks, find variables and come up with theories of quantification, subsequent correlation and ultimately explanation (Bluhm et al. 2011; Connelly et al. 2010). It is these explanations that can later be put into recommendations for policy-makers and businesses alike.

### *Types and utility functions of crowd investors*

Using the 'crowd' to obtain ideas, feedback and solutions in order to develop corporate activities (Brabham 2008; Howe 2006; Kleemann et al. 2008) is nothing new. The widely available access to social media and networks makes it easy to tap a large number of people instantly. A distinct feature of the crowd was carved out in the previous paragraphs as consisting of a large number of people, each contributing little, but with a possible high combined impact (Belleflamme et al. 2010b; Whitla 2009). It has been examined that such a crowd is behaving in unforeseen, chaotic and complex manners (Drury and Reicher 1999; Drury and Stott 2011; Ivancevic et al. 2010; Massink et al. 2010) and that small activities by the company (including the omission of certain actions) can lead to a hyperbolic response by the crowd. However, what we do not know is what motivates the individuals being part of the crowd. Do these motivations differ for certain types of offered crowd investments? Previous research seems to hint at that, as there is a distinctiveness in the handling of investors between CF for donations, projects or equity (Larralde and Schwienbacher 2012).

Kozinets et al. (2008) distinguish between four types of online consumer communities, Crowds, Hives, Mobs and Swarms, and find that collective innovation is produced both as an aggregated byproduct of everyday information consumption and as a result of the efforts of talented and motivated groups of innovative e-tribes. Their proposed typology may provide a starting point to address types of collective investors from a macro-marketing perspective, as the difference between crowd consumers and investors in CF is often only marginal.

Motivational factors, such as financial reward systems or personal involvement, may well be positively correlated to one type, but deter others. Nicholls (2010a) identifies types of social investors and their respective investment logics and creates a matrix of nine distinct models. His scenarios, each based upon the dominance of a singular investor reality, will provide an interesting counterproposition to the rationale of the crowd, consisting of equal investors with various logics.

Research in this area should therefore look into the perspective of the crowd as an emancipated entity, as well as on the individual members and their motivations stemming from the psychological to the economical. Answers will allow SEs to serve a broader spectrum of approaches to attract and retain crowd investors and to increase efficiency through tailored approaches for target audiences.

### *Opportunity recognition and matchmaking*

OR is at the very heart of venture creation, some scholars regard OR even as the basis of entrepreneurship (Short et al. 2010). As Lehner and Kaniskas (2012) and Corner and Ho (2010) examine, existing SE literature on OR draws upon a multitude of theoretical frameworks for their research. Among others, theories from Austrian School economists such as Schumpeter, Kirzner and Hayek (Murphy and Coombes 2009; Zahra et al. 2009) are employed and the behavioural theory of the firm (Zahra et al. 2008) is applied. In addition, closely related concepts to OR, such as Bricolage or innovation, are used to integrate OR and exploitation into a broader perspective of SE (Archer et al. 2009; Corner and Ho 2010; Marialaura Di Domenico et al. 2010; Fuglsang 2010; Nicholls 2010c; Shaw and Carter 2007). Some scholars maintain that SE opportunities are different from those found in for-profit ventures (Corner and Ho 2010; Mair and Noboa 2006; Robinson 2006). Different views on OR exist, depending on the activeness of the entrepreneur and the dispersion of available information. In CF, another perspective is added. Not only the entrepreneurs have to identify an opportunity, but also the crowd has to recognize and evaluate it. This brings an additional hurdle to the actual exploitation. In traditional financing, entrepreneurs have to deal with few, relatively sophisticated investors and need to convince them, often using business plans and forecasts. In CF, opportunities need to be communicated to a great mass of heterogeneous people, using different instruments and strategies. The individual crowd members in this model can be either (a) passive listeners acting on the available information or (b) active seekers looking for opportunities. Future research in this area will need to address this dual OR of the entrepreneur and the crowd alike, and take an eye on the SE context of OR. Findings will deliver insights on how an OR transfer can take place, from the entrepreneurs' alertness or informedness, to the crowd.

### *Business models and corporate governance*

A distinct CG with a broad stakeholder inclusion is seen as one central and defining element in the SE literature (Beckmann 2011; Nicholls 2010b). Stakeholder participation, the division of control power not based on the number of shares, and community-based decision-making processes are part of everyday life for many social ventures (Borzaga et al. 2008; Defourny and Nyssens 2009a, 2009b; Mason et al. 2007; Travaglini 2009).

With the inclusion of the crowd, consisting of a multitude of (partly anonymous) individuals as stakeholders or even shareholders, new approaches to CG models in SE need to be addressed. It may be difficult to include the crowd in traditional decision-making processes; therefore, communication means and forms need to be created and adapted, often powered by Web-based services over the Internet. The impact of such a large number of involved people can nevertheless have several beneficial aspects. Among them are an increased legitimacy, bringing with a higher acceptance and attractiveness to invest and work for such a company (Lumpkin 2011; Patriotta et al. 2011), or a refined outlook of what is really needed through the feedback of the many. The interplay of organizational forms, types of involvement, stakeholder tailored reporting (Nicholls 2009) and means of participation in CF may be the foremost questions to be asked in this context.

CG structures differ between countries, based upon legal requirements as well as different cultures and mindsets. Therefore, careful longitudinal enquiries in the CG structures of crowd-funded social ventures, scrutinizing the hurdles and opportunities for CF within existing CG structures, as well as respective public acceptance in a comparative fashion will provide further insights into this theme. Carmel and Harlock (2008) examine governance in the 'third sector' and bring new perspectives on the governance of what they call the 'dispersed state', which may provide an interesting starting point in such discussions.

## Information economics, reporting and risk

A growing body of research literature on communication strategies in the field of investor relations (IR) is available (Bassen et al. 2010; Kirchhoff and Piwinger 2009). Different approaches to potential and existing investors are laid out, united by the commonly accepted ambitions to attract new and keep current investors, fulfil legal requirements concerning reporting and disclosure and reduce the perceived idiosyncratic risk (differing from systemic risk stemming from industry). Ultimately, the intent of these measures is to reduce the cost of capital (Millo and Mackenzie 2009) and provide a true and fair view on the risk/return ratio.

Specialized platforms on the Internet, such as Kickstarter, have been brought to life as distinct business models, addressing the perceived communication needs of ventures seeking for CF and slowly taking over the role of financial intermediaries. IR literature holds much about communication in the web-age (Singer and Cacia 2009) including the importance of network domino effects for the dispersion of information. The primacy of the simply understood socially desirable mission of a venture, however, is unique in CF IR, compared to the more ample capital market stories typically drawn up in traditional companies (Bassen et al. 2010).

Reporting practises of social entrepreneurs have been examined by Nicholls (2009, 2010b), which he describes as 'blended value accounting'. Not only financial performance is disclosed, but the reports also include discussions on the social and environmental impacts. Exactly how reporting will take place in the area of highly dispersed investors remains unclear so far. Research in this theme therefore needs to look at the role of risk and information dispersion, enquire about legal proceedings, examine the risk equivalents of crowd-investors and perhaps challenge agency theory as a whole (Heracleous and Lan 2012).

## Networking and the role of platforms

Crowd-funded ventures rely heavily upon networks, mainly brought together by the Internet. Networking theory has already proven to be highly predictive in modelling the flow of various resources, such as materials, workforce but also more generally capabilities, information, business partners and opportunities in various situations (Dobrow et al. 2011; Hoang and Antoncic 2003; Mahmood et al. 2011; Martinez and Aldrich 2011; Soh 2010; Sullivan and Marvel 2011). Early research in CF for example sees a distinct approach to geographical closeness, compared to other forms of venture financing (Agrawal et al. 2011). Geographical distance does not come with the expected risk premium in CF. Also the importance of structural holes in linking cycles of crowd investors (Batjargal 2010) in order to globally disperse information about the investment opportunity may provide a fascinating lens for enquiry.

Nodes in these networks will be the individual crowd members but more so the platforms and their respective followers. The examination of the role of these platforms as amplifiers and mediators, creating quasi super-nodes, as well as of the ties, ruled and regulated by payment providers will be crucial in getting the whole picture. Research thus would take existing networking theory and adapt it where possible in order to model the flow of communication and resources.

### Discourse and legitimacy of CF

Higher legitimacy of a venture (or better of its respective opportunity) increases acceptance of its activities and helps accessing resources such as materials or workforce. In the case of CF, the legitimacy of a venture will ultimately moderate the crowd's willingness to invest in it. Legitimacy, however, is built up in a complex, recursive process, involving the individuals' values, self-pictures, needs and wants and the perceptions of the venture created by public discourse (Cornelissen and Clarke 2010; Dart 2004; Nicholls 2010c; Patriotta et al. 2011), which is difficult to predict when targeting a large heterogeneous audience.

The success of social entrepreneurs dealing in between the market, civil and public sector already depends on positive communication and thus ultimately on perceived legitimacy of their doings (Di Domenico et al. 2010; Di Domenico 2009; Lehner 2011b).

Are crowds then *per se* democratic, and is the dispersion of control in such ventures therefore always a positive thing (Drury and Reicher 1999)? Does CF for example help overcome the criticism of leaving social welfare provision in the hands and decisions of a few; as has been raised in the literature (Meyer 2009; Palier 2010)?

Research in this theme needs to be downright interdisciplinary, borrowing from the interplay between the domains of sociology and psychology, looking at the diverse fields of politics, law, international relations, communication and business, applying and modifying a diverse range of theories such as new institutionalism or contract failure theory.

There is also a methodological challenge included, as Büscher and Urry (2009) see the need for new strategies of enquiry in the age of mobile devices, which allow access to 'information at your fingertips'. This information is however condensed and often reduced of the richness of context specifics. They examine and propose the 'mobilities' paradigm in how to conduct empirical studies that better grasp the nature of movements of people, objects, information and ideas.

### Challenging finance metrics and instruments in a CF environment

The capital asset pricing model (CAPM) in its various forms is still seen as a basis to many of the finance-related metrics and instruments (Andersen et al. 2007; Berger and Udell 2006; Hovakimian et al. 2001; Millo and Mackenzie 2009). The assumptions in the calculation of the weighted average cost of capital, influenced by the costs of equity based on CAPM, are still widespread accepted (Artiach and Clarkson 2011; Brown 2011; Kunc and Bhandari 2011) and serve as a guiding principle in making traditional investment decisions.

Theory claims that investors will make use of derived models to compute the necessary return on investment based on risk comparisons. However, early empirical evidence shows that in CF, most members of the crowd are more motivated by the either explicitly or implicitly proposed non-monetary value and return (Belleflamme et al. 2010b; Drury and Stott 2011). Literature suggests the further development and inclusion of the SROI as a metrics in social ventures (Flockhart 2005) to help investors choose the highest leverage of their (social) investment.

However, so far, it has remained unclear whether such complex investment metrics really provide a decision-making tool, or are rather used to maintain some form of rationalization after the investment – which was in fact originally based upon more intrinsic choices. Especially the public sector, however, needs such tools to have a rational answer to questions about their investments and grants to social initiatives (Hennala et al. 2011; Hood 2011; Patriotta et al. 2011).

In the CF field, especially when investing in equity shares, real-options logic (Husted 2005; Levitas and Chi 2010; Scherpereel 2008; Tong and Reuer 2007), which is derived from financial markets, can provide another frame of thinking to explain investors' choices. Such thinking leads to limiting potential losses to the price of the option (the small initial investment), allows holding a bundle of strategic investment options as an answer to uncertainty and ultimately enables investors to claim their stakes when some of the ventures later gain movement and the proof of concept has been made.

Research in this theme needs to address the adaption of traditional metrics and explore new ways to measure and predict investment decisions. Perspectives from Behavioural Finance, such as 'herding', may also provide insights into the inner rationale of crowd investors (Fairchild 2011; Lehner 2004; Shleifer 2000).

## Legal and regulatory perspectives in CF

Platforms addressing equity-based CF often come up with a complex scheme of control and partaking in order to avoid costly rules and regulations. Due to high public pressure in a reclining economy, the recently passed JOBS act is celebrated in media as a giant step for entrepreneurship in the USA, as it exempts some equity CF from excessive regulatory schemes (Heminway and Hoffman 2011; Parrino and Romeo 2012; Pope 2011). Such a scheme, as suggested in this act, allows smaller ventures to offer equity or securities via crowd activities, while the necessary regulations are held at a minimum. It is thus seen as a big alleviation for entrepreneurs and newly founded ventures to travel further down the growing path after the initial steps – before venture capitalists of all sorts would find the investment attractive.

Research in this theme needs to address the implications of such rules and regulations, costs being one side, but the diminished value of reporting and auditing may well be a backlash for the efforts to attract crowd-based equity investors due to rising information asymmetry, and the fear of moral hazards.

Besides international legal and comparative studies, it might also be fruitful to apply agency theory and identify for example lobbying groups and their motives (Heracleous and Lan 2012). Also the long-term impact of these new rules and regulations for crowd-funded initiatives on traditional finance market rulings for small ventures may provide further perspectives.

In addition, the role of intermediaries in CF, for example the platforms themselves, with their perceived fiduciary duties needs to be addressed in order to provide guidance to both investors and ventures (Rubinton 2011). It will be interesting to see case studies on how courts decide on the role of these intermediaries when the first moral hazards and cases of fraud appear. Is the legal system prepared for the complex scheme of CF with so many and often globally dispersed participants? A special focus might also be necessary on the payment providers. Besides taxation and currency exchange issues, their activities are under strict oversight and control by individual governments and thus politics may exert influence.

The choice and interplay of legal business forms with their inherent organizational forms has been seen to matter in capital formation (Belleflamme et al. 2010a; Dushnitsky and Shapira 2010; Edwards and Edwards 2008; Lambert et al. 2012). The SE sector shows tailored and often highly complex legal forms such as community interest companies (e.g. the CIC or L3C) with unusual organizational structures (Hill et al. 2010), providing interesting perspectives for future research in how the crowd perceives these as investment opportunities.

## Conclusion

This paper has reviewed extant literature on CF and its financial underpinnings in an SE context, and has outlined eight CF-related research themes that would provide valuable information for academics, policy-makers and practitioners.

Once more we see that the complex and ambiguous nature of SE provides a fascinating playground for researchers from various disciplines (Mair and Marti 2006). The almost undefined and disputed field of CF for donations, equity or debt, even increases this convolution of terms, concepts and actions. The proposed schema of the inner workings of CF shall thus reduce ambiguity and provide a framework for researchers to find a common ground.

We need to see rigorous and robust conceptual and empirical research, drawing and developing from existing proven theories from a multitude of disciplines. Such solid research endeavours ultimately need to address and inform policy-makers and practitioners likewise in order to increase the success of CF of new (social) ventures – a worthwhile scholarly pursuit.

## References

Agrawal, A. K., C. Catalini, and A. Goldfarb. 2010. "Entrepreneurial Finance and the Flat-World Hypothesis: Evidence from Crowd-Funding Entrepreneurs in the Arts." Working Papers.

Agrawal, A. K., C. Catalini, and A. Goldfarb. 2011. "The Geography of Crowdfunding." NBER Working Paper No. w16820. http://ssrn.com/abstract=1770375

Ahlstrom, D., and G. D. Bruton. 2010. "Rapid Institutional Shifts and the Co Evolution of Entrepreneurial Firms in Transition Economies." *Entrepreneurship Theory and Practice* 34 (3): 531–554.

Akerlof, G. A. 1970. "The Market for 'Lemons': Quality Uncertainty and the Market Mechanism." *The Quarterly Journal of Economics* 84: 488–500.

Altman, E. I., and G. Sabato. 2007. "Modelling Credit Risk for SMES: Evidence From the US Market." *Abacus* 43 (3): 332–357.

Amit, R., L. Glosten, and E. Muller. 1990. "Entrepreneurial Ability, Venture Investments, and Risk Sharing." *Management Science* 36 (10): 1232–1245.

Andersen, T. G., T. Bollerslev, P. Christoffersen, and F. X. Diebold. 2007. *Practical Volatility and Correlation Modeling for Financial Market Risk Management.* Chicago: University of Chicago Press.

Archer, G., T. Baker, and R. Mauer. 2009. "Towards an Alternative Theory of Entrepreneurial Success: Integrating Bricolage, Effectuation and Improvisation." *Frontiers of Entrepreneurship Research* 29 (6): 4–26.

Artiach, T. C., and P. M. Clarkson. 2011. "Disclosure, Conservatism and the Cost of Equity Capital: A Review of the Foundation Literature." *Accounting & Finance* 51 (1): 2–49.

Balakrishnan, S., and M. P. Koza. 1993. "Information Asymmetry, Adverse Selection and Joint-Ventures* 1: Theory and Evidence." *Journal of Economic Behavior & Organization* 20 (1): 99–117.

Baron, D. P. 2007. "Corporate Social Responsibility and Social Entrepreneurship." *Journal of Economics & Management Strategy* 16 (3): 683–717.

Bassen, A., H. Basse Mama, and H. Ramaj. 2010. "Investor Relations: A Comprehensive Overview." *Journal für Betriebswirtschaft* 60 (1): 49–79.

Batjargal, B. 2010. "The Effects of Network's Structural Holes: Polycentric Institutions, Product Portfolio, and New Venture Growth in China and Russia." *Strategic Entrepreneurship Journal* 4 (2): 146–163.

Bauer-Leeb, M., and E. Lundqvist. 2012. "Social Entrepreneurs and Business Angels – A Quest for Factors Facilitating Business Relationships." PhD thesis, Danube University Krems.

Beckmann, M. 2011. "The Social Case as a Business Case: Making Sense of Social Entrepreneurship from an Ordonomic Perspective." In *Corporate Citizenship and New Governance*, edited by I. Pies and P. Koslowski, 91–115. Heidelberg: Springer-Verlag.

Belleflamme, P., T. Lambert, and A. Schwienbacher. 2010a. "Crowdfunding: An Industrial Organization Perspective." Paper presented at Digital Business Models Conference: Understanding Strategies, Paris, France, June 25–26.

Belleflamme, P., T. Lambert, and A. Schwienbacher. 2010b. "Crowdfunding: Tapping the Right Crowd." CORE Discussion Paper No. 2011/32. http://ssrn.com/abstract=1578175

Berger, A. N., and G. F. Udell. 1998. "The Economics of Small Business Finance: The Roles of Private Equity and Debt Markets in the Financial Growth Cycle." *Journal of Banking and Finance* 22 (6–8): 613–673.

Berger, A. N., and G. F. Udell. 2006. "A More Complete Conceptual Framework for SME Finance." *Journal of Banking & Finance* 30 (11): 2945–2966.

Bielefeld, W. 2009. "Issues in Social Enterprise and Social Entrepreneurship." *Journal of Public Affairs Education* 15 (1): 69–86.

Block, J. H. 2012. "R&D Investments in Family and Founder Firms: An Agency Perspective." *Journal of Business Venturing* 27 (2): 248–265.

Bluhm, D. J., W. Harman, T. W. Lee, and T. R. Mitchell. 2011. "Qualitative Research in Management: A Decade of Progress." *Journal of Management Studies* 48 (8): 1866–1891.

Bonoli, G., and B. Palier. 2009. "How Do Welfare States Change? Institutions and Their Impact on the Politics of Welfare State Reform in Western Europe." *European Review* 8 (3): 333–352.

Borzaga, C., G. Galera, and R. Nogales. 2008. *Social Enterprise: A New Model for Poverty Reduction and Employment Generation. An Examination of the Concept and Practice in Europe and the Commonwealth of Independent States*. Bratislava: UNDP, EMES.

Brabham, D. C. 2008. "Crowdsourcing as a Model for Problem Solving an Introduction and Cases." *Convergence: The International Journal of Research into New Media Technologies* 14 (1): 75–90.

Brettel, M., R. Mauer, A. Engelen, and D. Küpper. 2012. "Corporate Effectuation: Entrepreneurial Action and Its Impact on R&D Project Performance." *Journal of Business Venturing* 27 (2): 167–184.

Brown, S. J. 2011. "The Efficient Markets Hypothesis: The Demise of the Demon of Chance?" *Accounting & Finance* 51 (1): 79–95.

Brown, H., and E. Murphy. 2003. *The Financing of Social Enterprises: A Special Report by the Bank of England. Domestic Finance Division, Bank of England, London*. London: Bank of England.

Bull, M., and H. Crompton. 2006. "Business Practices in Social Enterprises." *Social Enterprise Journal* 2 (1): 42–60.

Bull, M., R. Ridley-Duff, D. Foster, and P. Seanor. 2010. "Conceptualising Ethical Capital in Social Enterprise." *Social Enterprise Journal* 6 (3): 250–264.

Büscher, M., and J. Urry. 2009. "Mobile Methods and the Empirical." *European Journal of Social Theory* 12 (1): 99–116.

Carmel, E., and J. Harlock. 2008. "Instituting The 'Third Sector' as a Governable Terrain: Partnership, Procurement and Performance in the UK." *Policy &# 38; Politics* 36 (2): 155–171.

Cha, M.-S., and Z.-T. Bae. 2010. "The Entrepreneurial Journey: From Entrepreneurial Intent to Opportunity Realization." *Journal of High Technology Management Research* 21 (1): 31–42.

Chandler, G. N., D. R. Detienne, A. Mckelvie, and T. V. Mumford. 2011. "Causation and Effectuation Processes: A Validation Study." *Journal of Business Venturing* 26 (3): 375–390.

Chillemi, O., and B. Gui. 1991. "Uninformed Customers and Nonprofit Organization: Modelling Contract Failure Theory." *Economics Letters* 35 (1): 5–8.

Cho, A. H. 2006. "Politics, Values and Social Entrepreneurship: A Critical Appraisal." In *Social Entrepreneurship*, edited by J. Mair, J. Robinson, and K. Hockerts, 34–56. Hampshire: Palgrave.

Connelly, B. L., R. D. Ireland, C. R. Reutzel, and J. E. Coombs. 2010. "The Power and Effects of Entrepreneurship Research." *Entrepreneurship Theory and Practice* 34 (1): 131–149.

Cornelissen, J. P., and J. S. Clarke. 2010. "Imagining and Rationalizing Opportunities: Inductive Reasoning and the Creation and Justification of New Ventures." *Academy of Management Review* 35 (4): 539–557.

Cornelius, N., M. Todres, S. Janjuha-Jivraj, A. Woods, and J. Wallace. 2008. "Corporate Social Responsibility and the Social Enterprise." *Journal of Business Ethics* 81 (2): 355–370.

Corner, P. D., and M. Ho. 2010. "How Opportunities Develop in Social Entrepreneurship." *Entrepreneurship Theory and Practice* 34 (4): 635–659.

Cosh, A., D. Cumming, and A. Hughes. 2009. "Outside Enterpreneurial Capital." *The Economic Journal* 119 (540): 1494–1533.

Crowdsourcing, O. 2012. *Crowdfunding Industry Report*. New York: Ellenoff Grossman & Schole LLP.

Cuervo Cazurra, A., and C. Annique Un. 2010. "Why Some Firms Never Invest in Formal R&D." *Strategic Management Journal* 31 (7): 759–779.

Cumming, D. 2012. *The Oxford Handbook of Entrepreneurial Finance*. Oxford: Oxford University Press.

Dacin, P. A., M. T. Dacin, and M. Matear. 2010. "Social Entrepreneurship: Why We Don't Need a New Theory and How We Move Forward From Here." *The Academy of Management Perspectives* 24 (3): 37–57.

Dart, R. 2004. "The Legitimacy of Social Enterprise." *Nonprofit Management and Leadership* 14 (4): 411–424.

Deakins, D., and G. Hussain. 1994. "Risk Assessment with Asymmetric Information." *International Journal of Bank Marketing* 12 (1): 24–31.

Defourny, J., and M. Nyssens. 2009a. "Conceptions of Social Enterprise and Social Entrepreneurship in Europe and the United States." Paper presented at the international conference on Social Enterprise, Trento, July 16.

Defourny, J., and M. Nyssens. 2009b. "Conceptions of Social Enterprise and Social Entrepreneurship in Europe and the United States: Convergences and Divergences." Paper presented at the second EMES international conference on Social Enterprise, in Trento, Italy.

Delanoë, S. 2011. "An Individual-Level Perspective for Assessing Nascent Venturing Outcomes." *Journal of Small Business and Enterprise Development* 18 (2): 232–250.

Di Domenico, M. L. 2009. "The Dialectic of Social Exchange: Theorising Corporate-Social Enterprise Collaboration." *Organization Studies* 30 (8): 887–907.

Di Domenico, M., H. Haugh, and P. Tracey. 2010. "Social Bricolage: Theorizing Social Value Creation in Social Enterprises." *Entrepreneurship Theory and Practice* 34 (4): 681–703.

Dobrow, S. R., D. E. Chandler, W. M. Murphy, and K. E. Kram. 2011. "A Review of Developmental Networks: Incorporating a Mutuality Perspective." *Journal of Management* 38 (1): 210–242.

Drayton, B. 2006. "Everyone a Changemaker: Social Entrepreneurship's Ulimate Goal." *Innovations* 1 (1): 80–96.

Drury, J., and S. Reicher. 1999. "The Intergroup Dynamics of Collective Empowerment: Substantiating the Social Identity Model of Crowd Behavior." *Group Processes & Intergroup Relations* 2 (4): 381–402.

Drury, J., and C. Stott. 2011. "Contextualising the Crowd in Contemporary Social Science." *Contemporary Social Science* 6 (3): 275–288.

Duckett, S., and H. Swerissen. 1996. "Specific Purpose Programs in Human Services and Health: Moving from an Input to an Output and Outcome Focus." *Australian Journal of Public Administration* 55 (3): 7–17.

Dushnitsky, G., and Z. Shapira. 2010. "Entrepreneurial Finance Meets Organizational Reality: Comparing Investment Practices and Performance of Corporate and Independent Venture Capitalists." *Strategic Management Journal* 31 (9): 990–1017.

Edmondson, A., and S. Mcmanus. 2007. "Methodological Fit in Management Field Research." *Academy of Management Review* 32 (4): 1155–1179.

Edwards, J. M., and M. E. J. M. Edwards. 2008. *Hybrid Organizations: Social Enterprise and Social Entrepreneurship*. Honolulu: Lulu.Com.

Ekedahl, M., and Y. Wengström. 2010. "Caritas, Spirituality and Religiosity in Nurses' Coping." *European Journal of Cancer Care* 19 (4): 530–537.

Esping-Andersen, G. 2006. "The Three Worlds of Welfare Capitalism." In *The Welfare State Reader*. 2nd ed. Cambridge: Polity Press.

Fairchild, R. 2011. "An Entrepreneur's Choice of Venture Capitalist or Angel-Financing: A Behavioral Game-Theoretic Approach." *Journal of Business Venturing* 26 (3): 359–374.

Fayolle, A., P. Kyro, and J. Ulijn. 2005. "The Entrepreneurship Debate in Europe: A Matter of History and Culture?" In *Entrepreneurship Research in Europe: Outcomes and Perspectives*, edited by A. Fayolle, P. Kyrö, and J. Ulijn, 1–34. Cheltenham: Edward Elgar Publishing Limited.

Fedele, A., and R. Miniaci. 2010. "Do Social Enterprises Finance Their Investments Differently from For-Profit Firms? The Case of Social Residential Services in Italy." *Journal of Social Entrepreneurship* 1 (2): 174–189.

Ferrera, M., A. Hemerijck, and M. Rhodes. 2004. *The Future of European Welfare States: Recasting Welfare for a New Century*. Oxford: Oxford University Press.

Firth, N. 2012. "Crowdfunding Successes Show Value of Small Donations." *The New Scientist* 213 (2858): 1–22.

Flockhart, A. 2005. "Raising the Profile of Social Enterprises: The Use of Social Return on Investment (SROI) and Investment Ready Tools (IRT) to Bridge the Financial Credibility Gap." *Social Enterprise Journal* 1 (1): 29–42.

Fox, S. 2012. "The New Do-It-Yourself Paradigm: Financial and Ethical Rewards for Businesses." *Journal of Business Strategy* 33 (1): 21–26.

Frumkin, P., and M. T. Kim. 2001. "Strategic Positioning and the Financing of Nonprofit Organizations: Is Efficiency Rewarded in the Contributions Marketplace?" *Public Administration Review* 61 (3): 266–275.

Fuglsang, L. 2010. "Bricolage and Invisible Innovation in Public Service Innovation." *Journal of Innovation Economics* 1 (5): 67–87.

Galera, G., and C. Borzaga. 2009. "Social Enterprise: An International Overview of Its Conceptual Evolution and Legal Implementation." *Social Enterprise Journal* 5 (3): 210–228.

Gallego-Álvarez, I., J. M. Prado-Lorenzo, and I.-M. García-Sánchez. 2011. "Corporate Social Responsibility and Innovation: A Resource-Based Theory." *Management Decision* 49 (10): 1709–1727.

Gundry, L. K., J. R. Kickul, M. D. Griffiths, and S. C. Bacq. 2011. "Creating Social Change Out of Nothing: The Role of Entrepreneurial Bricolage in Social Entrepreneurs' Catalytic Innovations." *Social and Sustainable Entrepreneurship* 13: 1–24.

Gunn, R., C. Durkin, G. Singh, and J. Brown. 2008. "Social Entrepreneurship in the Social Policy Curriculum." *Social Enterprise Journal* 4 (1): 74–80.

Hansmann, H. 1987. "Economic Theories of Nonprofit Organization." In *The Nonprofit Sector: A Research Handbook*, edited by W.W. Powell, 27–42. New Haven: Yale University Press.

Haugh, H. 2006. "Nonprofit Social Entrepreneurship." In *The Life Cycle of Entrepreneurial Ventures*, edited by S. Parker, 401–436. Cambridge: University of Cambridge.

Heminway, J., and S. Hoffman. 2010–2011. "Proceed at Your Peril: Crowdfunding and the Securities Act of 1933." *Tennessee Law Review* (78): 879–922.

Hennala, L., S. Parjanen, and T. Uotila. 2011. "Challenges of Multi-Actor Involvement in the Public Sector Front-End Innovation Processes: Constructing an Open Innovation Model for Developing Well-Being Services." *European Journal of Innovation Management* 14 (3): 364–387.

Heracleous, L., and L. L. Lan. 2012. "Agency Theory, Institutional Sensitivity, and Inductive Reasoning: Towards a Legal Perspective." *Journal of Management Studies* 49 (1): 223–239.

Herman, R., and D. Renz. 2008. "Advancing Nonprofit Organizational Effectiveness Research and Theory: Nine Theses." *Nonprofit Management and Leadership* 18 (4): 399–415.

Hill, T., T. Kothari, and M. Shea. 2010. "Patterns of Meaning in the Social Entrepreneurship Literature: A Research Platform." *Journal of Social Entrepreneurship* 1 (1): 5–31.

Hmieleski, K. M., and R. A. Baron. 2008. "Regulatory Focus and New Venture Performance: A Study of Entrepreneurial Opportunity Exploitation Under Conditions of Risk Versus Uncertainty." *Strategic Entrepreneurship Journal* 2 (4): 285–299.

Hoang, H., and B. Antoncic. 2003. "Network-Based Research in Entrepreneurship: A Critical Review." *Journal of Business Venturing* 18 (2): 165–187.

Hood, C. 2011. "Public Management Research on the Road from Consilience to Experimentation?" *Public Management Review* 13 (2): 321–326.

Hovakimian, A., T. Opler, and S. Titman. 2001. "The Debt-Equity Choice." *Journal of Financial and Quantitative Analysis* 36 (1): 1–24.

Howe, J. 2006. "The Rise of Crowdsourcing." *Wired Magazine* 14 (6): 1–4.

Huarng, K.-H., and T. H. -K. Yu. 2011. "Entrepreneurship, Process Innovation and Value Creation by a Non-Profit SME." *Management Decision* 49 (2): 284–296.

Husted, B. W. 2005. "Risk Management, Real Options, Corporate Social Responsibility." *Journal of Business Ethics* 60 (2): 175–183.

Hynes, B. 2009. "Growing the Social Enterprise – Issues and Challenges." *Social Enterprise Journal* 5 (2): 114–125.

Irwin, D., and J. M. Scott. 2010. "Barriers Faced by SMEs in Raising Bank Finance." *International Journal of Entrepreneurial Behaviour & Research* 16 (3): 245–259.

Ivancevic, V. G., D. J. Reid, and E. V. Aidman. 2010. "Crowd Behavior Dynamics: Entropic Path-Integral Model." *Nonlinear Dynamics* 59 (1): 351–373.

Janney, J. J., and S. Gove. 2011. "Reputation and Corporate Social Responsibility Aberrations, Trends, and Hypocrisy: Reactions to Firm Choices in the Stock Option Backdating Scandal." *Journal of Management Studies* 48 (7): 1562–1585.

Kerlin, J. 2006. "Social Enterprise in the United States and Europe: Understanding and Learning from the Differences." *Voluntas: International Journal of Voluntary and Nonprofit Organizations* 17 (3): 246–262.

Kirchhoff, K. R., and M. Piwinger. 2009. *Praxishandbuch Investor Relations: Das Standardwerk der Finanzkommunikation*. Wiesbaden: Gabler.

Kittur, A. 2010. "Crowdsourcing, Collaboration and Creativity." *XRDS* 17 (2): 22–26.

Kleemann, F., G. G. Voß, and K. Rieder. 2008. "Un (der) Paid Innovators: The Commercial Utilization of Consumer Work Through Crowdsourcing." *Science, Technology & Innovation Studies* 4 (1): 5–26.

Korsgaard, S. 2011. "Opportunity Formation in Social Entrepreneurship." *Journal of Enterprising Communities: People and Places in the Global Economy* 5 (4): 265–285.

Kozinets, R. V., A. Hemetsberger, and H. J. Schau. 2008. "The Wisdom of Consumer Crowds Collective Innovation in the Age of Networked Marketing." *Journal of Macromarketing* 28 (4): 339–354.

Kreiser, P. M., L. D. Marino, P. Dickson, and K. M. Weaver. 2010. "Cultural Influences on Entrepreneurial Orientation: The Impact of National Culture on Risk Taking and Proactiveness in SMES." *Entrepreneurship Theory and Practice* 34 (5): 959–983.

Kunc, M., and M. R. Bhandari. 2011. "Strategic Development Processes During Economic and Financial Crisis." *Management Decision* 49 (8): 1343–1353.

Lam, W. 2010. "Funding Gap, What Funding Gap? Financial Bootstrapping: Supply, Demand and Creation of Entrepreneurial Finance." *International Journal of Entrepreneurial Behaviour & Research* 16 (4): 268–295.

Lambert, R. A., C. Leuz, and R. E. Verrecchia. 2012. "Information Asymmetry, Information Precision, and the Cost of Capital." *Review of Finance* 16 (1): 1–29.

Lambert, T., and A. Schwienbacher. 2010. "An Empirical Analysis of Crowdfunding." Working Paper, University de Louvain France.

Laratta, R. 2010. "Ethical Climate in Nonprofit and Government Sectors: The Case of Japan." *Social Enterprise Journal* 6 (3): 225–249.

Larralde, B., and A. Schwienbacher. 2012. "Crowdfunding of Small Entrepreneurial Ventures." In *The Oxford Handbook of Entrepreneurial Finance*, edited by D. Cumming. Vol. 369. New York: Oxford University Press.

Lehner, O. M. 2004. "A Survey of Behavioral Finance." *Journal of Banking and Finance in Austria* 1 (2): 1–22.

Lehner, O. M. 2011a. "The Phenomenon of Social Enterprise in Austria: A Triangulated Descriptive Study." *Journal of Social Entrepreneurship* 2 (1): 53–78.

Lehner, O. M. 2011b. *Social Entrepreneurship Perspectives: Triangulated Approaches to Hybridity. Studies in Business and Economics*, edited by T. Tuomo. Vol. 111. Jyväskylä: JSBE.

Lehner, O. M., and J. Kaniskas. 2012. "Opportunity Recognition in Social Entrepreneurship: A Thematic Meta Analysis." *Journal of Entrepreneurship* 21 (1): 25–58.

Levander, U. 2010. "Social Enterprise: Implications of Emerging Institutionalized Constructions." *Journal of Social Entrepreneurship* 1 (2): 213–230.

Levitas, E., and T. Chi. 2010. "A Look at the Value Creation Effects of Patenting and Capital Investment Through a Real Options Lens: The Moderating Role of Uncertainty." *Strategic Entrepreneurship Journal* 4 (3): 212–233.

Lim, D. S. K., E. A. Morse, R. K. Mitchell, and K. K. Seawright. 2010. "Institutional Environment and Entrepreneurial Cognitions: A Comparative Business Systems Perspective." *Entrepreneurship Theory and Practice* 34 (3): 491–516.

Lumpkin, G. T. 2011. "From Legitimacy to Impact: Moving the Field Forward by Asking How Entrepreneurship Informs Life." *Strategic Entrepreneurship Journal* 5 (1): 3–9.

Mahmood, I. P., H. Zhu, and E. J. Zajac. 2011. "Where Can Capabilities Come From? Network Ties and Capability Acquisition in Business Groups." *Strategic Management Journal* 32 (8): 820–848.

Mair, J., and I. Marti. 2006. "Social Entrepreneurship Research: A Source of Explanation, Prediction, and Delight." *Journal of World Business* 41 (1): 36–44.

Mair, J., and I. Marti. 2009. "Entrepreneurship in and Around Institutional Voids: A Case Study from Bangladesh." *Journal of Business Venturing* 24 (5): 419–435.

Mair, J., and E. Noboa. 2006. "Social Entrepreneurship: How Intentions to Create a Social Venture Are Formed." In *Social Entrepreneurship*, edited by J. Mair, J. Robinson, and K. Hockerts, 121–135. New York: Palgrave Macmillan.

Martin, T. 2012. "The Jobs Act of 2012: Balancing Fundamental Securities Law Principals with the Demands of the Crowd." Available at SSRN 2040953.

Martinez, M. A., and H. E. Aldrich. 2011. "Networking Strategies for Entrepreneurs: Balancing Cohesion and Diversity." *International Journal of Entrepreneurial Behaviour & Research* 17 (1): 7–38.

Mason, C., J. Kirkbride, and D. Bryde. 2007. "From Stakeholders to Institutions: The Changing Face of Social Enterprise Governance Theory." *Management Decision* 45 (2): 284–301.

Massink, M., D. Latella, A. Bracciali, and J. Hillston. 2010. "Combined Process Algebraic, Agent and Fluid Flow Approach to Emergent Crowd Behaviour." CNR-ISTI Technical Report.

Mcwilliams, A., and D. S. Siegel. 2010. "Creating and Capturing Value: Strategic Corporate Social Responsibility, Resource-Based Theory, and Sustainable Competitive Advantage." *Journal of Management* 37 (5): 1480–1495.

Meuleman, M., K. Amess, M. Wright, and L. Scholes. 2009. "Agency, Strategic Entrepreneurship, and the Performance of Private Equity Backed Buyouts." *Entrepreneurship Theory and Practice* 33 (1): 213–239.

Meyer, M. 2009. "Wie viel wirtschaft verträgt die zivilgesellschaft? Über möglichkeiten und grenzen wirtschaftlicher rationalität in npos." In *Bürgergesellschaft als projekt*, edited by I. Bode, A. Evers, and A. Klein, 127–144. Wiesbaden: VS Verlag für Sozialwissenschaften.

Meyer, K. E., S. Estrin, S. K. Bhaumik, and M. W. Peng. 2009. "Institutions, Resources, and Entry Strategies in Emerging Economies." *Strategic Management Journal* 30 (1): 61–80.

Meyskens, M., C. Robb-Post, J. A. Stamp, A. L. Carsrud, and P. D. Reynolds. 2010. "Social Ventures from a Resource-Based Perspective: An Exploratory Study Assessing Global Ashoka Fellows." *Entrepreneurship Theory and Practice* 34 (4): 661–680.

Millo, Y., and D. Mackenzie. 2009. "The Usefulness of Inaccurate Models: Towards an Understanding of the Emergence of Financial Risk Management." *Accounting, Organizations and Society* 34 (5): 638–653.

Moss, T. W., J. C. Short, G. T. Payne, and G. Lumpkin. 2011. "Dual Identities in Social Ventures: An Exploratory Study." *Entrepreneurship Theory and Practice* 35 (4): 805–830.

Muller, A., and R. Kräussl. 2011. "Doing Good Deeds in Times of Need: A Strategic Perspective on Corporate Disaster Donations." *Strategic Management Journal* 32 (9): 911–929.

Murphy, P., and S. Coombes. 2009. "A Model of Social Entrepreneurial Discovery." *Journal of Business Ethics* 87 (3): 325–336.

Nicholls, A. 2009. "'We Do Good Things, Don't We?': 'Blended Value Accounting' in Social Entrepreneurship." *Accounting, Organizations and Society* 34 (6–7): 755–769.

Nicholls, A. 2010a. "The Institutionalization of Social Investment: The Interplay of Investment Logics and Investor Rationalities." *Journal of Social Entrepreneurship* 1 (1): 70–100.

Nicholls, A. 2010b. "Institutionalizing Social Entrepreneurship in Regulatory Space: Reporting and Disclosure by Community Interest Companies." *Accounting, Organizations and Society* 35 (4): 394–415.

Nicholls, A. 2010c. "The Legitimacy of Social Entrepreneurship: Reflexive Isomorphism in a Pre-Paradigmatic Field." *Entrepreneurship Theory and Practice* 34 (4): 611–633.

Nyssens, M., S. Adam, and T. Johnson. 2006. *Social Enterprise: At the Crossroads of Market, Public Policies and Civil Society Routledge Studies in the Management of Voluntary and Non-Profit Organizations*. London and New York: Routledge.

Palier, B. 2010. *A Long Goodbye to Bismarck?: The Politics of Welfare Reform in Continental Europe*. Amsterdam: Amsterdam University Press.

Parrino, R. J., and P. J. Romeo. 2012. "Jobs Act Eases Securities-Law Regulation of Smaller Companies." *Journal of Investment Compliance* 13 (3): 27–35.

Patriotta, G., J.-P. Gond, and F. Schultz. 2011. "Maintaining Legitimacy: Controversies, Orders of Worth, and Public Justifications." *Journal of Management Studies* 48 (8): 1804–1836.

Perry, J. T., G. N. Chandler, and G. Markova. 2012. "Entrepreneurial Effectuation: A Review and Suggestions for Future Research." *Entrepreneurship Theory and Practice* 36 (4): 837–861.

Pope, N. 2011. "Crowdfunding Microstartups: It's Time for the Securities and Exchange Commission to Approve a Small Offering Exemption." *Journal of Business Law* 13 (4): 973–1002.

Qiongzhi, L. 2007. "Efficiency Measurement and Quantity Optimization of Public Outcome: Based on Objective of Social Justice Output ." http://en.cnki.com.cn/Article_en/CJFDTOTAL-NDSP200702007.htm

Reyes, L. F. M., and S. Finken. 2012. "Social Media as a Platform for Participatory Design." In *Proceedings of the 12th Participatory Design Conference: Exploratory Papers, Workshop Descriptions, Industry Cases-Volume 2*, 89–92. ACM, Roskilde, Denmark, August 12–16.

Ridley-Duff, R. 2008. "Social Enterprise as a Socially Rational Business." *International Journal of Entrepreneurial Behaviour and Research* 14 (5): 291–312.

Ridley-Duff, R. 2009. "Co-Operative Social Enterprises: Company Rules, Access to Finance and Management Practice." *Social Enterprise Journal* 5 (1): 50–68.

Ridley-Duff, R. 2010. "Communitarian Governance in Social Enterprises: Case Evidence from the Mondragon Cooperative Corporation and School Trends Ltd." *Social Enterprise Journal* 6 (2): 125–145.

Robinson, J., ed. 2006. *Navigating Social and Institutional Barriers to Markets: How Social Entrepreneurs Identify and Evaluate Opportunities*. New York: Palgrave Macmillan.

Rubinton, B. J., 2011. "Crowdfunding: Disintermediated Investment Banking." http://ssrn.com/abstract=1807204

Ruebottom, T. 2011. "Counting Social Change: Outcome Measures for Social Enterprise." *Social Enterprise Journal* 7 (2): 173–182.

Ruvinsky, J. 2012. "Making Businesses More Responsible." *Stanford Social Innovation Review*, no. Winter 2012: 7–10.

Scarlata, M., and L. Alemany, eds. 2012. *Philantrohpic Venture Capital from a Global Perspective*. Oxford: Oxford University Press.

Scherpereel, C. M. 2008. "The Option Creating Institution: A Real Options Perspective on Economic Organization." *Strategic Management Journal* 29 (5): 455–470.

Schnatterly, K., K. W. Shaw, and W. W. Jennings. 2008. "Information Advantages of Large Institutional Owners." *Strategic Management Journal* 29 (2): 219.

Schwienbacher, A., and B. Larralde. 2010. "Crowdfunding of small entrepreneurial ventures." In *The Oxford Handbook of Entrepreneurial Finance*, edited by Douglas Cumming, 369–392. Oxford: Oxford University Press.

SEC (Social Enterprise Coalition). 2004. *Unlocking the Potential: A Guide to Finance for Social Enterprises*. London: Social Enterprise Coalition.

Seghers, A., S. Manigart, and T. Vanacker. 2012. "The Impact of Human and Social Capital on Entrepreneurs' Knowledge of Finance Alternatives." *Journal of Small Business Management* 50 (1): 63–86.

SEL (Social Enterprise London). 2001. *Introducing Social Enterprise*. London: Social Enterprise London.

Sharfman, M. P., and C. S. Fernando. 2008. "Environmental Risk Management and the Cost of Capital." *Strategic Management Journal* 29 (6): 569–592.

Shaw, E., and S. Carter. 2007. "Social Entrepreneurship: Theoretical Antecedents and Empirical Analysis of Entrepreneurial Processes and Outcomes." *Journal of Small Business and Enterprise Development* 14 (3): 418–434.

Shleifer, A. 2000. *Inefficient Markets: An Introduction to Behavioral Finance*. Oxford: Oxford University Press.

Short, J., D. Ketchen, C. Shook, and R. Ireland. 2010. "The Concept of "Opportunity" in Entrepreneurship Research: Past accomplishments and Future Challenges." *Journal of Management* 36 (1): 40–65.

Singer, P., and C. Cacia. 2009. "The Role of Web Investor Relations for Mitigating and Manage Stock Exchange Liquidity and Enterprise Risks." Paper presented at 9th Global Conference on Business & Economics, Cambridge University, UK. October 16–17.

Soh, P. H. 2010. "Network Patterns and Competitive Advantage Before the Emergence of a Dominant Design." *Strategic Management Journal* 31 (4): 438–461.

Sullivan, D. M., and M. R. Marvel. 2011. "Knowledge Acquisition, Network Reliance, and Early-Stage Technology Venture Outcomes." *Journal of Management Studies* 48 (6): 1169–1193.

Tong, T. W., and J. J. Reuer. 2007. "Real Options in Strategic Management." *Advances in Strategic Management* 24: 3–28.

Travaglini, C. 2009. "Social Enterprise in Europe: Governance Models." In *Second EMES International Conference on Social Enterprise*. Trento: EMES.

Vaccaro, I. G., J. J. P. Jansen, F. A. J. Van Den Bosch, and H. W. Volberda. 2012. "Management Innovation and Leadership: The Moderating Role of Organizational Size." *Journal of Management Studies* 49 (1): 28–51.

Valenzuela, S., A. Arriagada, and A. Scherman. 2012. "The Social Media Basis of Youth Protest Behavior: The Case of Chile." *Journal of Communication* 62 (2): 299–314.

Van Slyke, D. M. 2006. "Agents or Stewards: Using Theory to Understand the Government-Nonprofit Social Service Contracting Relationship." *Journal of Public Administration Research and Theory* 17 (2): 157–187.

Wang, H., and S. S. Lim. 2008. "Real Options and Real Value: The Role of Employee Incentives to Make Specific Knowledge Investments." *Strategic Management Journal* 29 (7): 701–721.

Ward, C., and V. Ramachandran. 2010. "Crowdfunding the Next Hit: Microfunding Online Experience Goods." Paper presented at Computational Social Science and the Wisdom of Crowds, Whistler, Canada, December 10.

Whitla, P. 2009. "Crowdsourcing and Its Application in Marketing Activities." *Contemporary Management Research* 5 (1): 15–28.

Williamson, O. E. 1988. "Corporate Finance and Corporate Governance." *Journal of Finance* 43 (3): 567–591.

Yunus, M., and K. Weber. 2007. *Creating a World Without Poverty: Social Business and the Future of Capitalism*. New York: Public Affairs.

Zahra, S., E. Gedajlovic, D. Neubaum, and J. Shulman. 2009. "A Typology of Social Entrepreneurs: Motives, Search Processes and Ethical Challenges." *Journal of Business Venturing* 24 (5): 519–532.

Zahra, S., H. Rawhouser, N. Bhawe, D. Neubaum, and J. Hayton. 2008. "Globalization of Social Entrepreneurship Opportunities." *Strategic Entrepreneurship Journal* 2 (2): 117–131.

# Individual crowdfunding practices

Paul Belleflamme[a,b,c], Thomas Lambert[b,d] and Armin Schwienbacher[d]

[a]Center for Operations Research and Econometrics, Université catholique de Louvain, Louvain-la-Neuve, Belgium; [b]Louvain School of Management, Université catholique de Louvain, Louvain-la-Neuve, Belgium; [c]CESifo Research Network, Munich, Germany; [d]Université Lille Nord de France – SKEMA Business School, Lille, France

This study investigates characteristics of individual crowdfunding practices and drivers of fundraising success, where entrepreneurs can tailor their crowdfunding initiatives better than on standardized platforms. Our data indicate that most of the funds provided are entitled to receive either financial compensations (equity and profit-share arrangement) or nonfinancial benefits (final product and token of appreciation), while donations are less common. Moreover, crowdfunding initiatives that are structured as nonprofit organizations tend to be significantly more successful than other organizational forms in achieving their fundraising targets, even after controlling for various project characteristics. This finding is in line with theoretical arguments developed by the contract failure literature which postulates that nonprofit organizations may find it easier to attract money for initiatives that are of interest for the general community due to their reduced focus on profits.

## 1 Introduction

What determines the success chances of entrepreneurs to reach their capital targets through crowdfunding? Crowdfunding changes sharply how capital is allocated and represents a viable alternative in channeling outside capital to entrepreneurial ventures. Furthermore, the amount raised through crowdfunding increased dramatically in recent years.[1] Crowdfunding helped to raise about \$1.5 billion of capital in 2011, according to a global survey conducted by *Crowdsourcing.org*.[2] However, little is known about the characteristics of crowdfunding practices and which practices are associated with fundraising success.[3]

In this study, we derive characteristics of *individual crowdfunding* practices by means of hand-collected data of 44 initiatives and then we examine drivers of fundraising success. We deliberately excluded initiatives launched using crowdfunding platforms since they have received greater attention in the literature (see, e.g., Agrawal, Catalini, and Goldfarb 2011; Hildebrand, Puri, and Rocholl 2011). In our context, individual crowdfunding practices relate to practices in which entrepreneurs do not make use of a 'structured' crowdfunding platform – such as *Kickstarter, RocketHub, IndieGoGo, MyMajorCompany*, and *Prosper* – to fund their venture. In such platforms, the process of raising funds is standardized, in

---

A previous version of the paper circulated with the title 'An Empirical Analysis of Crowdfunding'.

contrast to individual initiatives where entrepreneurs can shape the process according to their specific needs. As will become clear below, this enables entrepreneurs to offer a greater variety of compensation to the crowd, including active involvement into the process itself.

Our hand-collected data are helpful in providing a better understanding of how such individual practices are structured and what motivates them. Perhaps surprisingly, only a limited fraction of initiatives is based on donations. In 91% of cases, crowdfunders receive either nonfinancial benefits (e.g., token of appreciation and right to receive the venture's product) or financial compensation (e.g., equity, revenue, and profit-share arrangements) in return for financial contributions. Individual crowdfunding initiatives take the form of pre-ordering of the product in more than one-third of our sample. Interestingly, nonprofit entrepreneurs represent 10% of individual initiatives covered by our study, while 36% of initiatives take place as a company.

In more than one-third of cases, crowdfunders' investments may be qualified as 'active', in the sense of financial contribution with a promise of compensation in addition to direct involvement in the venture they fund. This is a specific feature of individual practices where the crowdfunding process can be tailor-made. Direct involvement – for instance, participation in the decision-making, provision of time and expertise – allows entrepreneurs to extract more easily additional value from crowdfunders. This may in turn increase the level of community benefits provided to crowdfunders. We illustrate this with the following examples. The South African singer, *Verity Price*, produced her album through her own crowdfunding campaign. She set up a website where over 2000 crowdfunders participated in the creative content of her album by having a say regarding, e.g., songs recorded and artworks used. The crowdfunders of *MyFootballClub* are actively associated with the management of their football club by voting, among others, on budget, club officials, kit supplier contracts, and transfer deals. Furthermore, the crowdfunders' community is able to raise new ideas for activities at the club that are discussed and subject to approval via a vote by the community.

Another point worth stressing is that crowdfunding seems to involve relatively small amounts of capital. Although entrepreneurs raised on average around €150,000 from their crowdfunding campaign, the distribution is skewed; the median amount is merely around €6400. For the sake of comparison, seed capital invested by business angels is typically between $25,000 and $500,000, and deals involved by venture capitalists can be even larger (Linde and Prasad 2000).[4] In the theoretical part of this paper (see Section 4), we rationalize this stylized fact as follows. Compared with traditional funding, crowdfunding has the advantage of offering an enhanced experience to crowdfunders and, thereby, of allowing the entrepreneur to practice a behavior-based price discrimination and extract a larger share of the crowdfunder surplus; the disadvantage is that the entrepreneur is constrained in her choice of prices by the amount of capital that she needs to raise: the larger this amount, the more prices have to be twisted so as to attract a large number of crowdfunders in the first period, and the less profitable the price discrimination scheme.

In addition, entrepreneurs' motivations in using crowdfunding are further examined through a questionnaire sent to entrepreneurs of individually crowdfunded venture. This survey highlights, in particular, the significant role played by crowdfunding campaigns in getting public attention on the venture and/or on its products.

Finally, we examine what drives the success chances of crowdfunding. This is done through multivariate analyses. A striking result is that nonprofit organizations are significantly more likely to achieve their target level of capital in comparison with other organizational forms such as a corporation and freelance. This result appears robust to different econometric specifications. This finding is consistent with the notion that nonprofit entrepreneurs find it easier to attract capital by donors and other sources, since their focus is not purely profit-driven (Glaeser and Shleifer 2001). As theoretically shown in the latter paper, profit-driven organizations may be prone to focus too much on profits at the expense of other dimensions such as quality of the product or service provided. This in turn may not be desired by donors and other sources aimed at fostering specific initiatives.

We structure the paper as follows. The following section reviews the related literature. Section 3.1 discusses data collection and defines the variables used. Section 3.2 describes key characteristics of individual crowdfunding practices, based on our hand-collected data-set. Section 4 presents a model of individual crowdfunding pratices based on a simple extension of Belleflamme, Lambert, and Schwienbacher (2012; henceforth referred to as BLS). Section 5 provides the results of multivariate analyses on the determinants of crowdfunding success. Finally, Section 6 concludes.

## 2 Related literature

The literature on crowdfunding, and especially on individual crowdfunding practices, is still embryonic. BLS (2012) compare two dominant forms of individual crowdfunding practices (as shown in Section 3.1), where crowdfunders are offered either to pre-order the product or to advance an amount of money in exchange for a share of future profits. In either form, crowdfunders enjoy a community-based experience that confers them extra utility (community benefits) with respect to other consumers or investors. The authors show that entrepreneurs prefer pre-ordering if the initial capital requirement is relatively small, and the profit-sharing for larger capital amount. Their conclusions come from the crucial role played by the kind of community benefits that both forms of crowdfunding confer. In their case analysis of an equity-based individually crowdfunded start-up, Schwienbacher and Larralde (2012) also stressed the need for building a community of crowdfunders which enjoys additional utility from their participation. Both papers have implications for entrepreneurial ventures in attracting outside finance at their initial stage, beside other financing sources such as banks, friends & family, business angels, or even venture capital.

The literature on crowdfunding also extends to the study of platforms. Agrawal, Catalini, and Goldfarb (2011) study the geographic dispersion of investors in an online crowdfunding platform that enables musicians to raise money to produce their album. Although the geographic distance between the entrepreneur and the investors increases, they find that geography still plays a role at early financing stages. Along the same lines, Ward and Ramachandran (2010) estimate the extent to which demand for crowdfunding projects is driven by peer effects. They show that crowdfunders are influenced by the success or failure of related projects and use the actions of other crowdfunders as a source of information in their funding decisions.[5]

As mentioned in Section 1, *Crowdsourcing.org* provided an early survey analysis of crowdfunding platforms. They estimated the size of the crowdfunding market at $1.5 billion in 2011. Although somewhat impressive, the size of the crowdfunding market remains relatively smaller than other sources. The Global Entrepreneurship Monitor (GEM) 2009 report assessed the size of informal investment (i.e., entrepreneurs themselves, friends & family, and business angels) at 11.3% of Gross Domestic Product in China, 1.5% in the USA, and 0.8% in France, among others.[6] According to the GEM report, informal investment is far more important than venture capital (see also Wong 2010).

Most strikingly, this survey conducted by *Crowdsourcing.org* shows that equity-based crowdfunding models tend to raise larger amount of capital than reward-based crowdfunding models,[7] which is in line with BLS's (2012) predictions. However, reward-based models represent the majority of platforms.

Mollick (2012) provides another empirical study aiming at understanding the underlying dynamics of the recent rise of crowdfunding. Using data from *Kickstarter* (the largest crowdfunding platform at this date), the author examines, like us, the determinants of success in crowdfunding ventures, as well as their geographic distribution. Among the chances of success that the study highlights are the networks of founders and also the signals of the underlying quality of the project. Intermediary crowdfunding platforms, such as *Kickstarter*, are particularly helpful in these two matters. In contrast, individual entrepreneurs who launch their own crowdfunding initiatives, like the ones we consider in this paper, have a harder time in activating a network or in signaling the quality of their projects. This explains why these two variables are absent from our analysis. On the other hand, as individual crowdfunding initiatives are not as standardized as intermediated ones, entrepreneurs have a wider array of available strategies; this allows us to include into our analysis other variables related to the interaction between the entrepreneur and the crowd.

Finally, when crowdfunding practices emerge in nonprofit organizations, they can be related to the strand of the literature devoted to choice of an organizational form (for-profit vs nonprofit). Ghatak and Mueller (2011) develop a theoretical framework of labor donation theory to investigate under which conditions nonprofit organizations can provide a better alternative to motivated workers than other forms of organization. Their results built on Glaeser and Shleifer (2001), whose work models the incentives of an entrepreneur who chooses between a for-profit and nonprofit organizational form. Rooted in the contract failure literature, Glaeser and Shleifer (2001) argue that profit incentives might lead to undesirable outcomes from the point of view of donors who value the noncontractible outcome of the entrepreneurial venture. Motivating an agent on a contractible task (effort in reducing costs or boosting output) might lead to undesirable outcomes since another noncontractible task (effort in enhancing quality) might be neglected. They show that nonprofit is attractive for entrepreneurs because lower financial incentives in the nonprofit is compensated for by the increase in donations (see Bilodeau and Slivinski [2004] for a similar argument).

## 3 Empirical analysis of individual crowdfunding practices

In this section, we first describe our data-set and the variables that we use; then, we report a number of summary statistics.

### 3.1 *Data collection and variables*

To shed light on the structure and characteristics of individual crowdfunding practices, we hand-collected data from various sources on all crowdfunding initiatives that we could possibly identify on the Internet. Data collection took place at the end of 2009 and early 2010. Since there was no database available or even listing of individual initiatives, we relied on the Internet to construct our sample. One advantage is that entrepreneurs using crowdfunding as a way to collect funds typically use the Internet to do so, as well as social networks and blogs. This helped us identify cases to construct our sample.

Our focus is on individually crowdfunded ventures, which excludes all initiatives made by crowdfunding platforms. The identification of entrepreneurs relying on crowdfunding has been done in two steps. Initially, we made the Internet research on individually crowdfunded ventures that are explicitly associated with the word of 'crowdfunding'. This search did not allow us to find a sufficient number of such entrepreneurs. In a second step, we decided to revisit the definition of crowdfunding.[8] That is, we selected all entrepreneurs who use the Web 2.0 to generate funds for their investments via a large number of Internet users. This step was essential because some entrepreneurs have recourse to crowdfunding without knowing that their own fundraising is a kind of 'crowdfunding'. In total, we identified 69 cases and we managed to collect sufficient (but still partially incomplete) information on 44 of them.

We also complemented our data-set through a questionnaire sent to the 69 cases identified, during the months of December 2009 and January 2010. In total, we received 19 completed questionnaires (some only partially). The response rate in this survey is therefore around 32%. Despite the high response rate, the total sample remains relatively small, which inevitably raises some statistical concerns. In particular, this may induce some small-sample bias for which it is difficult to control; however, crowdfunding is a nascent phenomenon so that our data-set of 44 initiatives converges towards the entire population at the beginning of 2010.

All the variables employed in the analysis are defined in Table 1. We use two measures that reflect the funding outcome: *funds raised* is the total funds raised by the entrepreneur since the starting date of her crowdfunding campaign; and *success*, which scales *funds raised* by the amount of funds targeted. These variables capture the extent to which the personal crowdfunding campaign of an entrepreneur is successful. We then identify the type of organizational form adopted by the entrepreneur. Dummy variables *company* and *nonprofit* capture the type of organizational form – namely for-profit company and nonprofit association, respectively; other organizational forms (observed but not measured) are typically freelance and project-based initiatives. More precisely, *company* and *nonprofit* differ on the use of profits. The former may distribute them to persons who exercise control over the firm (e.g., limited liabilities companies), while the latter barred from distributing them to their controlling members or boards (e.g., charitable foundations and NGOs). Nonprofit organizations may instead use profits as perquisites and, so, do not allow enrichment from persons exercising control over the organization.[9]

We include in our analysis a set of variables reflecting key characteristics of individual crowdfunding practices: *pre-ordering* is equal to one if the entrepreneur presales the product/service before production takes place; *active implication* is equal to one if crowdfunders are involved in the venture they fund in one way or another (e.g., in the management and in the creative process); *social networks* is equal to one if at least one online social network or blog is used by the entrepreneur besides her own website; *product* is equal to one if the entrepreneur provides a product as opposed to a service; and *number of crowdfunders* is the number of crowdfunders having participated in the funding of the venture.

To explore the influence of the type of crowdfunding model, we include three dummy variables capturing whether the individual crowdfunding practice is equity-, reward-, or donation-based. This is the same classification adopted in the report of *Crowdsourcing.org*. Equity-based crowdfunding is defined as a model in which crowdfunders receive a financial compensation (e.g., equity, revenue, and profit-share arrangements). In contrast, reward-based crowdfunding allows crowdfunders to receive a nonfinancial benefit in return to their financial contributions (e.g., credit on an album, pre-ordering of products or services). In donation-based crowdfunding, crowdfunders make only donation without any kind of return.[10] We therefore differentiate the type of organizational form from the crowdfunding model, which is defined below. That is, nonprofit organizations do not imply necessarily donation-based crowdfunding model,

Table 1. Definition of variables.

| Variable | Definition |
|---|---|
| **Funding outcome:** | |
| Funds raised | Total funds raised (in at 2009 market prices) by the entrepreneur between the starting date of her crowdfunding campaign until the beginning of 2010. |
| Funds targeted | Total funds expected initially (in € at 2009 market prices) from the crowdfunding campaign by the entrepreneur. |
| Success | Ratio of *funds raised* to *funds targeted*. |
| **Organizational form:** | |
| Nonprofit | Dummy = 1 if entrepreneur is working on behalf of a nonprofit-making association. |
| Company | Dummy = 1 if the crowdfunding initiative is structured as a company. |
| **Crowdfunding characteristics:** | |
| Pre-ordering | Dummy = 1 if entrepreneurs presale the product/service before production takes place. |
| Active implication | Dummy = 1 if crowdfunders are involved in any way whatsoever in the venture they fund. |
| Social networks | Dummy = 1 if at least one of the following communication methods is used: Facebook, Twitter, blogs, LinkedIn, MySpace; these methods are characterized by facilitating social networking. |
| Product | Dummy = 1 if the goal of the venture is the making of a product (conversely a service). |
| Number of crowdfunders | Total number of crowdfunders per 100 crowdfunders. |
| **Crowdfunding models:** | |
| Equity-based model | Dummy = 1 if crowdfunders receive compensation in the form of equity in the venture they fund, revenue, or profit-share arrangements. |
| Reward-based model | Dummy = 1 if crowdfunders receive a nonfinancial benefit in return for financial contributions. Nonfinancial benefits often take the form of a token of appreciation or the pre-ordering of products or services. |
| Donation-based model | Dummy = 1 if crowdfunders make only donation without any kind of return (i.e., philanthropic or sponsorship-based incentive). |
| **Date of establishment and start of crowdfunding campaign:** | |
| Starting year | Year at which the crowdfunding campaign started. |
| Starting after 2007 | Dummy = 1 if the crowdfunding campaign started in 2007 or later. |
| Age | The time span between the starting date of the crowdfunding campaign and the establishment date of the organizational form. |
| **Country of registration:** | |
| USA | Dummy = 1 if the registered office of entrepreneur is located in the USA. |
| Europe | Dummy = 1 if the registered office of entrepreneur is located in a European country. |

and vice versa. Nonprofit organizations may indeed reward their crowdfunders through nonfinancial compensation.

Another category captures the age of the crowdfunding practice. We identify the year at which the crowdfunding campaign started by the inclusion of the variable *starting year*. The variable *starting after 2007* is equal to one if the crowdfunding campaign does not start prior 2007, and zero otherwise. *Age* measures the time span between the starting date of the crowdfunding campaign and the establishment date of the organizational form. Finally, we look at the region of the world where the registered office of the entrepreneurial venture is located with the inclusion of the following dummies: *USA* and *Europe*; other regions are captured in the constant.

## 3.2   *Characteristics of individual crowdfunding practices*

Table 2 reports summary statistics (in Panel A) and survey outputs (in Panel B). Not surprisingly, summary statistics confirm that crowdfunding is a recent phenomenon. Over 84% of the entrepreneurs have used crowdfunding for their venture most recently only (variable *starting after 2007*), i.e., since 2007. Entrepreneurs start on average their crowdfunding campaign 1.5 years after having started their business/activity (mean value of *age* equals 1.54). Thirty percent of entrepreneurs are from the USA and 55% from Europe.

In terms of funding outcome, entrepreneurs have raised on average around €150,000 through their individual crowdfunding campaign; the median value is however substantially lower, namely close to €6400. Hence, amounts pledged by crowdfunders remain rather limited as compared with business angels or venture capitalists (e.g., Linde and Prasad 2000). Although the large discrepancy observed between the minimum and the maximum amount raised via crowdfunding, entrepreneurs have reached on average 62% of the amount they initially targeted.

Of interest are also the organizational forms adopted by entrepreneurs resorting to crowdfunding: 10% of crowdfunding initiatives are nonprofit organizations, while 36% are structured as a company; the remaining initiatives (representing 54% of our sample) stem from entrepreneurs who have recourse to crowdfunding, for instance, as freelance or in connection with a specific project only.

Interestingly, in 36% of cases, crowdfunders are offered to pre-order the product or the service. In more than one-third of our sample, crowdfunders act as active players in the venture they fund through involvement in the creative process, in the decision-making, or in various operating tasks. This variable *active implication* captures crucial characteristics of individual practices. On the one hand, active involvement by the crowd may increase the level of community benefits. On the other hand, the entrepreneurs' preference for individual crowdfunding practice as compared with standardized crowdfunding platform may be motivated by its ability to extract value from crowdfunders more easily. Indeed, it allows the entrepreneurs to involve their crowdfunders in tasks with value added – such as time and expertise – whose implementation via a standardized platform is not adapted whereas the flexibility of the individual practice makes it possible.

Regarding media usage, 78% of entrepreneurs used specific communication methods that facilitate social networking. The goal of the venture is the making of a product in half the initiatives. It is worth noting that individual crowdfunding initiatives attracted the participation of about 1700 crowdfunders on average.

Our study distinguishes different crowdfunding models. Pure donation constitutes 9% of our sample. Other models provide (financial or nonfinancial) return to their crowdfunders. The equity-based crowdfunding model is used in 30% of the cases, whereas reward-based crowdfunding model is adopted in 61% of the cases. This pattern is in line with the survey conducted by *Crowdsourcing.org*.

Our survey provides further characteristics. Panel B of Table 2 depicts that 63.2% of individual crowdfunding practices are managed by a single founder, 15.8% by two founders, and 21.1% by three founders (the highest number of founders observed in our sample). Seventy percent of these founders hold a university degree, while 10% are still attending university.

Table 2.  Characteristics of crowdfunded projects: summary statistics and survey output.

*Panel A: summary statistics*

| Variables | Mean | SD | Median | Min. | Max. | No of obs. |
|---|---|---|---|---|---|---|
| Funding outcome: | | | | | | |
| Funds raised | 149,406.10 | 307,682.30 | 6431.13 | 35.73 | 1,123,563.00 | 30 |
| Funds targeted | 596,286.90 | 1,045,869.00 | 90,000.00 | 59.55 | 5,359,272.00 | 35 |
| Success | 0.62 | 0.85 | 0.43 | 0.00 | 4.50 | 30 |
| Organizational form: | | | | | | |
| Nonprofit | 0.10 | 0.29 | 0.00 | 0.00 | 1.00 | 44 |
| Company | 0.36 | 0.49 | 0.00 | 0.00 | 1.00 | 44 |
| Crowdfunding characteristics: | | | | | | |
| Pre-ordering | 0.36 | 0.49 | 0.00 | 0.00 | 1.00 | 44 |
| Active implication | 0.36 | 0.49 | 0.00 | 0.00 | 1.00 | 44 |
| Social networks | 0.78 | 0.42 | 1.00 | 0.00 | 1.00 | 44 |
| Product | 0.50 | 0.51 | 0.50 | 0.00 | 1.00 | 44 |
| Number of crowdfunders | 17.27 | 43.51 | 0.80 | 0.03 | 210 | 31 |
| Crowdfunding models: | | | | | | |
| Equity-based model | 0.30 | 0.46 | 0.00 | 0.00 | 1.00 | 44 |
| Reward-based model | 0.61 | 0.49 | 1.00 | 0.00 | 1.00 | 44 |
| Donation-based model | 0.09 | 0.29 | 0.00 | 0.00 | 1.00 | 44 |
| Date of establishment and start of crowdfunding campaign: | | | | | | |
| Starting year | 2007.84 | 1.67 | 2008 | 2002 | 2009 | 32 |
| Starting after 2007 | 0.84 | 0.37 | 1.00 | 0.00 | 1.00 | 32 |
| Age | 1.54 | 2.23 | 1.00 | 0.00 | 9.00 | 26 |
| Country of registration: | | | | | | |
| USA | 0.30 | 0.46 | 0.00 | 0.00 | 1.00 | 44 |
| Europe | 0.55 | 0.50 | 1.00 | 0.00 | 1.00 | 44 |

*Panel B: additional statistics based on survey output*

| Questions | Answers (%) | No of obs. |
|---|---|---|
| *1. Number of founders* | | |
| One founder only | 63.2% | 19 |
| Two founders exactly | 15.8% | 19 |
| Three founders exactly | 21.1% | 19 |
| *2. Question: 'Do founders hold a university degree?'*[a] | | |
| Yes | 70.0% | 19 |
| No | 20.0% | 19 |
| Still attending university | 10.0% | 19 |

*3. Question: 'Do crowdfunders expect to receive return or reward from their investment?'*

| | |
|---|---|
| Yes | 76.5% | 17 |
| No, they only make a donation | 23.5% | 17 |

*3. bis. Sub-question: 'If yes, what kind?'*

| | | |
|---|---|---|
| Direct cash payment (other than dividends from shares) | 22.2% | 9 |
| Shares/stock, including dividends in the future | 33.3% | 9 |
| Right to receive own product | 66.7% | 9 |
| Other | 66.7% | 9 |

*4. Question: 'If you give investors shares, do you allocate using voting rights to them?'*

| | | |
|---|---|---|
| Yes | 18.2% | 11 |
| No | 81.8% | 11 |

*5. Question: 'If other sources of finance than crowdfunding are used, please specify which one(s).'*

| | | |
|---|---|---|
| Bank loan | 0.0% | 9 |
| Contributions from family and/or friends | 18.8% | 9 |
| Business angel | 18.8% | 9 |
| Founder's own money | 25.0% | 9 |
| Government subsidy | 18.8% | 9 |
| Other | 43.8% | 9 |

*6. Question: 'What constitutes your main motivations for using crowdfunding?'[a,b]*

| | High relevant | Relevant | Neutral | Somewhat relevant | Not relevant at all |
|---|---|---|---|---|---|
| Raise money | 92.9% | 7.1% | 0.0% | 0.0% | 0.0% |
| Getting public attention for my company/project | 64.3% | 21.4% | 7.1% | 0.0% | 7.1% |
| Validate my product/service before selling it (market survey) | 35.7% | 21.4% | 7.1% | 0.0% | 35.7% |

Note: All the variables in Panel A are defined in Table 1. Information shown in Panel B was collected through the survey.
[a] If more than one founder involved, we consider each founder separately.
[b] No of obs. = 14 for all the three motivations listed. Respondents could also cite other motivations; they are not listed here explicitly.

Raising money was a strong motivation for all respondents, getting public attention was relevant (or highly relevant) for over 85%, and obtaining feedback for the product/ service offered was relevant (or highly relevant) for about 60% of the respondents. Many of them combine crowdfunding with other sources of finance, notably with own money, friends & family money, business angel and government subsidy. Consistently with Panel A, 76.5% offer their crowdfunders a reward, mostly in the form of right to receive the product (66.7% of the cases of these 76.5% of the sample) or shares that may yield dividends in the future (33.3%). Direct cash payment is expected in 22.2% of the cases where a reward/return is promised. We note that, in 66.7% of the cases, other forms of reward are offered, e.g., being credited on an album or a film, receiving the possibility to transfer money to a charity of one's choice.

Several of these variables are correlated with each other, as evidenced in Table 3. While some correlations are intuitive, others are worth being discussed. Individual crowdfunding initiatives taking place as a company tend to involve more often active implication from crowdfunders; companies are more likely to enable crowdfunders to provide input or vote on the project. One possible reason is that projects done outside a company may be smaller and simpler; also, interacting with the crowd for a particular task requires an organizational structure that companies possess. This correlation is also in line with the notion that investors may require more control than for other organizational forms; our simple correlation, however, does not offer any conclusive evidence on whether this is actually a main driver. Conversely, nonprofit organizations offer active involvements of crowdfunders less often; this lends to think that their projects require little input from crowdfunders; also, conversely to companies, crowdfunders may put more trust into nonprofit organizations; but again, this claim is highly speculative here. An interesting positive correlation exists between *active implication* and *reward-based model*, whereas the correlation is negative with *equity-based model*. This suggests that reward-based models are more conducive to integrate crowdfunders within the organization than equity-based models.

Lastly, Table 3 shows that the correlation between *company* and *funds raised* is positive and statistically significant, suggesting that companies tend to generate higher amounts of money from their crowdfunding campaign. Compellingly, the variable *success* is positive and significantly correlated with the dummy variable *nonprofit*. Though suggestive, this evidence does not allow us to ascertain that nonprofit organizations are drivers of success of crowdfunding initiatives and even less to say something on the channel through which nonprofit organizations operate as drivers of success. The following two sections explore these issues further, respectively, from theoretical and empirical viewpoints.

## 4  Theoretical framework

In this section, we propose a simple theoretical model that allows us to explain why *nonprofit organizations may be more successful in using crowdfunding* while incorporating important findings of the survey analysis as ingredients for the modeling set-up. We also compare the choice of opting for crowdfunding with the outcome of traditional funding, in order to investigate scenarios in which crowdfunding is an optimal choice for entrepreneurs. The model is adapted from BLS (2012) where it is assumed that the crowdfunders enjoy some additional utility with respect to the other consumers of the venture's product. This assumption reflects the fact (which we have amply documented above) that entrepreneurs resorting to crowdfunding use the Internet to maintain an interaction with their funders so as to provide them with so-called 'community benefits'. Moreover, we incorporate the

Table 3. Correlation matrix.

| | (1) | (2) | (3) | (4) | (5) | (6) | (7) | (8) | (9) | (10) | (11) | (12) |
|---|---|---|---|---|---|---|---|---|---|---|---|---|
| (1) Funds raised | 1.00 | | | | | | | | | | | |
| (2) Success | 0.32* | 1.00 | | | | | | | | | | |
| (3) Nonprofit | 0.02 | 0.49*** | 1.00 | | | | | | | | | |
| (4) Company | 0.68*** | −0.01 | −0.24 | 1.00 | | | | | | | | |
| (5) Active implication | 0.16 | −0.08 | −0.24 | 0.41*** | 1.00 | | | | | | | |
| (6) Social networks | 0.03 | 0.07 | −0.02 | 0.13 | 0.01 | 1.00 | | | | | | |
| (7) Product | 0.31* | 0.29 | 0.00 | 0.09 | 0.00 | 0.07 | 1.00 | | | | | |
| (8) Number of crowdfunders | 0.36* | 0.27 | 0.17 | 0.35* | 0.38** | −0.25 | −0.07 | 1.00 | | | | |
| (9) Equity-based model | 0.20 | 0.01 | −0.20 | 0.03 | −0.28* | 0.23 | −0.15 | −0.31* | 1.00 | | | |
| (10) Reward-based model | −0.11 | 0.01 | −0.24 | 0.11 | 0.41*** | −0.09 | 0.14 | 0.34* | −0.82*** | 1.00 | | |
| (11) Donation-based model | −0.15 | −0.03 | 0.73*** | −0.24 | −0.24 | −0.22 | 0.00 | −0.06 | −0.20 | −0.40*** | 1.00 | |
| (12) Age | 0.42* | −0.08 | 0.14 | −0.03 | −0.39** | −0.25 | 0.11 | −0.30 | 0.05 | −0.19 | 0.19 | 1.00 |

Notes: All the variables are defined in Table 1. Significance levels: *** for 1%, ** for 5%, and * for 10%.

following additional key findings of the previous section into our analysis. We focus on crowdfunding experiences where consumers are invited to pre-order the product. The advantage of this form of crowdfunding is that advanced sales allow the entrepreneur to identify (and reward) the most eager consumers, and thereby to practice price discrimination. The drawback is that the revenues collected through advanced sales must be large enough to cover the initial capital requirement, which may actually restrict the scope for profitable price discrimination. This is the trade-off that we address in this model. The main result of the analysis is that crowdfunding is preferred to traditional funding as long as the capital requirement stays below some upper bound, which increases with the level of community benefits. Insofar as nonprofit entrepreneurs are more likely to offer larger community benefits than for-profit entrepreneurs (in the spirit of Glaeser and Shleifer 2001), it can be concluded that nonprofit entrepreneurs are also more likely to prefer crowdfunding over traditional funding.[11] We now develop this argument in details.

### 4.1 Set-up

An entrepreneur needs an amount of capital equal to $K$ to launch a new product. There is a unit mass of consumers who are identified by $\theta$, with $\theta$ uniformly distributed on [0,1]. The parameter $\theta$ is a taste parameter that measures the consumer's willingness to pay for one unit of the product (by assumption, consumers buy one or zero unit). If the unit price of the product is $p$, then a consumer of type $\theta$ derives surplus $U = \theta - p$.[12]

The entrepreneur can choose between the two ways of financing the initial capital requirement: traditional funding or crowdfunding. Our modeling of the former encompasses a wide array of financing sources such as equity financing (venture capital, business angel, and friends & family) and bank loans as long as they do not involve extra nonmonetary benefits similar to what the crowd would obtain.

If the firm chooses *traditional funding*, then the sequence of decisions is as follows. In period 1, the entrepreneur incurs the fixed cost $K$, which is financed through, e.g., a bank loan. Then, in period 2, the entrepreneur sets a uniform price for its product, and consumers decide to buy or not. Denoting by $p_t$ this uniform price, the indifferent consumer would be such that $\theta - p_t = 0$. The entrepreneur would then choose $p_t$ to maximize $p_t(1 - p_t)$, where we assume that the marginal cost of production is equal to zero.[13] Consequently, the entrepreneur would set $p_t = 1/2$, all consumers with $\theta \geq 1/2$ would purchase the product, and gross profits would be equal to 1/4. We record for further reference that under traditional funding, the entrepreneur achieves a net profit equal to

$$\Pi_t = \frac{1}{4} - K. \tag{1}$$

This constitutes a worthwhile benchmark for comparison with crowdfunding.

The alternative to traditional funding is *crowdfunding based on pre-ordering*. The timing of the game is now as follows. In the first period, the entrepreneur sets the pre-ordering price $p_c$ (with subscript letter $c$ for 'crowdfunders') and consumers decide whether or not to pre-order at that price. If they do, they are offered some rewards by the entrepreneur, which increase their willingness to pay for the product. In particular, a consumer of type $\theta$ who pre-orders the product is willing to pay up to $\theta(1 + \sigma)$, where $\sigma$ measures the magnitude of the community benefits stemming from the crowdfunding experience. Let $n_c$ denote the mass of crowdfunders. If $n_c p_c < K$, insufficient capital has been collected and the game stops. The crowd then receives its money back. Otherwise, if $n_c p_c \geq K$, the game moves to the second period where the entrepreneur sets $p_r$, the price for consumers who did not pre-order in period 1 (with subscript letter $r$ for 'regular consumers'). Those consumers then decide to buy or not (observing all the previous steps).

### 4.2 Optimal choice of financing source

As we solve the game backward for its subgame-perfect Nash equilibrium, we start by analyzing the second period. Suppose that $n_c p_c \geq K$. Then the indifferent consumer between pre-ordering and not is identified by a taste parameter $\theta_c = 1 - n_c$. Consumers who can potentially buy the product at period 2 are such that $\theta \in [0, \theta_c]$. Facing $p_r$, they buy iff $\theta \geq p_r$. Hence, the entrepreneur chooses $p_r$ to maximize $p_r(\theta_c - p_r)$. The optimal price and second-period profit are easily found as $p_r(\theta_c) = \theta_c/2$ and $\pi_2(\theta_c) = \theta_c^2/4$.

We can now move to the first period and identify the indifferent consumer between pre-ordering and not as the consumer for whom $\theta_c(1 + \sigma) - p_c = \theta_c - p_r$. Using the value of $p_r$ that we have just derived, we find: $\theta_c = 2p_c/(1 + 2\sigma)$. We can then write the entrepreneur's maximization program in period 1 as

$$\max_{p_c} p_c \left( 1 - \frac{2p_c}{1 + 2\sigma} \right) + \frac{1}{4} \left( \frac{2p_c}{1 + 2\sigma} \right)^2,$$

under the following constraints

$$\pi_1 \equiv p_c \left( 1 - \frac{2p_c}{1 + 2\sigma} \right) \geq K, \text{ and } 0 \leq \frac{2p_c}{1 + 2\sigma} \leq 1.$$

The unconstrained optimum is given by the first-order condition: $p_c^* = (1 + 2\sigma)^2/2(1 + 4\sigma)$. [14] The first constraint is satisfied if $\pi_1 \geq K$, which can be rewritten as

$$K \leq \frac{\sigma(1 + 2\sigma)^2}{1 + 4\sigma^2} \equiv \bar{K}.$$

We have thus two cases to distinguish. First, if $K \leq \bar{K}$, then the entrepreneur can set the price $p_c^*$. The total profit at the unconstrained optimum is then computed as

$$\Pi_c = \pi_1 + \pi_2 - K = \frac{1}{4} + \frac{\sigma^2}{1 + 4\sigma} - K. \tag{2}$$

Second, if $K > \bar{K}$, then the unconstrained optimal price and number of crowdfunders are insufficient to cover the capital requirement. Then $p_c$ is computed as the solution to $\pi_1 = K$. This equality defines a polynomial of the second degree in $p_c$ that has real roots as long as $K < (1 + 2\sigma)/8 \equiv \hat{K}$. Put differently, there is a threshold for the initial capital requirement above which the entrepreneur is unable to finance her venture through crowdfunding and pre-ordering. In BLS (2012), we show that the entrepreneur is then constrained to charge a lower price to crowdfunders: $\bar{p}_c = \frac{1}{4}(1 + 2\sigma + \sqrt{(1 + 2\sigma)(1 + 2\sigma - 8K)}) < p_c^*$. It follows that $\bar{\pi}_1 = K$, while $\bar{\pi}_2$ (which is equal to the total profit) is computed as

$$\bar{\Pi}_c = \bar{\pi}_2 = \left(\frac{\bar{p}_c}{1 + 2\sigma}\right)^2 = \frac{1}{16}\left(1 + \sqrt{1 - \frac{8K}{1 + 2\sigma}}\right)^2. \tag{3}$$

We are now in a position to *compare the two funding mechanisms*. First, it is obvious from expressions (1) and (2) that crowdfunding is preferred to traditional funding for $K \leq \bar{K}$. Second, for $K > \bar{K}$, we compute from expressions (1) and (3) that

$$\bar{\Pi}_c \geq \Pi_t \Leftrightarrow K \leq \frac{2\sigma(2\sigma + 1)}{(4\sigma + 1)^2} \equiv \hat{K}.$$

Collecting the previous results, we can state the following:

**Proposition 1.** (Optimal Financing Source) The entrepreneur prefers to finance the initial capital requirement $K$ through crowdfunding as long as $K$ is not larger than $K_{up} = \max\{\hat{K}, \bar{K}\}$. Otherwise (and if $K < 1/4$), she opts for traditional funding.

We check that $K_{up} < \hat{K}$, $K_{up} = \hat{K}$ for $\sigma \leq 1/2$, and $K_{up} = \bar{K}$ for $\sigma > 1/2$. The intuition behind Proposition 1 is quite simple. On the one hand, crowdfunding has the advantage of offering an enhanced experience to some consumers and, thereby, of allowing the entrepreneur to practice a form of behavior-based price discrimination, which has the potential to increase profits by extracting a larger share of the consumer surplus. On the other hand, the disadvantage is that the entrepreneur is constrained in the first period by the amount of capital that she needs to raise. This distorts the price discrimination strategy of the entrepreneur. The larger this amount, the larger the number of consumers that have to be attracted to cover it, which eventually reduces the profitability of the pre-ordering scheme. Empirical observations presented in Sections 2 and 3.2 confirm this prediction.

### 4.3 For-profit versus nonprofit organizations

We now enrich our model by considering that before choosing her source of financing (crowdfunding vs traditional funding), the entrepreneur also decides upon the organizational form of her venture: for-profit status or nonprofit status. The status of the firm has the following implication: under the nonprofit status, the entrepreneur is restricted in her ability to distribute profits to herself. In particular, we make the following set of assumptions. As in the so-called 'contract failure literature' and, especially, in Glaeser and Shleifer (2001), we assume that regardless of the status of the firm, the entrepreneur's utility is an increasing function of the quality of the community benefits that she provides to her crowdfunders. That is, the entrepreneur gets a higher (lower) utility if the quality $\sigma$ of the community benefits that she provides exceeds (falls short of) some exogenously determined level $\bar{\sigma}$. This can be justified either by referring to some altruistic preference of the entrepreneur (her desire to provide better quality than what is available on average) or as a reduced form of some reputation mechanism that would be at work in a richer model with asymmetric information and repeat purchases.

More precisely, we adopt the following framework. We focus on cases where crowdfunding allows the venture to achieve the optimal price discrimination scheme. That is, we take $K \leq \bar{K}(\sigma) = \sigma(1 + 2\sigma)^2/(1 + 4\sigma)^2$. Net profits are then given by $\Pi_c(\sigma) = \frac{1}{4} + \frac{\sigma^2}{1+4\sigma} - K$, which are higher than under traditional funding. It is easily checked that $\Pi_c'(\sigma) > 0$ and $\Pi_c''(\sigma) > 0$.

We assume that the cost of community benefits for the entrepreneur is given by $C(\sigma)$ with $C' > 0$ and $C'' > 0$. We also let $b > 0$ denote the marginal utility for the entrepreneur of increasing the quality of the community benefits. We posit then the following utility functions. If the venture is for-profit, the entrepreneur earns the venture's profits as income; she then chooses $\sigma$ to maximize the quasi-linear utility function:

$$U_F = \Pi_c(\sigma) - C(\sigma) + b(\sigma - \bar{\sigma}).$$

In contrast, if the venture is nonprofit, the entrepreneur is forced, because of the nondistribution constraint, to consume profits as perquisites. We assume that the entrepreneur strictly prefers cash to perquisites; her utility from perquisites is thus modeled as a fraction $0 < \delta < 1$ of the profits, which leads to the following utility function

$$U_N = \delta(\Pi_c(\sigma) - C(\sigma)) + b(\sigma - \bar{\sigma}).$$

Maximizing utility with respect to $\sigma$ allows us to define the optimal level of community benefits for a for-profit ($\sigma_F$) entrepreneur and for a nonprofit ($\sigma_N$) entrepreneur, respectively, as

$$\begin{cases} \Pi_c'(\sigma_F) - C'(\sigma_F) + b = 0, \\ \delta\big(\Pi_c'(\sigma_N) - C'(\sigma_N)\big) + b = 0. \end{cases}$$

As $\delta < 1$, we have that $C'(\sigma_N) - \Pi_c'(\sigma_N) = b/\delta > b = C'(\sigma_F) - \Pi_c'(\sigma_F)$. Then, a sufficient condition to have $\sigma_N > \sigma_F$ is that $C'(\sigma) - \Pi_c'(\sigma)$ increases with $\sigma$, or that $C''(\sigma) > \Pi_c''(\sigma)$. Take, for instance, $C(\sigma) = (\gamma/2)\sigma^2$; then, the condition $C''(\sigma) > \Pi_c''(\sigma)$ is equivalent to $\gamma > 2/(4\sigma + 1)^3$, which is certainly satisfied if $\gamma \geq 2$.

This result (which mirrors Proposition 1 in Glaeser and Shleifer 2001) shows that if the cost of providing community benefits increases faster than the venture's profit, then *a nonprofit entrepreneur using crowdfunding will choose a larger level of community benefits than a for-profit entrepreneur.* The intuition is clear: because the nonprofit entrepreneur has to consume profits as perquisites, which she values less than cash, she puts a relatively larger weight than the for-profit entrepreneur on the noncash benefit of raising the quality of community benefits, which leads her to provide larger community benefits.

Now, remark that $\bar{K}'(\sigma) > 0$, i.e., the threshold under which crowdfunding is always preferred to traditional funding increases with the level of community benefits. Then, $\sigma_N > \sigma_F$ implies that $\bar{K}(\sigma_N) > \bar{K}(\sigma_F)$. There exists therefore a range of capital requirements, $K \in [\bar{K}(\sigma_F), \bar{K}(\sigma_N)]$, that nonprofit entrepreneurs are able to finance through crowdfunding while for-profit entrepreneurs are not.[15]

The former result may explain why *nonprofit organizations tend to be more successful than for-profit organizations in using crowdfunding:* by credibly committing to provide larger community benefits to crowdfunders, they extend the range of initial capital requirements that can be financed through crowdfunding.

## 5 Empirical analysis of determinants of crowdfunding success

The previous sections derived empirical predictions on drivers of crowdfunding success, in particular with respect to the organizational form adopted by the entrepreneurial firm. The theoretical model concludes that, ceteris paribus, nonprofit organizations should be able to raise larger amounts and thereby be more successful in attaining their targeted funds. In this section, we empirically investigate these predictions based on our collected sample of individual crowdfunding initiatives.

Table 4. Nonprofit organizations and the amount of funds raised: OLS regressions.

| Variables | (1) | (2) | (3) | (4) | (5) | (6) | (7) | (8) | (9) | (10) |
|---|---|---|---|---|---|---|---|---|---|---|
| Nonprofit[a] | 2.62* | 1.19 | 1.80 | 3.69* | 3.58** | 3.29*** | 2.08** | 3.04** | 3.67** | 4.09*** |
| | (1.45) | (1.18) | (1.45) | (2.01) | (1.38) | (1.11) | (0.96) | (1.14) | (1.50) | (1.05) |
| Company[a] | | | | | | 3.78*** | 2.87*** | 3.60*** | 4.16*** | 3.30*** |
| | | | | | | (0.86) | (0.74) | (0.85) | (0.94) | (0.91) |
| Active implication | 4.26*** | 2.15*** | 3.33*** | 4.32*** | 5.68*** | 2.61*** | 1.45* | 2.36*** | 2.17** | 3.86*** |
| | (1.01) | (0.93) | (1.08) | (1.08) | (1.07) | (0.86) | (0.76) | (0.85) | (0.94) | (0.95) |
| Social networks | −0.01 | −0.56 | 0.47 | −0.45 | −1.20 | −0.63 | −0.88 | −0.45 | −0.58 | −1.58* |
| | (1.08) | (0.85) | (1.05) | (1.22) | (1.13) | (0.83) | (0.68) | (0.82) | (0.91) | (0.86) |
| Product | 3.10*** | 2.58*** | 3.10*** | 3.23*** | 2.94*** | 3.19*** | 2.78*** | 3.03*** | 3.13*** | 3.23*** |
| | (0.86) | (0.68) | (0.82) | (0.89) | (091) | (0.65) | (0.54) | (0.62) | (0.67) | (0.69) |
| ln (Funds targeted) | | 0.46*** | | | | | 0.34*** | | | |
| | | (0.11) | | | | | (0.09) | | | |
| Number of crowdfunders | | | 0.02* | | | | | 0.01 | | |
| | | | (0.01) | | | | | (0.01) | | |
| Equity-based model | | | | 1.72 | | | | | 0.44 | |
| | | | | (2.14) | | | | | (1.62) | |
| Reward-based model | | | | 1.12 | | | | | 1.27 | |
| | | | | (1.96) | | | | | (1.46) | |
| Age | | | | | 1.18 | | | | | 0.61* |
| | | | | | (0.36) | | | | | (0.32) |
| Test diff. (p value) | | | | | | 0.71 | 0.46 | 0.66 | 0.79 | 0.55 |
| F statistics (p value) | 0.00 | 0.00 | 0.00 | 0.00 | 0.00 | 0.00 | 0.00 | 0.00 | 0.00 | 0.00 |
| Adjusted $R^2$ | 0.50 | 0.70 | 0.64 | 0.47 | 0.65 | 0.71 | 0.81 | 0.75 | 0.71 | 0.80 |
| No of obs. | 30 | 30 | 29 | 30 | 22 | 30 | 30 | 29 | 30 | 22 |

Notes: The dependent variable in all the regressions is the natural logarithm of *funds raised*. All the variables are defined in Table 1. The method of estimation is OLS. A constant term is included in all the regressions, whose coefficient is not reported. Numbers in parentheses are standard errors. The row for the test of difference reports the $p$ values for the null hypothesis of equality of coefficients on *nonprofit* and *company*. Significance levels: *** for 1%, ** for 5%, and * for 10%.

Table 5. Nonprofit organizations and fundraising success: Tobit regressions.

| Variables | (1) | (2) | (3) | (4) | (5) | (6) | (7) | (8) |
|---|---|---|---|---|---|---|---|---|
| Nonprofit[a] | 1.29*** | 0.99** | 2.67*** | 1.00* | 1.34*** | 0.99** | 2.67*** | 1.06** |
| | (0.45) | (0.46) | (0.47) | (0.52) | (0.45) | (0.47) | (0.47) | (0.51) |
| Company[a] | | | | | 0.20 | −0.01 | 0.04 | 0.35 |
| | | | | | (0.34) | (0.35) | (0.30) | (0.44) |
| Active implication | 0.01 | −0.29 | −0.02 | −0.28 | −0.06 | −0.27 | −0.02 | −0.46 |
| | (0.31) | (0.34) | (0.25) | (0.40) | (0.34) | (0.35) | (0.29) | (0.46) |
| Social networks | −0.08 | 0.08 | −0.56* | 0.08 | −0.11 | 0.09 | −0.55* | 0.05 |
| | (0.33) | (0.33) | (0.29) | (0.42) | (0.33) | (0.34) | (0.29) | (0.42) |
| Product | 0.40 | 0.49* | 0.53** | 0.57 | 0.39 | 0.48* | 0.52** | 0.59* |
| | (0.26) | (0.26) | (0.21) | (0.34) | (0.26) | (0.26) | (0.21) | (0.34) |
| Number of crowdfunders | | 0.01 | | | | 0.01 | | |
| | | (0.00) | | | | (0.00) | | |
| Equity-based model | | | 2.18*** | | | | 2.15*** | |
| | | | (0.50) | | | | (0.51) | |
| Reward-based model | | | 1.81*** | | | | 1.80*** | |
| | | | (0.46) | | | | (0.46) | |
| Age | | | | −0.12 | | | | 0.52 |
| | | | | (0.14) | | | | (0.39) |
| Test diff. (p value)[a] | 0.04 | 0.03 | 0.00 | 0.12 | 0.04 | 0.06 | 0.00 | 0.28 |
| LR χ² (df) (p value) | | | | | 0.06 | 0.04 | 0.00 | 0.15 |
| Pseudo $R^2$ | 0.14 | 0.17 | 0.33 | 0.15 | 0.14 | 0.18 | 0.33 | 0.16 |
| No of obs. | 30 | 29 | 30 | 22 | 30 | 29 | 30 | 22 |

Notes: The dependent variable in all the regressions is *success*. All the variables are defined in Table 1. The method of estimation is Tobit. A constant term is included in all the regressions, whose coefficient is not reported. Numbers in parentheses are standard errors. The row for the test of difference reports the $p$ values for the null hypothesis of equality of coefficients on *nonprofit* and *company*. Significance levels: *** for 1%, ** for 5%, and * for 10%.

We examine two dimensions of crowdfunding outcome: the total amount raised by the entrepreneur (the variable *funds raised*), and the total amount raised as compared with the entrepreneur's initial target (the variable *success*). Our findings are summarized in Tables 4 and 5. We focus particularly on the relationship between the nonprofit organizational form and fundraising outcome, controlling for other potential determinants of funds raised.

Table 4 shows Ordinary Least Squares (OLS) regressions on the natural logarithm of *funds raised*. This table exhibits that nonprofit organizations tend to attract larger amounts of money than other forms (columns 1–5), although the coefficient is not always statistically significant. When controlling for *company*, our other important form of organization, *nonprofit* clearly becomes strongly significant. However, this compares *nonprofit* with forms other than companies. The latter form also raises significantly more money than these other forms and the difference between *nonprofit* and *company* is never statistically significant [see the row *Test diff. (p value)* at the bottom of the table]. These results change little across specifications.[16] In contrast, Table 5 provides evidence in support of our main theoretical prediction that nonprofit entrepreneurs are more successful than for-profit entrepreneurs, including those organized as a company. We estimate Tobit models because the dependent variable, *success*, is left censored by construction (i.e., the lower limit is equal to zero). The coefficient of *nonprofit* is large (columns 1–8) and also statistically different from the coefficient of *company* in all specifications (columns 5–8). The effect is also economically meaningful: compared with other organizational forms, nonprofits tend to raise 129% more funds than targeted through crowdfunding (using the coefficient in column 1). Compared with for-profit entrepreneurs structured as company (the variable *company*), the economic impact is given by the difference between the two coefficients, which represents 114% more than targeted funds (using coefficients in column 5). This is remarkable and, as shown in Section 4, can be interpreted in line with the contract failure theory that these organizations are better at attracting outside funds because of their possible stronger focus on the social outcome than on monetary gains. Although we cannot exclude a possible bias due to the self-reporting of targeted amounts, any bias is likely to occur for all the initiatives; therefore, there is no specific reason to expect that entrepreneurs of nonprofit organizations are prone to understate more than entrepreneurs of other organizational forms. In other words, such a bias would inflate values of the variable *success* but it is likely to be similar across all initiatives.

According to Tables 4 and 5, other potential determinants appear to affect the amount raised in crowdfunding initiatives and success. For instance, the variable *active implication* enters positively and significantly in all the regressions in Table 4, implying that direct involvement by the crowd exerts an important role on the amount of funds raised. Hence, by involving crowdfunders into venture's activities, which confers them higher community benefits, entrepreneurs extend the levels of capital that are financed through crowdfunding. However, this result is not supported in the alternative measure, as shown in Table 5. Next, the use of social networks does not seem to enhance the amount of funds raised, while entrepreneurial initiatives that make a product tend to attract larger amounts of capital than those that offer a service (in Table 5 only significant in some specifications). This result may be mechanical, as activities that make a product will on average require larger investments than for providing a service. Indeed, the former may require significant production facilities that lead to major capital expenditures upfront. A second possible explanation for this positive effect may stem from the fact that the crowdfunders may be more tempted to provide money if they expect a tangible outcome; one reason could be that the provision of a product is contractible and thus less subject to uncertainty about quality (Hart and Moore 1988). In this case, they may favor initiatives that make a product as opposed to a service.

These results are generally robust to the inclusion of additional control variables. For instance, including *funds targeted* (in italic) into the regression of Table 4 does not affect our diagnostics on differences (or the lack thereof) between nonprofits and for-profits. However, the variable is positive and significant, in line with intuition. Indeed, this variable is likely to capture financial needs of the entrepreneur. Age of the firm (captured by the variable *age*) does not affect amounts raised nor success of the crowdfunding initiative.[17] This suggests that delaying the crowdfunding campaign from the establishment date of the entrepreneurial activity has no effect on the amount collected. Finally, the choice of crowdfunding model (*equity-based model* and *reward-based model*) seems to affect success rate of the initiative (Table 5), but not the amount raised (Table 4). Compared with donation-based models (captured by the constant term), we therefore conclude that the effect of model choice on outcome is unclear in our analysis, or at best weakly against donation-based models.

These tests should be viewed as weak tests for one of the predictions of our theoretical model. Given the small sample size and limitations in the control variables available, these results should be taken with care. Still, they provide useful insights on what drives the success of crowdfunding initiatives and on the specificities of nonprofit organizations.

## 6 Conclusion

This paper examines characteristics of individual crowdfunding practices and drivers of fundraising success. To our knowledge, this is the first study directly dealing with individual crowdfunding practices based on a hand-collected data-set. We document evidence that the individual crowdfunding practice is a way to develop venture's activities through the process of fundraising, where entrepreneurs may tailor their crowdfunding campaign better than on standardized platforms. This enables entrepreneurs to offer a large variety of compensation to the crowd, including active involvement in terms of time and expertise. We also find that such individual initiatives generate on average small amounts of capital comparatively to other financing sources. Furthermore, the questionnaire sent to entrepreneurs highlights that crowdfunding allows them to attract attention on their own venture. This can become a vital asset, especially for artists or entrepreneurs in need to present their talent and product to the 'crowd' (as potential customers). In other cases, it is a unique way to validate original ideas in front of a specifically targeted audience. This may in turn provide insights into market potential of the product offered.

We also document that nonprofit organizations positively affect the success chances of entrepreneurs to reach their capital targets. The empirical evidence from multivariate analyses supports our theoretical predictions that nonprofit entrepreneurs tend to be more successful in using crowdfunding. In our setting, the reduced focus on profits by such entrepreneurs is viewed by crowdfunders as a credible commitment to provide larger community benefits and, thereby, extends the range of initial capital requirements that can be pledged through crowdfunding.

## Acknowledgements

We are grateful to all the participants in this survey. We wish to thank Grégoire Krieg for his excellent research assistance. Any remaining errors are the authors' alone.

**Notes**

1.  The potential of crowdfunding in boosting economic activity led, in April 2012, the US Congress to pass the Jumpstart Our Business Startups Act, designed to make easier for start-ups and small businesses to raise funds by, among other measures, protecting crowdfunders (i.e., the individuals who participate to the crowdfunding mechanism).
2.  The report "Crowdfunding Industry Report: Market Trends, Composition and Crowdfunding Platforms" (May 2012) is released by Crowdsourcing LLC and Massolution. An abridged version is available at www.crowdsourcing.org.
3.  At the exception of Mollick (2012), see the literature review below.
4.  Sohl (2003) reports that the typical angel early-stage round (seed or start-up) ranges between $100,000 and $2 million, while venture capitalists are in the $10 to $15 million range. This is in line with Ibrahim (2008), see also Freear, Sohl, and Wetzel (2002), Wong (2010), and Goldfarb et al. (2012).
5.  Relatedly, there are several papers on the peer-to-peer lending platform *Prosper* (see, e.g., Hildebrand, Puri, and Rocholl 2011; Lin, Prabhala, and Viswanathan 2012; Zhang and Liu 2012).
6.  Global Entrepreneurship Monitor: www.gemconsortium.org.
7.  See Table 1 for a definition of equity- and reward-based crowdfunding models.
8.  A detailed definition is provided in BLS (2012).
9.  See, for instance, Hansmann (1996) for extensive developments.
10. The report of *Crowdsourcing.org* also identifies lending-based models. Our sample does not contain such models. This is expected since lending-based crowdfunding is better suited for platforms, which are beyond the scope of our analysis.
11. In BLS (2012), we also consider crowdfunding initiatives that compensate crowdfunders by offering them a share of the venture's profits. Qualitatively similar results to those presented here can be obtained for this alternative form of crowdfunding (namely that crowdfunding is preferred to traditional funding when the required capital is relatively small, and that nonprofit organizations are more likely to be successful in raising funds through crowdfunding).
12. This problem was initially examined by Mussa and Rosen (1978).
13. In this linear model, this assumption is made without loss of generality. Prices can simply be reinterpreted as markups above a constant marginal cost.
14. We check that the second set of constraints is satisfied. We compute indeed $\theta_c^* = (1 + 2\sigma)/(1 + 4\sigma)$, which is clearly positive and smaller than unity.
15. The same result holds for initial capital requirements between $\bar{K}$ and $\tilde{K}$ (where the entrepreneur is constrained in her price discrimination scheme). We check indeed that $\bar{\Pi}_c''(\sigma) < 0$ (meaning that the condition $C''(\sigma) > \Pi''(\sigma)$ is always satisfied) and that $\tilde{K}'(\sigma) > 0$.
16. Untabulated regressions also show that these results do not change if we use bootstrap method for estimating standard errors. The statistics were obtained from 200 replications resampled from the actual data-set.
17. The number of observations drops, however, due to data availability.

**References**

Agrawal, A., C. Catalini, and A. Goldfarb. 2011. "The Geography of Crowdfunding." NBER Working Paper, No. 19820.

Belleflamme, P., T. Lambert, and A. Schwienbacher. 2012. "Crowdfunding: Tapping the Right Crowd." Working Paper.

Bilodeau, M., and A. Slivinski. 2004. "Rational Nonprofit Entrepreneurship." *Journal of Economics & Management Strategy* 7: 551–571.

Freear, J., J. E. Sohl, and W. Wetzel. 2002. "Angles on Angels: Financing Technology-Based Ventures – A Historical Perspective." *Venture Capital – An International Journal of Entrepreneurial Finance* 4: 275–287.

Ghatak, M., and H. Mueller. 2011. "Thanks for Nothing? Not-for-Profits and Motivated Agents." *Journal of Public Economics* 95: 94–105.

Glaeser, E. L., and A. Shleifer. 2001. "Not-for-Profit Entrepreneurs." *Journal of Public Economics* 81: 99–115.

Goldfarb, B., G. Hoberg, D. Kirsch, and A. Triantis. 2012. "Does Angel Participation Matter? An Analysis of Early Venture Financing." Working Paper.

Hansmann, H. 1996. *The Ownership of Enterprise*. Cambridge: Harvard University Press.

Hart, O., and J. Moore. 1988. "Incomplete Contracts and Renegotiation." *Econometrica* 56: 755–785.

Hildebrand, T., M. Puri, and J. Rocholl. 2011. "Skin in the Game: Incentives in Crowdfunding.", Working Paper.

Ibrahim, D. M. 2008. "The (Not So) Puzzling Behavior of Angel Investors." *Vanderbilt Law Review* 61: 1405–1452.

Lin, M., N. Prabhala, and S. Viswanathan. 2012. "Judging Borrowers by the Company They Keep: Social Networks and Adverse Selection in Online Peer-to-Peer Lending." forthcoming at *Management Science*.

Linde, L., and A. Prasad. 2000. *Venture Support Systems Project: Angel Investors*. Cambridge: MIT Entrepreneurship Center.

Mollick, E. 2012. *The Dynamics of Crowdfunding: Determinants of Success and Failures*. Working Paper.

Mussa, M., and S. Rosen. 1978. "Monopoly and Product Quality." *Journal of Economic Theory* 18: 301–317.

Schwienbacher, A., and B. Larralde. 2012. "Crowdfunding of Small Entrepreneurial Ventures." In *The Oxford Handbook of Entrepreneurial Finance*, edited by D. J. Cumming. Oxford: Oxford University Press.

Sohl, J. E. 2003. "The US Angel and Venture Capital Market: Recent Trends and Developments." *Journal of Private Equity* 6: 7–17.

Ward, C., and V. Ramachandran. 2010. "Crowdfunding the Next Hit: Microfunding Online Experience Goods.", Working Paper.

Wong, A. 2010. "Angel Finance: The Other Venture Capital." In *Venture Capital: Investment Strategies, Structures, and Policies*, edited by D. J. Cumming. New Jersey: John Wiley & Sons.

Zhang, J., and P. Liu. 2012. "Rational Herding in Microloan Markets." *Management Science* 58: 892–912.

# A conceptualized investment model of crowdfunding

Alan Tomczak and Alexander Brem

*Department of Idea and Innovation Management, Friedrich Alexander Universität
Erlangen-Nürnberg, Nürnberg, Germany*

Crowdfunding is growing in popularity as a new form of both investment opportunity
and source of venture capital. This article takes a view on whether crowdfunding is a
replacement or an addition to traditional seed capital sources in the early stages of a
new venture. With access to angel investment decreasing since the financial crisis of
2008, crowdfunding is of great importance to start-ups seeking starting capital.
However, little effort has been made to define the investment model of crowdfunding
with both crowdfunder and crowdfundee in mind. Drawing on an in-depth review of
current literature on crowdfunding, this article creates an investment model of
crowdfunding with various reward models available to investor and investee in mind.
This article provides an extensive survey of the environment of crowdfunding based
on current literature. It offers a jumping off point and a thorough literature review for
researchers of crowdfunding, providing a detailed examination of the current
landscape of crowdfunding based on available literary sources.

## 1.  Introduction

Crowdfunding has quickly become a popular avenue of funding for investment, seed money
and start-up funding. The growth rates have been astounding over its short life span.
However, this article argues that what has been lacking is the construction of a
crowdfunding investment model. This is of great importance as almost $1.5 billion was
raised in over 1 million crowdfunding campaigns in 2011 (Crowdfunding Industry Report,
2012, 14). This sum was projected to double for 2012 (Crowdfunding Industry Report, 2012,
14). The Daily Crowdsource, an industry publication, gave $123 million as the total for 2011
(Burke, 2012). Although lower than the $1.5 billion figure, this number is still impressive as
the figure given that two years prior it was only $32 million, making it a quadruple increase
in crowdfunding investment in a two-year span (Burke, 2012). But certain questions have
arisen, such as: In what ways can funds be raised? What rewards are offered to investors in
crowdfunding? And what factors make up crowdfunding?

This article will review all available rewards offered through crowdfunding to show
the theoretical basis for the two-sided market of crowdfunding and crowdfunding
investment and to show how all elements of crowdfunding interact through a
conceptualized investment model for crowdfunding that is developed by the authors.

## 1.1. Motivation

The motivation behind this article is the lack of a coherent article in current academic journals showing all relevant options and reward models for crowdfunding. The authors of this article undertook a thorough analysis of the most widely cited research based on number of citations from the period of 2009–2012 from Google Scholar and the EBSCO e-journal database, working papers and industry publications along with other sources. During this undertaking, a need was recognized for one paper that collected all relevant detail regarding crowdfunding investment. This article is an attempt at fulfilling this gap in contemporary literature.

## 1.2. How crowdfunding can fill gaps in capital for new ventures

One of the hardest things for any small entrepreneur to come by is start-up capital. Lavinsky (2010) says:

> [...] the vast majority of entrepreneurs have failed to raise venture capital. There are two key reasons for this. First, most entrepreneurs don't qualify for venture capital since they can't scale fast enough, nor do they have the potential for a large enough exit. And second, there are too few venture capitalists versus the masses of entrepreneurs who need money.

A study by Dutch bank ABN AMRO found that entrepreneurs have difficulty obtaining funding between €35,000 and €150,000 (Voorbraak, 2011, 2). A similar study by the New York Federal Reserve found the denial rate for loans of less than $100,000 was more than twice as high as it was for bigger loans (Pagliery, 2012).

The best possible option for entrepreneurs seeking capital, especially at the earliest stages of their development, is through business angels or angel investment. Angel investment can be described as '[...] the first round of external independent investment' (McKaskill, 2009, 9). These investments generally take place once the founding members of a start-up have exhausted their personal funds as well as tapped out capital available from friends and family. In a general sense, angel investment follows after or along with the friends, family and fools (FFF) stage of financing. Fools denote the high risk associated with investment in emerging stage firms (Cumming and Johan, 2009). Figure 1 shows the stages of entrepreneurial firm development with crowdfunding added in italics in its applicable areas.

Typically in the seed capital and early stages as represented above, ventures are not developed to the point where they can stand on their own and often are not appealing enough to outside investors to attract venture capital funding. These ventures are in between a stage of potential failure or success. The following are two opportunities that crowdfunding can provide seed capital:

> [...] [o]ne is the initial seed money to start a business, where friends and family finance may be unavailable or insufficient, and amounts required are too small for business angels to get involved [and] [...] also the gap above the level where business angles [sic] are usually active, but where the capital required is too small for venture capitalists to get involved. (Collins and Pierrakis, 2012, 18)

These phases provide ample opportunity for raising seed capital with crowdfunding to offset the risks of personal guarantees for bank loans from the company's founders and when FFF and personal savings have been drained. This is of special importance today as the rates of angel investment have been steadily decreasing since their roughly 10-year peak in 2008 according to a study by PwC MoneyTree (Rannala, 2013).

Hemer (2011) also draws a parallel between angel investing and crowdfunding:

> [...] crowdfunding could be one informal financing alternative to close the early-stage gap which represents one of the major obstacles when getting start-up projects off the ground.

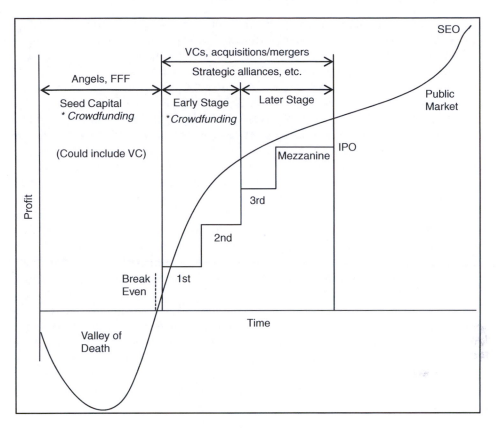

Figure 1. Stages of entrepreneurial firm development.
*Source*: Cumming and Johan (2009, 6).

> Business angel financing is a good reference here and fuels the hope that crowdfunding may also be able to tap into hidden informal capital resources. (28)

Pope (2011) offers crowdfunding as a means to raise funds for micro start-ups. This article will not attempt to convince the reader of the capabilities of crowdfunding for funding entrepreneurs as this has been done many times over by articles such as Burkett (2011), Gennari (2012), Steinberg and DeMaria (2012), Watts (2012) and Wroldsen (2013), to name just a few.

The starkness of the early stage investment environment becomes even stronger when we look to literature. 'Less than three percent of the thousands of entrepreneurs seeking funding from angel investors actually get funding [ . . . ]' (Pope, 2011, 122–123). In addition, it appears that many angels only consider investing in businesses looking to raise larger amounts of funding with the majority of rounds raised from business angels in 2009/2010 greater than £100,000 (Collins and Pierrakis, 2012, 17). Crowdfunding can also help counter the historically low yield rates of angel investment. The yield rate is '[t]he percentage of investment opportunities that are brought to the attention of investors that result in an investment' (Sohl, 2012, 2). Historically, this average is between 10% and 15% (Sohl, 2012, 2). Crowdfunding provides a potential opportunity to combat this extreme competitiveness.

The potential of crowdfunding is becoming even more pronounced as we are seeing not only decreasing angel investment but also the 'Series A Crunch'. The Series

A Round is financing that usually occurs after the seed stage of venture capital. The crunch refers to recent drops in available funding for these funding rounds. Although it has been perhaps rightfully suggested that crowdfunding alone will not solve the Series A Crunch (Caldbeck, 2013), it does provide an additional avenue for potentially raising seed capital for very early stage ventures. Additionally, businesses may require a small tranche of funds between seed and Series A in the form of crowdfunding to fill in funding gaps or until the current Series A Crunch ends and liquidity increases. Shontell (2012, 2013) highlights several examples of companies that were effectively killed by the lack of access to Series A financing. It appears there is an overall decrease in risk appetite and liquidity from larger investors. Moreover, the industry is witnessing the very first evidence of a consolidation of some angel investors into angel network-supported crowdfunding platforms. One example of this is MicroVentures, a US-based crowdfunding platform, which advertises itself as 'connecting angel investors and startups' (MicroVentures, 2013). There is also Crowdfunder.com which connects local start-ups in the USA and Mexico with select groups of local qualified investors depending on where they are geographically located (Crowdfunder, 2013). Additionally, there is the investment platform, AngelList, which maintains a team of select Silicon Valley investors (AngelList, 2013).

The first step this article will take is defining what crowdfunding is, who the applicable players are and how the crowdfunding market operates. Immediately following each section will be a small piece of the greater crowdfunding investment model, labeled Parts 1–5, along with a description of its individual pieces thereafter. This is then followed by the entire model presented at once toward the end of this article. The article will highlight concepts established in crowdfunding research to create a process model of the investment procedure using flowcharting.

## 2.  Definition of crowdfunding

There are numerous definitions of crowdfunding; however, there is no accepted or universal definition. It must be mentioned first that there are several terms used for crowdfunding such as crowdfinancing and crowdinvesting. From this point forward, this article will use the term 'crowdfunding'. Before various definitions of crowdfunding can be given, one must first define the root word that crowdfunding originates from, which is 'crowdsourcing'. The term crowdsourcing was originally coined by *Wired* magazine writer Jeff Howe (Unterberg, 2010, 121). Howe defines it as '[ . . . ] the act of taking a job traditionally performed by a designated agent (usually an employee) and outsourcing it to an undefined, generally large group of people in the form of an open call' (Unterberg, 2010, 122).

One can easily take Howe's definition of crowdsourcing and replace the word 'job' with *loan/funding* to define crowdfunding, 'the act of taking a *loan/funding* traditionally performed by a designated agent and outsourcing it to an undefined, generally large group of people in the form of an open call'. To begin to get a more well-rounded sense of what crowdfunding is, it is beneficial to look to literature for other definitions.

In the basest sense, crowdfunding is '[r]aising funds by tapping a general public (or the crowd) [ . . . ]' (Lambert and Schwienbacher, 2010, 4). Lambert and Schwienbacher go one step further, defining it as '[ . . . ] an open call, essentially through the Internet, for the provision of financial resources either in form of donation or in exchange for some form of reward and/or voting rights in order to support initiatives for specific purposes' (4). There must be some caution and clarification when referring to the 'open call' utilizing the internet because '[ . . . ] making a general solicitation for equity offering is limited to publicly listed equity' (Belleflamme, Lambert, and Schwienbacher 2010, 5) in the case of an actual security being exchanged for money.

Voorbraak defines it as '[ . . . ] the process of one party requesting and receiving money and other resources from many individuals for financing a project, in exchange for a monetary or non-monetary return on investment' (2011, 1).

The consensus by most authors seems to be that crowdfunding is raising money from the general public, or the 'crowd', via an intermediary platform that is typically web-based. This article defines crowdfunding as the act of acquiring third-party financing from the general public via an intermediary, generally in the form of a web-based platform.

### 2.1.  Defining user roles in crowdfunding

There are three roles to fulfill in any crowdfunding effort. First, there is the intermediary '[ . . . ] who serves as a matchmaker between promoters and funders' (Burkett, 2011, 68). The central role of the intermediary, also known as the platform, is as '[ . . . ] matchmaker between promoters and funders' (Burkett, 2011, 68). Next, there are the fundraisers, entrepreneurs and others, raising funds via a crowdfunding platform. These fundraisers use crowdfunding to '[ . . . ] get direct access to the market and to gather financial support from truly interested supporters' (Ordanini et al., 2009, 5). Finally, there are the investors themselves, also defined as the 'crowd' from the term crowdfunding, who '[ . . . ] decide to financially support these projects, bearing a risk and expecting a certain payoff' (Ordanini et al., 2009, 5).

### 2.2.  Two-sided market dynamics of crowdfunding

Crowdfunding is the classic example of a two-sided market. Two-sided markets '[ . . . ] tie together two distinct groups of users in a network' (Eisenmann, Parker, and Alstyne 2006, 2). They are a direct extension of multisided platforms which aim to '[ . . . ] bring together two or more distinct but interdependent groups of customers' (Osterwalder and Pigneur, 2010, 77). In order to perform properly, they must operate under a platform which brings groups of users together (Eisenmann, Parker, and Alstyne 2006). A platform could be either a digital marketplace or website to exchange funds or even an intermediary or broker who connects investors with investees. This article will not discuss the technology behind digital crowdfunding platforms and will not discuss the associated technologies, for instance web programming, behind it because the disciplines involved are outside the realm of its focus. Additionally, there were no references found by this article's authors in literature to the programming architecture of crowdfunding platforms. There are some sources available on the programming behind crowdsourcing platforms, however, such as Aparicio, Costa, and Braga 2012 and Franklin et al., 2011.

The simplest analogy to describe a two-sided market is the real estate industry. There are home buyers and home sellers, served by the same property market. Overseeing the process as an intermediary is the real estate agent (platform) who connects sellers with buyers and vice versa. The fundraiser is comparable to the 'seller', and the 'buyer' to the investors (crowd).

There are three distinct roles in a typical two-sided network. As was previously discussed, there is the role of the platform or intermediary who introduces investor to investee; in the case of this article, a web platform or broker would fulfill this role. The other two roles aside from the intermediary are explained in the following:

[ ... ] two-sided networks have a 'subsidy side', that is, a group of users who, when attracted in volume, are highly valued by the 'money side', the other user group. (Eisenmann, Parker, and Alstyne 2006, 3)

In the context of crowdfunding, the subsidy side generally consists of the investors who pay no fees to platforms or to fundraisers for investing in crowdfunded projects. The money side is the entrepreneur or organization that is raising funds. For example, Kickstarter (2012b) charges fundraisers a flat 5% fee from the project's funding total but charges individual investors nothing. Another popular site, Indiegogo (2012), charges fundraisers a fee of 4% of the money raised if a certain fundraising goal is met or 9% if a fundraising goal is unmet and again investors pay nothing. Therefore, the fundraiser, or the money side, are charged a fee based on the amount of money raised on a crowdfunding platform and subsidize investors, or the subsidy side, who pay no fees to invest their money in different projects.

Utilizing Eisenmann, Parker, and Alstyne's (2006) description of two-sided markets, additional elements from Osterwalder and Pigneur (2010) and additional elements provided by the authors of this article, a modified triangular model of a two-sided market representing crowdfunding was created (Figure 2).

As seen in Figure 2 and as explained beforehand, a crowdfunding platform would fulfill the role of intermediary or platform provider. Project investors would satisfy the role of the subsidy side as they will be allowed to invest for free since their use of the platform will be financially supported by the money side fundraisers that pay fees based on their raised funds. Between the parties shown in Figure 1, rules are '[ ... ] the protocols, rights, and pricing terms that govern transactions' (Eisenmann, Parker, and Alstyne 2006, 5). For this model of crowdfunding, the rules would govern and oversee transactions via the platform from both the investor and fundraiser sides. These rules deal, in particular, with how and when funds can be released to the fundraiser, which is discussed later in this article.

Furthermore, '[t]he platform creates value by *facilitating interactions* between the different groups' (Osterwalder and Pigneur, 2010, 77). These interactions, particularly in the field of crowdfunding, take the form of network effects. Hendler and Golbeck (2008,

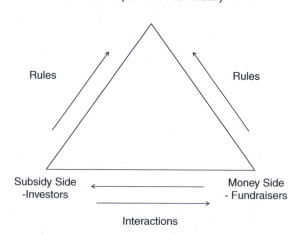

Figure 2. Two-sided market of crowdfunding.
*Source*: Based on Osterwalder and Pigneur (2010) and Eisenmann, Parker, and Alstyne (2006).

14) define them as '[...] the value of a service to a user that arises from the number of people using the service. At its core, it captures that value increases as the number of users increases [...]'. These interactions and accompanying network effects were not a part of Eisenmann, Parker, and Alstyne's (2006)original hypothetical model; however, Osterwalder and Pigneur (2010, 77) correctly pointed out that '[a] multi-sided platform grows in value to the extent that it attracts more users, a phenomenon known as the *network effect*'. This synergetic relationship between investors and fundraisers is extremely important to the model created in Figure 2. In the case of crowdfunding, this means an increase in the number of investors should lead to an increase in the number of fundraisers and vice versa. This is of importance to crowdfunding platforms as they require a sufficiently large crowd from which to draw investment from and enough crowdfunding projects posted to attract an adequate number of investors.

## 3.   Process flowcharting

The flowchart this article uses will feature several different symbols to represent different tasks in the investment process. This article will follow Harrington's (1991) general setup for flowcharting. 'The rectangles represent activities, and the lines with arrows connect the rectangles to show the direction of information flow and/or the relationships among the activities' and the rectangles themselves should '[i]nclude a short phrase within each rectangle describing the activity being performed' (88). Furthermore, flowcharting uses '[...] circle start and stop symbols to indicate where the flowchart begins and where it ends' (88). Additional elements will be added where needed from other literary sources and will be properly cited as such.

### 3.1.   *Flowcharting for business process modeling*

Flowcharting is another way to describe business process modeling, whereas the latter is currently the preferred nomenclature. 'The current generation of business process analysts prefers the term "process modeling" rather than flowcharting or mapping' (Rosemann, 2006, 250). Additionally, the benefits of flowcharting must be briefly covered to show its aid in creating the investment model of crowdfunding:

> The advantages of flowcharts centre on their ability to show the overall structure of a system, to trace the flow of information and work, to depict the physical media on which data are input, output and stored, and to highlight key processing and decision points. (Giaglis, 2001, 214)

Due to this ability to show the overall structure of a system, this article has chosen to utilize flowcharting to create its investment model of crowdfunding.

Flowcharting is quite often used as the tool to compose business process modeling. Havey (2005, 22) states that '[t]he design of a business process is intuitively a flowchart that outlines the steps performed over time in the resolution of a business problem'. Laguna and Marklund (2011, 110) reiterated this by stating that '[f]lowcharts are a fundamental tool for designing and redesigning processes'. Nysetvold and Krogstie (2006) said that business process modeling is based on a flowchart technique. An and Jeng (2005, 2069)go a step further, referring to business process modeling as 'business process flowchart modeling'. They call it one of the '[...] most prominent approaches to simulate the behavior of business processes [...]' (Jeng 2005, 2069).

This article's flowchart is created from a functional perspective (Giaglis, 2001). 'The functional perspective represents what process elements (activities) are being performed' (Giaglis, 2001, 212). In addition, this article applies the top-down approach of flowcharting.

This works as follows: '[a]s each layer of the model is specified, substeps within each process are delineated at greater and greater levels of detail, until sufficient detail is reached [ . . . ]' (Kangarloo et al., 1999, 547). This article, as will be seen at the beginning of the model, has created a business process model of crowdfunding investment that will become increasingly more complex toward the end as opposed to the more simplistic beginning. This fits better with the chosen top-down approach as opposed to a bottom-up approach.

### 3.2. Crowdfunding investment model – flow

The model will begin with a traditional START and finish with an END terminal. Terminals indicate '[ . . . ] the start or end of a process. The beginning terminal shape generally is labeled "start" or "begin". The ending terminal shape is labeled "stop" or "end"' (Mazumder, Bhattacharya, and Yadav 2011, 371). By following the arrows moving away from START, one can work its way through the entire model by following the flow along the arrows.

This article will use the American National Standards Institute standardized flowcharting symbols and elements from Business Process Modeling Notation 2.0 where needed. There appear to be no uniform global standards in flowcharting symbols, or the author of this article was not able to uncover any information pointing toward a universal standard. All symbols, in light of this article, appeared to be standardized and merely separated by some rare symbols that will not be used in its flowchart. The fully constructed model will be presented toward the end of this article. The individual parts of the model will be highlighted and discussed after each of the succeeding sections, immediately following the sections describing the sum of their individual pieces.

## 4. Direct versus indirect crowdfunding

There are two different types of fundraising in crowdfunding campaigns, collectively known as direct and indirect. Direct crowdfunding is when the fundraiser makes a direct appeal to a specific audience via their own fundraising platform (for example, the fundraiser's own website) or to their own supporters (for example, a band raising money from its fans). Indirect crowdfunding is, on the other hand, a general appeal for funding to the unknown general public or 'crowd'. This is typically accomplished via an intermediary platform. Numerous platforms have appeared on the crowdfunding scene '[ . . . ] such as Fundable, Kickstarter, Kiva, Sandawe, and SellaBand' (Lambert and Schwienbacher, 2010, 4). Their function is to '[ . . . ] intermediate between entrepreneurs and potential crowd-funders' (4).

The distinction between direct and indirect is important because '[ . . . ] at times entrepreneurs make use of [ . . . ] crowdfunding platforms instead of seeking direct contact with the crowd' (Belleflamme, Lambert, and Schwienbacher 2010, 5). Burkett (2011, 86) reinforces this direct versus indirect distinction as well, describing how a fundraiser can either make '[ . . . ] a pitch directly on its own website or indirectly through a crowdfunding intermediary [ . . . ]'.

The purpose of pointing out the distinction is to show that there is an option outside of using established crowdfunding intermediaries. However, if a fundraiser chooses to exploit direct fundraising, they would need to have a large enough crowd to raise funds from. Although there is no established minimum number of participants comprising the crowd in successful crowdfunding found in literature reviewed for this article, Howe mentioned 5000 as the minimum number of contributors for successful crowdsourcing campaigns (Accardi-Petersen, 2011, 211). In the opinion of this article's authors, this number would be too high to associate with crowdfunding. Kickstarter, arguably the world's most popular

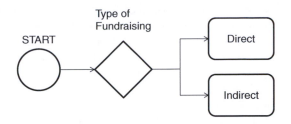

Figure 3.    Part 1: crowdfunding investment model.
*Source*: Own illustration.

crowdfunding platform, states that '[t]he average pledge is $71' and '[t]he average project is raising around $5,000' (Kickstarter, 2012b). By dividing the average amount raised by the average pledge, we can come to a rough estimation of 70 investors per project on average, far lower than the 5000 users mentioned by Howe for successful crowdsourcing. This is obviously a very loose way of calculating; however, the British crowdfunding platform Crowdcube (2012) claims a similar number of 73 investors per project and German website Seedmatch (2012) asserts 163 as the average number.

### 4.1.    *Crowdfunding investment model – Part 1*

**Figure** 3 shows the first part of the crowdfunding investment model. Going to the right from the START terminal on the left, where the crowdfunding process begins, the model comes to a diamond labeled 'Type of Fundraising'. This is the first decision of the investment model where a choice is made between one of the two types of fundraising: direct or indirect. The diamond shape was chosen to represent decisions that are to be made in the crowdfunding investment process, in this case whether the investor wants to invest directly with the crowdfundee (direct) or through an intermediary (indirect). Mazumder, Bhattacharya, and Yadav (2011, 371) say diamonds are used to indicate decisions signifying '[ . . . ] a point at which a decision must be made'. In general, flow lines point in indicating that options are given to the user when using decision diamonds (371).

    This type of split with a decision diamond and then two alternative choices is called an exclusive choice pattern:

> The Exclusive Choice pattern is defined as being a location in a process where the flow is 'split' into two or more exclusive alternative paths. The pattern is exclusive in that only one of the alternative paths may be chosen for the process to continue. (White, 2004, 5)

In this sense, the choice is mutually exclusive on either path of direct or indirect and they cannot be combined as an investment opportunity as a crowdfundee can only offer either a direct investment or an indirect investment.

    The rectangles labeled 'Direct' and 'Indirect' represent activities in the model. Activities correspond to '[ . . . ] any type of process or activity [ . . . ]' (Mazumder, Bhattacharya, and Yadav 2011, 371). These refer specifically to what type of fundraising the crowdfundee can choose to offer in this case.

### 5.    Baseline funding models

The two general models of funding at the core of crowdfunding are ex post facto and ex ante. Ex post facto funding is '[ . . . ] when a product is offered after financing is provided [ . . . ]' (Belleflamme, Lambert, and Schwienbacher 2010, 10). Kappel (2009, 375) describes it as a situation '[...] where financial support is offered in exchange for a completed product [...]'. In general, this means that the crowdfundee plans on giving the investor a proposed product in exchange for their investment. Often there is an existing prototype, blueprint or tentative design in place for a product that is awaiting manufacture prior to investment. This initial seed funding can then be used toward production costs. A famous example of this was the wildly popular Kickstarter crowdfunding campaign for the Pebble E-Paper watch, which is a watch that can sync with various smart phones using Bluetooth (Kickstarter, 2012e). For their financial support of the Kickstarter campaign to produce the timepieces, investors were to be given the watches in exchange for investments over $99 (Kickstarter, 2012e).

The other type of funding, ex ante, is when '[...] investors finance a project that has not been completed' (Rubinton, 2011, 5). Kappel (2009, 375) says ex ante crowdfunding is when '[...] financial support is given on the front end to assist in achieving a mutually desired result'. This means that a crowdfundee is not beyond the investigational stage of creating their desired product or service. A popular example of this is the Lowline Park project in New York City. Funding was raised to turn an 'abandoned New York City trolley terminal into a vibrant community green space' (Kickstarter, 2012c). It was obviously not possible to make a full-scale prototype park prior to an attempt at creating the actual park. So, money was raised in order to fully fund the project.

By funding before a product is completed, investors have a direct relationship with the realization of the product as opposed to ex post funding where a product or trial product has already been completed in advance of receiving funding. In contrast to ex post funded projects, ex ante funded projects '[...] do not require an established track record to work' (Kappel, 2009, 385), meaning that a fundraiser is less likely to need a certain performance history as a business or organization to receive funding from investors. Ex ante funding has been '[...] increasingly used in the entertainment industry by independent filmmakers, artists, writers, and performers to bypass traditional keepers of the purse' (376). It is also frequently used for other as-of-yet unmade creative services and products. Additionally, it appears that '[...] most crowdfunding is "ex ante"' (Burkett, 2011, 63).

### 5.1. *Crowdfunding investment model – Part 2*

The activities, direct and indirect, are a carryover from the aforementioned Part 1 (Figure 4). After the crowdfundee has chosen their fundraising type, the process comes to the next decision marked 'Investment Type'. Again the choice is mutually exclusive on either path of ex post or ex ante and cannot be combined as an investment opportunity either *has* an existing product (ex post) or *does not* (ex ante). The double

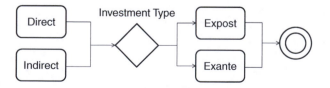

Figure 4. Part 2: crowdfunding investment model.
*Source*: Own illustration.

circle object immediately following ex post and ex ante is an intermediate event. Owen and Raj (2006) describe intermediate events as such:

> [o]ftentimes an event happens while a particular process is being performed, causing an interrupt to the process, and triggering a new process to be performed. Or, a process will complete, causing an event to start, and a new process to be performed. You can model these intermediate events by placing an [intermediate] event symbol directly on the process that it is associated with. (14)

This is essentially a point in which a large piece of the process has been completed and a new portion of the process model will now begin; however, the full process has not been completed at this point. This first portion of the crowdfunding investment model is named 'Type of Crowdfunding'.


## 6.  Payout modes of crowdfunding

From the literature found for this article, there are four payout models of crowdfunding. These 'Payout Modes' are the rules regulating how and when crowdfunding platforms release funds pooled from investors to the fundraiser. This can potentially be a serious hurdle when funds are not allowed to be released to the fundraiser and in some cases the investment model can stop at this stage.

Under a normal crowdfunding project, the fundraiser sets a goal or ultimate amount of money they are attempting to raise with their campaign. Many platforms employ the all-or-nothing funding model, whereby the total amount of money set as the fundraising goal by the fundraiser when posting the campaign must be met or exceeded in order for the funds to be released. If this minimum amount of money is not pledged by investors then no money is given to the fundraiser. This is also known as the threshold pledge model (Belleflamme, Lambert, and Schwienbacher 2010, 15).

The main principle is that:

> '[...] the platform and the project initiator agree on a concrete pledging period (between two weeks and several months) and a so-called threshold, a targeted sum of money that must be reached via the contributions of the backers or crowdfunders before any financial transaction is generated. Below this threshold, there is no flow of funds. (Hemer, 2011, 15)

Perhaps more simply described as the process '[...] whereby all pledges are voided unless a minimal amount is reached before some deadline [...]' (Belleflamme, Lambert, and Schwienbacher 2010, 11). If the funding goal is not met, then the '[...] money is returned to investors' (Collins and Pierrakis, 2012, 15).

Typically, pledged investments are held in a special account until the funding minimum is reached and the campaign is over. The money raised on the platform is '[...] transferred to and parked in an escrow account, which is managed by either the platform or by a partner bank' (Hemer, 2011, 15). For instance Kickstarter uses Amazon Payments to handle all transactions and escrow accounts on its web platform (Kickstarter, 2012a).

Kickstarter (2012a) described their all-or-nothing process as such:

> every project has a funding goal (a dollar amount) and a time limit (from 1–60 days) set by the project creator. When the deadline is reached, there are either of two results: (If) Funding Successful: If a project has met or surpassed its funding goal, all backers' credit cards are instantly charged and funds go directly to the project creator. Project creators are then responsible for completing the project and delivering rewards as promised. (If) Funding Unsuccessful: If a project has NOT met its funding goal, all pledges are canceled. That's it.

One of the most important aspects of the all-or-nothing model, from the investors' perspective, is that it ultimately protects them from being overzealous investors. 'The all-or-nothing condition also protects the most optimistic and foolhardy investors from their own improvidence. Unless the entrepreneur can convince other, more rational, investors to participate, the foolhardy are not at risk' (Bradford, 2012, 140). Moreover, it makes fundraisers carefully choose a realistic goal of financing appropriate for the project. 'Since overreaching could cause the offering to fail, the entrepreneur has an incentive to request only the true minimum amount needed to fund the project. This should lead to more careful budgeting before the funding request is posted' (140).

It is also suggested that the all-or-nothing model also prevents fraudulent campaigns by fundraisers. The minimum funding requirement itself is a sort of pseudo-fraud vetting system. 'The theory here is that the more people that have performed checks for fraud, the more likely a potentially fraudulent proposal will be identified as such' (Collins and Pierrakis, 2012, 24).

The next payout mode is 'holding'. This mode 'involves the platform operator creating a subsidiary company as an individual holding for each of the crowdfunding ventures that are to be funded' (Hemer, 2011, 16). Hemer further clarifies the holding process as when '[e]ach holding owns the above mentioned shares of "its" venture and sells them to the crowd. It acts as a single investor in the crowdfunding venture, alongside other potential investors from the conventional capital market' (16).

Kappel (2009) explains the holding model through British music production crowdsoucing platform Bankstocks. 'Bandstocks [ ... ] is owned and operated in the United Kingdom by Civilian Industries PLC ("Civilian"). Bandstocks is also the name for the securities (loan stocks) offered to investors on terms approved by the Financial Services Authorsity' (380). Every artist sets a target amount of money, similar to the all-or-nothing model, which is then divided into bandstocks, essentially stock shares which can be purchased by investors (380). Once enough funding is received, '[c]ivilian creates a subsidiary company (Albumco) specific to the recording project' (381).

The next mode is what Gerber, Hui, and Kuo (2012) refer to as the all and more model. In this model of funding, '[ ... ] creators can keep the money they raise even though their funding goals are not achieved' (Gerber, Hui, and Kuo 2012b, 3). It is also referred to as the keep-what-you-raise funding model (Gerber, Hui, and Kuo 2012).

RocketHub employs this fundraising system as well as Indiegogo (Gerber, Hui, and Kuo 2012b). In order to motivate fundraisers to not set arbitrary funding goals, there are different fees based on whether the goal is met, not met or exceeded:

> If creators reach or exceed their funding goals, RocketHub will offer an additional benefit, which is to waive the submission fees (4%) for creators' first five projects launched [ ... ] Indiegogo uses the keep-what-you-raise funding model. However, a higher fee will be charged from creators if they don't realize the funding goals. (Gerber, Hui, and Kuo 2012, 4)

This higher fee for partially funded projects seems to be an industry standard: 'a number of platforms charge higher commissions for partially-funded campaigns [ ... ]' (Crowdfunding Industry Report, 2012, 23).

The club mode was created as a way to offer pseudo-securities while avoiding securities regulations. 'A third group of companies has stayed away from offering securities and has offered club membership [ ... ]' (Watts, 2012, 4). This can be done by '[ ... ] recruiting potential funders from the crowd as members of a closed circle, which acts like an investment club' (Hemer, 2011, 17). With a simple change of language being used, saying *club member* instead of *shareholder*, the club mode has been able to avoid any complicated legalities. '[T]he crowdfunding participation is often structured in the form of making the participating crowd a member instead of a shareholder, such as BeerBankroll and MyFootballClub' (Schwienbacher and Larralde, 2010, 12).

A successful example of the club model was the purchase and takeover of British football club, Ebbsfleet United, by MyFootballClub, a members-only club:

> [M]embers of MyFootballClub (who own the football club Ebbsfleet United in United Kingdom) are completely involved in the management of the club through their voting right. The contribution of fans (a membership fee of £35) allowed them to complete the takeover of the club and form a community with real decision power. (Schwienbacher, Belleflamme, and Lambert 2011, 7)

Also, another members club, BeerBankroll, raised '[...] $2.5 million from its 5000 members' to start a community-owned beer company that intended to share profits with its members (Lambert and Schwienbacher, 2010, 2).

Although it must be noted that the line between offering a type of club membership and crossing over into the sale of actual securities can often be blurred. This was proven in 2009 during an attempt to raise money via crowdfunding to purchase American beer company Pabst Blue Ribbon. Forza Migliozzi saw that the Pabst Brewing Company was for sale for $300 million; he launched BuyABeerCompany.com to raise money from the general public, to purchase it (Sacks, 2012, 40). He '[...] [promised] investors "certificates of ownership" and beer with a value equal to the amount invested [...] [and] reportedly received $200 million in pledges from over five million individuals in the six-month period before the Securities and Exchange Commission ("SEC") shut them down for failing to register' as a security under the Securities Act of 1933 (Bradford, 2012, 6).

### 6.1. Crowdfunding investment model – Part 3

Part 3 of the model begins with a choice of payout mode (Figure 5). The diamond with four activities directly proceeding is a data-based exclusive choice decision gateway.

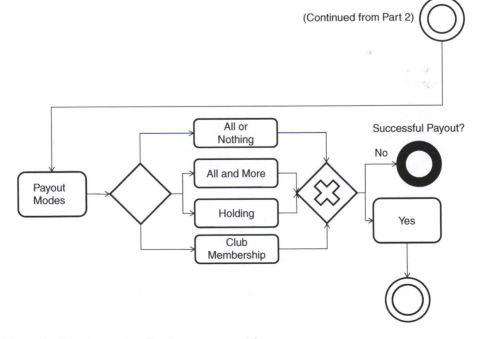

Figure 5.   Part 3: crowdfunding investment model.
*Source*: Own illustration.

In this type of gateway there are multiple but exclusive pathways determined by the process itself. White (2004) explains as follows:

> [T]he expressions will be evaluated (in a predetermined order) and for the first expression that is determined to be true, the corresponding Sequence Flow will be chosen and the Token will continue down that path. Only one Token will exit the Gateway for each Token that arrives at the Gateway. (5)

The only change this article would make to the preceding quote would be to replace the term *token* with *flow*.

The next decision following the payout modes is an event-driven exclusive decision. In this case, whether or not the crowdfunding campaign is funded or not, this 'event' determines which path the process takes. 'An event-based XOR gateway represents a branching point where the alternatives are based on an event that occurs at that point in the process flow' (Owen and Raj, 2006, 18). This step is of great importance because if funding is not successful, the entire process stops as represented by the black circle. The black circle is called a final flow node and it signifies that these processes are now finished. The final flow node '[ . . . ] is an indicator that a particular path has completed [ . . . ]' (White, 2004, 13). However, it is only this particular path where the process is stopped.

For example, Mollick (2013, 4) found in a study that out of 48,526 crowdfunding projects posted on Kickstarter, only 23,719 (or about 48% of those posted) were successfully funded. Kickstarter's own published statistics show that only 46% of projects were successfully funded in 2011 and 43% in 2010 (Kickstarter, 2012f). In the case of this article's model, the investment would not be able to proceed forward if, for example, while using the *all-or-nothing model*, the quota or required amount for funds to be release was not reached. In a sense, the investment process is held in queue until this stage is completed. However, if funding is secured, the process continues to an intermediate event and it goes forward from there.

## 7. General modes of investment of crowdfunding

There are three different general modes of investment in crowdfunding initiatives: passive investment, active investment and donation. Both Schwienbacher and Larralde (2010) and Metzler (2011) identified these three modes of investment. In addition to the three modes of investment found in the literature reviewed, this article leaves room open for other modes.

When an investor gives money to a fundraiser but is not active in decisions the company makes, this is known as a passive investment. Passive investment is a situation in which the investing firm is not seeking influence over the activities of the firm that it is investing in (Gilo, 2000). The best example of a passive investment is a regular bank loan. Although the success of the borrower is in the bank's best interest, banks are not likely to be as actively involved with specific decisions the borrower takes. Most passive investments '[ . . . ] do not offer any possibility to investors to become actively involved in the initiative, such as voting for selected characteristics of the final product or provide working time to the company' (Schwienbacher and Larralde, 2010, 13). Therefore, any entrepreneur who is seeking out passive investors is '[ . . . ] solely interested in raising money but not using the crowd as active consumers or giving up some control' over the product (Schwienbacher and Larralde, 2010, 13). According to a study from Lambert and Schwienbacher (2010, 9), passive investments account for 60% of total crowdfunding initiatives.

CROWDFUNDING AND ENTREPRENEURIAL FINANCE; ED. BY
RICHARD HARRISON.
Cloth    142 P.
LONDON: ROUTLEDGE, 2016


ED: U. EDINBURGH. SPECIAL ISSUE: VENTURE CAPITAL:
INTL JRNL OF ENTREPRENEURIAL FINANCE; V. 15:4.

  **ISBN** 1138927562     **Library PO#** SLIP ORDERS
                              **List**    160.00  USD
  6207 UNIV OF TEXAS/SAN ANTONIO    **Disc**     17.0%
  **App. Date** 11/11/15  FIN.BKS.PS 6108-09 **Net**   132.80  USD

SUBJ: 1. VENTURE CAPITAL. 2. CROWD FUNDING.


CLASS HG4751        DEWEY# 658.15224    LEVEL ADV-AC

**YBP Library Services**


CROWDFUNDING AND ENTREPRENEURIAL FINANCE; ED. BY
RICHARD HARRISON.
Cloth    142 P.
LONDON: ROUTLEDGE, 2016


ED: U. EDINBURGH. SPECIAL ISSUE: VENTURE CAPITAL:
INTL JRNL OF ENTREPRENEURIAL FINANCE; V. 15:4.

  **ISBN** 1138927562     **Library PO#** SLIP ORDERS
                              **List**    160.00  USD
  6207 UNIV OF TEXAS/SAN ANTONIO    **Disc**     17.0%
  **App. Date** 11/11/15  FIN.BKS.PS 6108-09 **Net**   132.80  USD

SUBJ: 1. VENTURE CAPITAL. 2. CROWD FUNDING.


CLASS HG4751        DEWEY# 658.15224    LEVEL ADV-AC

Active investments, on the other hand, '[ ... ] differ from passive investments by granting investors the ability to directly affect the results of the entrepreneur's project' via their ability to allow investors '[ ... ] to actively participate in the project' (Rubinton, 2011, 6, 9). The best example of an active investment is a stock purchase whereby the purchaser or investor now actively owns a portion of the company he/she invested in and may have voting rights. In terms of crowdfunding, established companies tend to offer active investment over passive investment as they often have the organizational structures in place to allow investors a more active voice in the direction of their efforts. Active investments account for around 30% of crowdfunding (Lambert and Schwienbacher, 2010, 9).

The third mode of investment is donation-based and as the name implies, this is when an investor donates his or her money to a crowdfunding initiative. In this case, the investor is giving money to a cause without expecting monetary reward and the investment itself does '[ ... ] not yield the donor any tangible reward' (Rubinton, 2011, 6). In the case of donation-based investments, '[ ... ] the financial return seems to be of secondary concern for those who provide funds. This suggests that crowdfunders care about social reputation and/or enjoy private benefits from participating in the success of the initiative' (Lambert and Schwienbacher, 2010, 12). Lehner (2012, 3) says when it comes to the subject of social reputation that 'crowd investors typically do not look much at collaterals or business plans, but at the ideas and core values of the firm [ ... ] and thus at its legitimacy'.

After investors have donated their money to a crowdfunding cause, '[ ... ] there is no continuing involvement by contributors, but this technique invites larger numbers of contributors to make small contributions, hopefully amounting to a meaningful gift in the aggregate, in part as a show of personal support for the individual' (Hanley and Bork, 2012, 44). In order to achieve donations, fundraisers need to limit monetary incentives to more easily attract donations (Belleflamme, Lambert, and Schwienbacher 2010). By putting more weight on the outcome, fundraisers are indicating to investors that the cause itself is more important than monetary goals. Unsurprisingly, '[ ... ] the majority of donation sites are for charities and non-profit institutions [ ... ]' (Griffin, 2013, 6). Pure donations constitute about 20% of crowdfunding initiatives (Lambert and Schwienbacher, 2010, 9). Though, this is not as popular a type of funding as active or passive investing, several large crowdfunding platforms offer it including '[ ... ] RocketHub, Indiegogo, Crowdrise, and Peerbackers' (Fink, 2012, 10).

There is certainly the possibility that other options are not covered in current literature or that other forms will appear in the future. Considering this, a fourth option of 'other' has been added. There are opportunities for hybridization; for instance, a donation could turn into an active investment, if the fundraiser also gives investors the ability to help determine project decisions. Another example of an alternative might be crowdsponsoring. Sponsoring, in this article's opinion, is not to be confused with donation. Sponsoring entails that a fundraiser would need to advertise or represent the product or service of the investing organization or person. Donation typically entails no reciprocation of action, meaning that in the prototypical donation case, the donator gives the money freely without expectation of a return of any sort. Additionally, a further difference in this article's opinion is that sponsorships are typically used to fund nonprofit ventures, whereas donations could be used in profit-oriented ventures.

Kaltenbeck (2011, 8) refers to crowdsponsoring as 'crowdsupporting' and calls it a '[ ... ] method for sponsorship with a non-financial return'. Hemer (2011) also identifies crowdsponsoring as an extension of crowdfunding. An ongoing example of crowd sponsoring is the Solar Impulse project. The Solar Impulse project is an effort to make a solar-powered airplane solely through sponsorship money. The project is partially funded through the solicitation of donations in the form of direct sponsorships from the general public through its Angels Program (Solar Impulse, 2011). In addition, they also have several corporate sponsors including Deutsche Bank (Banking on Green, 2012). Since crowdsponsoring is an as-of-yet unestablished form of crowdfunding in the current literature reviewed for this article, aside from the aforementioned references, it is included merely as a potential example of other forms of crowdfunding investment.

### 7.1. Nonequity rewards

One of the most important issues involving the finance model of crowdfunding is how investors are rewarded for their investments. Since crowdfunding is not always operated in the same manner as traditional investments like stock and bond purchases, most investors are looking for tangible, guaranteed rewards, monetary or otherwise, from fundraisers in exchange for their investment in crowdfunded projects. These come in different forms, often inhibited by legal restraints depending on where the fundraisers are based or the type of fundraising.

An important thing to note specifically for entrepreneurs is that:

> crowdfunding enables entrepreneurs to more quickly and easily identify supporter-investors who are willing and able to fund their businesses or projects. These investors may be more likely to be engaged with, and even passionate about, the ventures they are funding than repeat players in the seed, angel, or venture capital game. (Heminway and Hoffman, 2011, 931)

First, intrinsic motivation is most readily associated with the donation style of investment whereby investors are not expecting a tangible reward in exchange for their money. Sometimes investors are not wholly motivated by a financial goal but rather want to '[ . . . ] participate into [*sic*] innovative projects, be able to say 'I did it', obtain recognition and personal satisfaction. These are intrinsic motivations' (Schwienbacher and Larralde, 2010, 17). Kleemann, Voß, and Rieder (2008, 17) say '[a]n intrinsically motivated person, on the other hand, takes up an activity for its own sake − or for fun's sake' rather than purely for financial reasons. Hemer (2011, 14) identifies the following intrinsic motivations in crowdfunding:

> [ . . . ] personal identification with the project's subject and its goals; contribution to a societally [*sic*] important mission; satisfaction from being part of a certain community with similar priorities; satisfaction from observing the realisation and success of the project funded; enjoyment in being engaged in and interacting with the project's team; enjoying contributing to an innovation or being among the pioneers of new technology or business; the chance to expand one's own personal network; or the expectation of attracting funders in return for one's own crowdfunding project.

This article will delve no further into the psychology of why people donate as it is outside the scope of its purpose, but it is important to note it as a possible motivation for donation incentive in crowdfunding. Some examples of resources on the reasoning behind donations are Van Slyke and Brooks (2005), Vesterlund (2006) and Aaker and Akutsu (2009).

Patronage style rewards are an alternative form of reward; they are compensation for investment in the form of gifts or products associated with the fundraiser, hence the word 'patron' in the term. Burkett (2011, 64) describes patronage rewards as follows: '[i]n exchange for a contribution, most current crowdfunding sites only allow promoters to reward funders with nominal perks or "thank-you" gifts. Because the contributions are effectively donations, this is called "patronage crowdfunding"'. A popular example of this type of reward is through German-based website Sellaband, where supporters can fund the production of records for independent musicians. In exchange for financially supporting musicians, users are entitled to items such as '[...] free downloads, signed T-shirts and backstage passes' (Sellaband, 2012). These rewards are also sometimes referred to as patronage perks. In the entertainment industry, for example, they can include things such as '[...] film credits or album liner notes, advanced autographed copies of the work, or backstage access at a performer's show' (Burkett, 2011, 64) in exchange for investment. The advantage of the patronage model is that it is not regulated by securities laws as no equity is being exchanged for funding, merely various perks offered by the fundraisers in exchange for investments. From the investors' perspective they are both supporting a cause they feel is worthy and receiving a tangible reward in exchange for their financial support.

The next mode of reward is the prepurchase or preorder model. This is rather uncomplicated; investors purchase an as-of-yet unproduced product, that is, they preorder it in exchange for an investment of a certain amount as set by the fundraiser. Essentially, investors '[...] receive the product that the entrepreneur is making' (Bradford, 2012, 16). A contemporary example from Kickstarter is the Ouya game console which rose over $2.3 million of funding from investors in its first 24 hours of offering (Kickstarter, 2012d). The makers of the console promise to give each investor one of the gaming devices before it is released to the general public, in exchange for investments of $99 or more (Kickstarter, 2012d). In the case of Ouya and most preorder campaigns, the price of the investment is lower than the price the product will sell to the general public once produced, in other words the investment price is '[...] below the planned retail price' (Bradford, 2012, 17).

This is an excellent way for an organization to gauge interest in its potential product and to cover the costs of initial production. One of the associated advantages is signaling which is described by Hemer:

> [h]aving found a large number of supporters – which is visible to everybody who consults the CF-website – means, on the one hand, that these already form a core market and, on the other hand, that they can be easily mobilised as multiplicators and sales agents within their personal (social) networks. (2011, 28)

The downside of this mode is that the product may never be produced, nor is there any penalty if the product is not produced. Funders might not only lose their money but may also not receive the promised product if a fundraiser is unsuccessful in producing their promised creation. Even given the potential downsides, the prepurchase model is currently '[...] the most common type of crowdfunding [...]' (Bradford, 2012, 16). An additional advantage for prepurchase is that it does 'not involve securities for purposes of federal law' (32) along with the patronage style and donation; these investment perks are merely gifts in exchange for investment.

## 7.2. *Equity-based rewards*

The last type of compensation is equity-based. This is when a fundraiser sells an equity stake, or shares in their company, in exchange for investment from crowdfunders. First, it must be mentioned that investors in the USA will find it very difficult to participate in crowdfunding in exchange for equity. '[I]t is illegal in the United States to offer or sell a "security" without either complying with arduous registration requirements or wading through the difficult process of obtaining an exemption' (Burkett, 2011, 64). Any organization offering the sale of a security in the USA must be registered under the

Securities Act of 1933 (Bradford, 2012). The main issue is that general solicitations to the public for equity offerings are limited to companies that are publicly listed (Belleflamme, Lambert, and Schwienbacher 2010). Crowdfunding in and of itself qualifies as a general solicitation, making it very hard for US-based crowdfunders to list equity-based deals for investors from the general public. It must be noted, however, that recent legislation in the USA is expected to lower requirements for the sale of equity, specifically in regard to crowdfunding, making it possible for crowdfunders to sell securities. This article will not discuss legal issues in depth. There are ample resources dealing with the legal aspects of crowdfunding including Burkett (2011), Heminway and Hoffman (2011), Bradford (2012) and Hazen (2012).

There has been a massive growth in equity-based crowdfunding, particularly in Europe with an increase of 114% in equity-based offerings between 2007 and 2011 (Crowdfunding Industry Report, 2012, 17). This expansion was mainly attributed to 'growth in the number of European platforms' (17).

One form of equity-based reward is patronage plus, an extension of the aforementioned patronage model, which takes the patronage model one step further. This is typically when an investor is entitled to not only rewards but also monetary compensation:

> [...] [T]he website Bandstocks allows residents in the UK to contribute money to help bands produce new albums. Like with patronage crowdfunding, Bandstocks funders receive certain in-kind perks, such as a copy of the recording or VIP privileges. Unlike patronage crowdfunding, however, Bandstocks' funders acquire a financial interest in the recording. In other words, they are entitled to a share of the net receipts generated by the album. (Burkett, 2011, 74–75)

Additionally, investors on the Sellaband platform are sometimes '[...] rewarded with a royalty on future sales' (Ordanini et al., 2009, 24). The benefit from this model is that the financial success of the venture has a direct correlation with evangelism from financial backers and vice versa. This means that funders are more likely to advertise the product to the general public when they know that they will benefit monetarily by the increased popularity in the form of increased sales of the product. It is a popular view that the patronage plus model will be more successful in the long term because '[...] fans become literally invested in the success [...]' of the artist or product (Kappel, 2009, 376).

Another reward mode is profit sharing. This is where an investor receives a share of profit from the fundraiser in exchange for investment. Lambert and Schwienbacher (2010, 5) included this in their reward options: '[...] cash, bonds, stocks [and] profit sharing [...]'. An example of profit sharing is through Hong Kong-based Grow VC. The platform requires users to 'pay a subscription fee – between $25 and $140 a month, depending on how much equity that member wants [...] [then pools together] [...] 75% of these fees in a community investment fund' (Burkett, 2011, 75). Subscribers then 'allocate a portion of the community investment fund to particular entrepreneurial projects that they think have the most potential for return' (Burkett, 2011, 75). This investment is then held for three years, at which point Grow VC takes '25% of profits from the investment [...] [then] [...] those members who invested their portion of the fund into a successful project receive a certain percentage of the profits' (Burkett, 2011, 76).

In the light of some literature, and in the opinion of this article's authors, profit sharing is a form of equity-based security. Heminway and Hoffman (2011, 906) said, '[c]rowdfunding interests that include revenue-sharing or profit-sharing benefits appear to be equity-type capital investment vehicles'. Securities law also tend to include '[...]

any profit-sharing agreement [...]' (Hazen, 2012, 1740) as a security just like equity-based investments.

An additional type of reward model that is related to equity tenders is private placement offering. 'In a private placement, an issuer puts out an offer to a select (private) group of qualifying recipients' (Watts, 2012, 8). This is similar to crowdfunding in that crowdfunding is also limited to a select group of individuals that are engaged in crowdfunding investments; however, in crowdfunding campaigns the crowd is typically unknown to the fundraiser. Qualified recipients, also known as qualified or sophisticated investors, are typically investors that have an existing relationship with the fundraiser and/ or are considered to be well experienced in investing. Though they are different, this does not mean that a crowdfunding project cannot qualify as a private placement offering if the crowdfunding offer is only tendered to a select group of crowdfunders.

In the case of private placement, '[...] the "crowd" would be comprised of friends and family' (Burkett, 2011, 77), or more simply put, '[...] those [investors] who have a "substantial, pre-existing relationship"' with a known fundraiser (77). The reason for this focus on investors with preexisting relationships is that this is a way around existing US and EU law regarding securities regulations. Although fundraisers investing in US-based offers must keep in mind that '[...] the SEC's Division of Trading and Markets warns that anyone finding investors for a company, including venture capital, angel financings, and private placements, may need to register as a broker' (Bradford, 2012, 55).

An example of this type of scheme is ProFounder, 'which functions as a matchmaker between promoters seeking capital in the United States and those who have a "substantial, pre-existing relationship" with a given promoter' (Burkett, 2011, 77). In the case of ProFounder, the crowd is '[...] comprised of friends and family [...]' and is self-described as a '[...] "*community*-based crowdfunding platform," as opposed to the normal crowdfunding platform where promoters appeal to the masses without the need for a preexisting relationship' (77).

### 7.3. *Crowdfunding investment model – Part 4*

The first decision of Part 4 has mutually exclusive paths to follow based on the four general modes of investment (Figure 6). This is a fairly simplistic procedure; each path leads directly to their accompanying reward models on the other end of the arrows. Donation has only one type of reward identified in literature reviewed for this article, intrinsic value, and therefore ends at this point on the final flow node. Since 'Other' is nonspecific in terms of rewards, its path also ends here. At this point, all elements of the crowdfunding investment model have been fulfilled for these types of investment modes and the model ends here.

Passive investment and active investment have multiple reward types and as such are succeeded by decision diamonds which represent the multiple reward options available to fundraisers. The diamond after passive investment represents nonequity-based reward options. The diamond after active investment represents equity-based reward options.

Starting with the two rewards on the top, prepurchase and patronage, they all filter into the black final flow node as these reward systems do not have any legal issues associated with them in regard to financial transaction or securities regulations, or at least none that were found in the literature this article reviewed. Hence, the crowdfunding investment model ends for them here. Equity, private placement offer, profit sharing and patronage plus all lead toward an intermediate event that will continue to Part 5 of the model.

(Continued from Part 3)

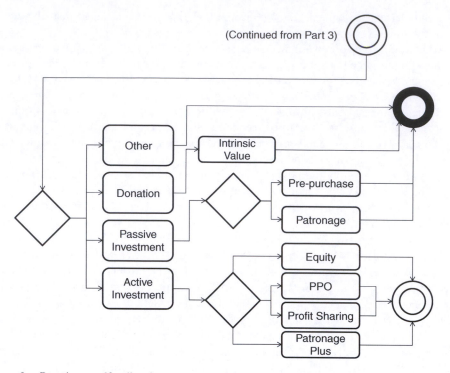

Figure 6. Part 4: crowdfunding investment model.
*Source*: Own illustration.

## 8. Crowdfunding investment model – Part 5

The first symbol is known as an event-driven gateway (Figure 7). The purpose of this type of gateway is to show that '[t]he first Event that occurs will trigger the path that will be taken to the exclusion of any other path from the Gateway [ . . . ]' (White, 2004, 17). For the purposes of this article's model, it means that when there is an equity-based transaction, sometimes it is known in advance that the transaction was in fact a securities transaction, but not always. 'The actual decision on which branch is activated is made by the environment and is deferred to the latest possible moment [ . . . ]' (Russell et al., 2006, 4). This means that in the event it is known that a security has been invested in and needs no confirmation, they would continue to the securities exemptions stage to look for applicable exemptions.

The last decision determines whether the equity investment was successful or not due to legal or other issues. If unsuccessful, the process stops here on the final flow node. If successful, the user proceeds to reinvest and determines whether to reinvest; if he/she chooses to reinvest, he/she proceeds back to the START terminal. This final point will be added in the complete flowchart shown in Figure 8.

## 9. Crowdfunding investment model

Here the completed model of crowdfunding investment can be seen with all of the 'Parts' mentioned in the previous sections put together. The notable aspects of the completed model are the swim lanes, pools and the reinvestment arrow which was described in the previous section.

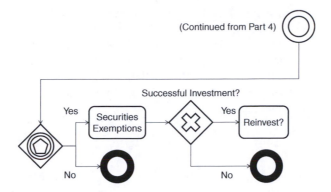

Figure 7.    Part 5: crowdfunding investment model.
*Source*: Own illustration.

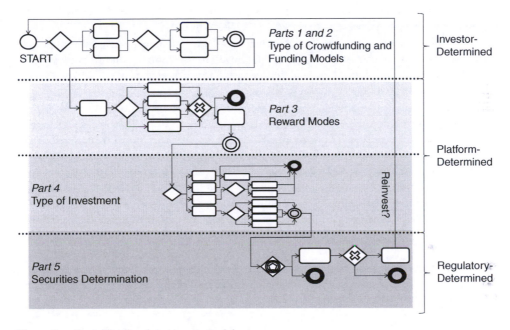

Figure 8.    Crowdfunding investment model.
*Source*: Own illustration.

Kosalge and Chatterjee (2011, 518) say that swim lanes are '[ . . . ] a commonly used visual representation in process flow diagrams, where vertical lines are drawn on paper to demarcate the domain of a person, a group, or an object'. In the model above, they represent the four gray-shaded areas separated with dotted lines. Parts 1 and 2 combine to represent the type of crowdfunding and funding models. They together are represented by the pool called 'Investor-Determined', meaning they are noteworthy as areas where investors have the most influence. Pools are used to '[ . . . ] specify "who does what" by placing the events and processes into shaded areas called pools that denote who is performing a process [ . . . ] [a] pool typically represents [ . . . ] things such as functions [ . . . ]' (Owen and Raj, 2006, 9). In the model above, they differentiate the crowdfunding investment processes into the relevant players: investors, platform and regulators. The swim lanes are used to further partition pools (Owen and Raj, 2006, 9) as mentioned earlier.

Part 3 in the second swim lane represents the reward modes of crowdfunding. Part 4 in the third lane signifies the type of investment. Both Part 3 and Part 4 represent areas that are platform-determined. In this sense, the platform is representing the interests of the crowdfundee as they have the power to make decisions on the process via the platform. Part 5 represents equity-based crowdfunding as denoted by the swim lane name 'Securities Determination'. This area is determined by the regulatory structure surrounding the crowdfunding deal.

## 10. Conclusion

This article's model appears to be the first and only conceptualized crowdfunding investment model, in light of the present literature on crowdfunding. It also seems to be the first attempt at accumulating all relevant subject matter involving the crowdfunding finance process from existing literature.

Two important findings of this article involved the identification of bottlenecks in the investment process that were not recognized in literature reviewed for this article. First, in Part 4 of the model, the delays concerning the payout models are critically important to crowdfunding investment. This is a stage where the entire funding process can stop. Furthermore, in Figure 5, it is also imperative to recognize how varied legal issues can both help and hinder the equity-based crowdfunding offer.

In the opinion of this article's authors, future investigation should be concentrated on identifying the various legal aspects of the crowdfunding process that impact its model. There are many open aspects on the end of the model, especially in regard to legal issues and reinvestment as well as other gaps that can be filled in. Moreover, the current literature that was reviewed for this article did not focus on elements of successful or unsuccessful crowdfunding from the investor's standpoint and how that would affect reinvestment rates. It is important that future research focuses on reiterations of the model it proposes as well as filling in the holes that are certainly present.

## Acknowledgements

This research was generously funded by the Ludwig-Erhard-Forschungszentrum für Kooperative Wirtschaft at the Friedrich-Alexander-Universität Erlangen-Nürnberg (FAU).

## References

Aaker, J., and T. Akutsu. 2009. "Why do People Give? The Role of Identity in Giving." *Journal of Consumer Psychology* 19: 267–270.

Accardi-Petersen, M. 2011. *Agile Marketing*. New York: Springer Science + Business Media.

An, L., and J.-J. Jeng. 2005. "On Developing System Dynamics Model For Business Process Simulation." *Proceedings of the 2005 Winter Simulation Conference*, 2068–2077.

AngelList. 2013. "Investors." Accessed July 1. https://angel.co/people/investors

Aparicio, M., C. J. Costa, and A. S. Braga. 2012. "Proposing a System to Support Crowdsourcing." *Proceedings of the Workshop on Open Source and Design of Communication*, 13–17.

Banking on Green. 2012. "Deutsche Bank and Solar Impulse: A Perfect Team for Sustainable Innovation." Accessed September 8. http://www.banking-on-green.com/en/content/sustainability_projects_initiatives/deutsche_bank_and_solar_impulse_3662.html

Belleflamme, P., T. Lambert, A. Schwienbacher, and 2010. *Digital Business Models: Understanding Strategies* 1–30.

Bradford, C. S. 2012. "Crowdfunding and the Federal Securities Laws." *Columbia Business Law Review* 2012 (1): 1–150.

Burke, A. 2012. "$123 Million Crowdfunding Market Nearly Quadrupled in a Year, Report Says." Accessed December 12. http://www.forbes.com/sites/techonomy/2012/03/30/123-million-crowdfunding-market-nearly-quadrupled-in-a-year-report-says/

Burkett, E. 2011. "A Crowdfunding Exemption? Online Investment Crowdfunding and U.S. Securities Regulation." *Transactions: The Tennessee Journal of Business Law* 13: 63–106.

Caldbeck, R. 2013. "Crowdfunding Won't Solve the Venture Capital Series A Crunch." Accessed on January 25, 2013. http://www.forbes.com/sites/ryancaldbeck/2013/01/23/crowdfunding-wont-solve-the-venture-capital-series-a-crunch/

Collins, L., and Y. Pierrakis. 2012. "The Venture Crowd: Crowdfunding Equity Investment into Business." Working Paper R2/2011. London: Nesta.

Crowdcube. 2012. "A New Way to Raise Finance for Your Business." Accessed August 21. http://www.crowdcube.com/pg/businessfinance-3

Crowdfunder. 2013. "Homepage." Accessed July 1. http://www.crowdfunder.com/

Crowdfunding Industry Report. 2012. *Market Trends, Composition and Crowdfunding Platforms*. 1–30. Los Angeles, California: Crowdsourcing LLC.

Cumming, D. J., and S. A. Johan. 2009. *Venture Capital and Private Equity Contracting: An International Perspective*. Burlington, MA: Academic Press.

Eisenmann, T., G. Parker, and M. W. Van Alstyne. 2006. "Strategies for Two- Sided Markets." *Harvard Business Review* 84 (10): 1–11.

Fink, A. C. 2012. "Protecting the Crowd and Raising Capital Through the CROWDFUND Act." *University of Detroit Mercy Law Review* 90: 1–141.

Franklin, M. J., D. Kossmann, T. Kraska, S. Ramesh, and R. Xin. 2011. "CrowdDB: Answering Queries with Crowdsourcing." *Proceedings of the* 2011: 61–72.

Gennari, A. N. 2012. "The Determinants of SMEs Capital Structure: Overcoming Supply Constraints." MA thesis, NOVA – School of Business and Economics, Lisbon.

Gerber, E. M., J. S. Hui, and P. Kuo. 2012a. *Crowdfunding: Why People are Motivated to Post and Fund Projects on Crowdfunding Platforms*. Illinois: Creative Action Lab, Northwestern University.

Gerber, E., J. Hui, and P. -Y. Kuo. 2012b. *Crowdfunding: Why People are Motivated to Participate*, Technical Report 12-02. Evanston, Illinois: Northwestern University Segal Design Institute.

Giaglis, G. M. 2001. "A Taxonomy of Business Process Modeling and Information Systems Modeling Techniques." *The International Journal of Flexible Manufacturing Systems* 13 (2): 209–228.

Gilo, D. 2000. "The Anticompetitive Effect of Passive Investment." *Michigan Law Review* 99 (1): 1–47.

Griffin, Z. J. 2013. "Crowdfunding: Fleecing the American Masses." *Case Western Reserve Journal of Law, Technology & the Internet*, Forthcoming.

Hanley, B. D. F., and P. Bork. 2012. "Crowdfunding: A New Way to Raise Capital, or a Cut-Back in Investor Protection." *INSIGHTS* 26 (6): 44–50.

Harrington, H. J. 1991. *Business Process Improvement: The Breakthrough Strategy for Total Quality, Productivity, and Competitiveness*. Cambridge, UK: Cambridge University Press.

Havey, M. 2005. *Essential Business Process Modeling*. Sebastopol, CA: O'Reilly Media, Inc.

Hazen, T. L. 2012. "Crowdfunding or Fraudfunding? Social Networks and the Securities Laws: Why the Specially Tailored Exemption Must Be Conditioned on Meaningful Disclosure." *North Carolina Law Review* 90: 1735–1770.

Hemer, J. 2011. "A Snapshot on Crowdfunding." Fraunhofer ISI Working Paper. Working Paper R2/2011.

Heminway, J. M., and S. R. Hoffman. 2011. "Proceed at Your Peril: Crowdfunding and the Securities Act Of 1933." *Tennessee Law Review* 78 (879): 879–972.

Hendler, J., and J. Golbeck. 2008. "Metcalfe's Law, Web 2.0, and the Semantic Web." *Journal of Web Semantics* 6 (1): 14–20.

Indiegogo. 2012. "FAQ: Learn More." Accessed August 10. http://www.indiegogo.com/learn/faqs

Kaltenbeck, J. 2011. "Crowdfunding und Social Payments: Im Anwendungskontext von Open Educational Resources." *Contributions to Open Education Resources*, Vol. 1, 1–97.

Kangarloo, H., J. D. Dionisio, U. Sinha, D. Johnson, and R. K. Taira. 1999. "Process Models for Telehealth: An Industrial Approach to Quality Management of Distant Medical Practice." *Journal of the American Medical Informatics Association* 545–549.

Kappel, T. 2009. "Ex Ante Crowdfunding and the Recording Industry: A Model for the U.S." *Loyola of Los Angeles Entertainment Law Review* 29 (3): 375–385.

Kickstarter. 2012a. "FAQ: Creators." Accessed July 4. http://www.kickstarter.com/help/faq/creators#HowDoIContAmazPaymWithAQues

Kickstarter. 2012b. "How Kickstarter Works." Accessed July 23. http://www.kickstarter.com/start/

Kickstarter. 2012c. "LowLine: An Underground Park on NYC's Lower East Side." Accessed June 30. http://www.kickstarter.com/projects/855802805/lowline-an-underground-park-on-nycs-lower-east-sid

Kickstarter. 2012d. "2012d. "OUYA: A New Kind of Video Game Console." Accessed August 15. http://www.kickstarter.com/projects/ouya/ouya-a-new-kind-of-video-game-console

Kickstarter. 2012e. "Pebble: E-Paper Watch for iPhone and Android." Accessed July 25. http://www.kickstarter.com/projects/597507018/pebble-e-paper-watch-for-iphone-and-android

Kickstarter. 2012f. "2011: The Stats." Accessed July 7. http://www.kickstarter.com/blog/2011-the-stats

Kleemann, F., G. G. Voß, and K. Rieder. 2008. "Un(der)paid Innovators: The Commercial Utilization of Consumer Work through Crowdsourcing." *Science Technology Innovation Studies* 4 (1): 6–26.

Kosalge, P., and D. Chatterjee. 2011. "Look Before You Leap into ERP Implementation: An Object-Oriented Approach to Business Process Modeling." *Communications of the Association for Information Systems* 28: 509–536.

Laguna, M., and J. Marklund. 2011. *Business Process Modeling, Simulation and Design*. New Delhi, India: Dorling Kindersley (India) Pvt. Ltd.

Lambert, T., and A. Schwienbacher. 2010. *An Empirical Analysis of Crowdfunding*. Louvain-la-Neuve: Louvain School of Management, Catholic University of Louvain.

Lavinsky, D. 2010. "Funding Fathers." Accessed December 14, 2012. http://www.sbnonline.com/Local/Article/20471/65/0/Funding_fathers.aspx

Lehner, O. M. 2012. "A Literature Review and Research Agenda for Crowdfunding of Social Ventures." Paper presented at the 2012 Research Colloquium on Social Entrepreneurship, University of Oxford, July 16–19.

Mazumder, B., S. Bhattacharya, and A. Yadav. 2011. "Total Quality Management in Pharmaceuticals: A Review." *International Journal of PharmTech Research* 3 (1): 365–375.

McKaskill, T. 2009. *An Introduction to Angel Investing: A Guide to Investing in Early Stage Entrepreneurial Ventures*. Melbourne: Breakthrough Publications.

Metzler, T. 2011. *Venture Financing by Crowdfunding*. Munich, Germany: GRIN Verlag.

MicroVentures. 2013. "Homepage." Accessed July 1. http://www.microventures.com/

Mollick, E. R. 2013. "The Dynamics of Crowdfunding: Determinants of Success and Failure." *Journal of Business Venturing*. Forthcoming.

Nysetvold, A. G., and J. Krogstie. 2006. "Assessing Business Process Modeling Languages Using a Generic Quality Framework." In *Advanced Topics in Database Research*, edited by K. Siau. Vol. 5, 79–93. Hershey, Pennsylvania: Idea Group.

Ordanini, A., L. Miceli, M. Pizzetti, and A. Parasuraman. 2011. "Crowd-Funding: Transforming Customers into Investors through Innovative Service Platforms." *Journal of Service Management* 22 (4): 443–470.

Osterwalder, A., and Y. Pigneur. 2010. *Business Model Generation*, 1–288. Hoboken, NJ: Wiley.

Owen, M., and J. Raj. 2006. *BPMN and Business Process Management: An Introduction to the New Business Process Modeling Standard*, 1–34. http://www.osiris-consultores.cl/Telelogic/6_BPMN%26BPM.pdf

Pagliery, J. 2012. "Construction Firms Fare Worst in Loan Crunch." Accessed December 13. http://money.cnn.com/2012/08/15/smallbusiness/construction-loan/index.html

Pope, N. D. 2011. "Crowdfunding Microstartups: It's Time for the Securities and Exchange Commission to Approve Small Offering." *University of Pennsylvania Journal of Business Law* 13 (4): 101–129.

Rannala, E. 2013. "Riding on the Wings Of Angels, VCs Avoid the So-Called Series A Crunch." Accessed March 3. http://techcrunch.com/2013/03/02/are-angels-getting-crunched-but-not-vcs/

Rosemann, M. 2006. "Potential Pitfalls of Process Modeling: Part A." *Business Process Management Journal* 12 (2): 249–254.

Rubinton, B. J. 2011. "Crowdfunding: Disintermediated Investment Banking." *Munich Personal RePEc Archive*. (MPRA) Paper No. 31649. http://mpra.ub.uni-muenchen.de/31649/

Russell, N., A. H. M. Ter Hofstede, W. M. Van der Aalst, and P. Wohed. 2006. "On the Suitability of UML 2.0 Activity Diagrams for Business Process Modelling." *Proceedings of the Third Asia-Pacific Conference on Conceptual Modelling* 53: 1–10.

Sacks, D. 2012. "Shaking up Crowdfunding." *Fast Company*, June 2012.

Schwienbacher, A., P. Belleflamme, and T. Lambert. 2011. *Crowdfunding: Tapping the Right Crowd*, No. 2011032, CORE Discussion Papers, Université catholique de Louvain, Center for Operations Research and Econometrics (CORE).

Schwienbacher, A., and B. Larralde. 2010. "Crowdfunding of Small Entrepreneurial Ventures." In *Handbook of Entrepreneurial Finance*, edited by D. Cumming, 1–23. Oxford: Oxford University Press.

Seedmatch. 2012. "Statistik Q2-12." Accessed September 13. http://blog.seedmatch.de/wp-content/uploads/2012/07/Statistik-Q2-12_final.png

Sellaband. 2012. "How It Works." Accessed August 28. https://www.sellaband.com/en/pages/how_it_works

Shontell, A. 2012. "And Now Were at the Point Where Startups Are Running Out of Cash." Accessed November 20. http://www.businessinsider.com/startup-cash-crunch-2012-11

Shontell, A. 2013. "The Series A Crunch Has Claimed Another Startup." Accessed February 23. http://www.businessinsider.com/startup-turf-geography-club-shuts-down-2013-2

Sohl, J. 2012. *The Angel Investor Market In 2011: The Recovery Continues*, 1–2. Center for Venture Research.

Solar Impulse. 2011. "Angels." Accessed September 9, 2012. http://www.solarimpulse.com/en/team/angels/

Steinberg, S., and R. DeMaria. 2012. *The Crowdfunding Bible: How to Raise Money for Any Startup, Video Game, or Project*, edited by J. Kimmich, 1–80. Cincinnati, OH: ReadMe Publishing.

Unterberg, B. 2010. "Kapitel 8 Crowdsourcing (Jeff Howe)." In *Social Media Handbuch: Theorien, Methoden, Modelle*. 1st ed., 121–135. Baden-Baden, Germany: Nomos Verlagsgesellschaft.

Van Slyke, M. David, and Arthur C. Brooks. 2005. "Why do People Give? New Evidence and Strategies for Nonprofit and Public Managers." *American Review of Public Administration* 35 (3): 199–222.

Vesterlund, L. 2006. "Why do People Give?" In *The Nonprofit Sector: A Research Handbook*, edited by W. Powell, and R. S. Steinberg. 2nd ed., 568–587. New Haven, CT: Yale University.

Voorbraak, K. J. M. 2011. *Crowdfunding for Financing New Ventures: Consequences of the Financial Model on Operational Decisions*. Eindhoven: Eindhoven University of Technology.

Watts, T. 2012. "Crowdfunding: Raising Funds from Those You Know." *Keynotes*. 1–10. http://opencoffee.3783750.n2.nabble.com/attachment/5040633/3/Crowdfunding%20Keynotes.pdf

White, S. A. 2004. "Process Modeling Notations and Workflow Patterns." In *Workflow Handbook 2004*, edited by L. Fischer, 1–24. Lighthouse Point, FL: Future Strategies.

Wroldsen, J. S. 2013. "The Social Network and the Crowdfund Act: Zuckerberg, Saverin and Venture Capitalists' Dilution of the Crowd." *Vanderbilt Journal of Entertainment and Technology Law* 15: 1–45.

# Exploring entrepreneurial legitimacy in reward-based crowdfunding

Denis Frydrych, Adam J. Bock, Tony Kinder and Benjamin Koeck

*University of Edinburgh Business School, Edinburgh, UK*

Venture financing through social networks has become a global phenomenon. The processes and drivers of crowdfunding require careful study to identify similarities and distinctions from traditional venture finance. The demonstration of project legitimacy is especially interesting because online crowdfunding limits investors' access to the entrepreneur and organisation. How do rewards-based crowdfunding projects establish and demonstrate legitimacy in this virtual, impersonal context? We employ a novel data-set collected from the Kickstarter crowdfunding platform to explore the characteristics of successful projects, including legitimating signals and content. The data reveal numerous findings linking project characteristics to legitimacy and success. First, lower funding targets and shorter duration signal legitimacy by setting modest, achievable expectations. Rewards structures, such as traditional equity investment terms, appear to generate a sense of legitimate investment returns. Finally, narrative legitimacy in the online crowdfunding context may derive more from the online platform community than the visual pitch. Our study reveals a more nuanced picture of legitimacy formation during rewards-based crowdfunding, with implications for theories of resource assembly and the practice of venture finance.

## 1. Introduction

Early stage venture funding is difficult. Accelerating rates of innovation and market adoption increase the attractiveness of distributed online financing for new ventures. Although online social networking emerged as a consumer-driven service, entrepreneurs have now begun to exploit formal and informal networks for capital assembly.

Crowdfunding, a form of crowdsourced venture funding, is an online ecosystem experiencing rapid growth. Resource deficient entrepreneurs utilise crowdfunding as an innovative capital management mechanism to bypass early stage capital gaps by pre-funding production and sales (Harrison 2013). Entrepreneurs target 'amateurs' or affinity-based consumers to pre-finance a service or product, rather than pitch professional investors. Crowdfunding helps entrepreneurs and investors reduce the risk of underfunding a project, since investments are not executed unless the minimum funding amount is met.

Crowdfunding may facilitate legitimacy development for nascent ventures. The market-facing funding approach offers entrepreneurs a 'tailor-made' solution to assemble and allocate finance (Belleflamme, Lambert, and Schwienbacher 2013). Crowdfunding engages prospective customers and investors in the funding, (pre-) launch or growth of entrepreneurial projects and firms (Burtch, Ghose, and Wattal 2011; Mollick 2014). Entrepreneurs can establish strong networks in the market and utilise traction from the distributed group of individuals to increase organisational legitimacy and facilitate financial capital assembly.

As Reuber and Fischer (2011) note, online reputation and brand communities support entrepreneurial activities in Internet-enabled markets by attracting investors: the firm's reputation with customers is co-created with legitimacy in an online environment.

Online brand communities may confer market validity, encouraging investors and customers to engage with an entrepreneurial venture. Crowdfunding enables entrepreneurs to create, develop and foster online reputation and community using social-psychological incentives (Lehner 2013). Some entrepreneurs exploit these heterogeneous communities to mobilise socially embedded financial capital.

Legitimacy may be an important driver of financial resource assembly for these ventures (Mollick 2013). As crowdfunding is a recent phenomenon, our understanding of the drivers of legitimacy during crowdfunding and venture development has not been investigated. This study explores (1) how entrepreneurs facilitate organisational legitimacy creation during crowdfunding and (2) how the process affects the financial outcome in reward-based crowdfunding. We discuss how entrepreneurs promote legitimacy through specific crowdfunding features. Our study reveals some of the narrative processes that entrepreneurs deploy to establish legitimacy in reward-based crowdfunding.

## 2.   Research motivation

### 2.1   Crowdfunding practice

The fundamental concept of crowdfunding – assembling financial capital from social networks – is not new. Historical examples of crowdfunding include the (family) partnership system in the late middle age (Lane 1944), charitable fund-raising (Bremner 1996; Ingenhoff and Koelling 2009) and micro-finance (Morduch 1999). However, recent developments in information and communication technology (ICT) facilitate the development and professionalisation of crowdfunding via distributed, open access, online systems. Specialised online crowdfunding platforms are at 'the heart of crowdfunding [and] drive the implementation of the crowdfunding model' (Ingram, Teigland, and Vaast 2013, 1).

Crowdfunding platforms are developing into capital intermediates (Harrison 2013; Lehner 2013). There were more than 800 active online crowdfunding platforms in 2012, listing more than 1.1 million crowdfunding projects and invested capital of US$2.7 billion (Massolution 2013). Kickstarter surpassed US$1 billion in funded projects in early 2014; crowdfunding's growth may ultimately impact the traditional venture capital market. The rapid growth of crowdfunding justifies research to better understand similarities and distinctions from traditional venture finance.

### 2.2   Crowdfunding theory

Nascent entrepreneurs and *de novo* firms face the disadvantage of small size and limited access to resources. Some entrepreneurs overcome the 'liability of newness' (Stinchcombe 1965) through a series of techniques and actions to facilitate resource assembly (Hitt et al. 2011; Ciabuschi, Perna, and Snehota 2012). It is unclear whether innovative ICT platforms are simply another tool in the entrepreneur's resource assembly toolkit, or an entirely distinct mechanism for capital formation processes. Rewards-based crowdfunding presents additional challenges to the traditional model because it may represent a mechanism for generating 'pre-production sales', reducing or eliminating the venture's initial working capital deficit.

Crowdfunding takes traditional 'offline' business processes into an online environment, enabling entrepreneurs to nurture and facilitate business development. Features such as online-based communities and interaction mechanisms generate new settings for capital assembly, suggesting the potential for distinctive or novel entrepreneurial processes and potentially different success drivers. The use of ICT-enabled tools may also introduce different investment dynamics effecting processes and activities associated with organisational legitimacy creation and resource assembly.

The links between venture creation, resource assembly and crowdfunding processes merit careful investigation. Crowdfunding, including rewards-based crowdfunding, may require new theories of resource assembly and venture heterogeneity. The drivers, processes and outcomes of venture capital activity may not be entirely applicable in the context of crowdsourced finance.

## 3. Literature review

Crowdfunding represents an apparently novel platform for early stage capital assembly. Its underlying practices and mechanisms have been examined in various literatures, including the resource-based view, social network theory and micro-economic pricing models. We examine the characteristics of crowdfunding through the lens of prior research to specify novel aspects and potential deviations from prior research.

### 3.1. Crowdfunding as transaction mechanism

Four models of crowdfunding have been observed: donation, reward, lending and equity-based. All rely on the crowdsourcing mechanism to obtain capital from a previously distributed and heterogeneous group (the crowd) who provide the capital injection in exchange for tangible or intangible returns.

Mollick (2014) argues that the difference between crowdfunding models lies in the goals of the entrepreneurs and supporters. Equity- and lending-based models rely on relatively traditional investment mechanisms. Lending-based models link founders and supporters in a debtor and lender relationship, and the equity-based models (similar to traditional venture capital) create an entrepreneur–investor relationship. In donation-based models, project creators are social entrepreneurs while supporters serve as philanthropists. In the case of reward-based crowdfunding, the predominant online model, entrepreneurs are characterised as 'creators' or 'project founders' and project supporters represent early customers or co-creators rather than investors.

The donation-based crowdfunding model is relatively well-aligned with models of social entrepreneurship (Lehner 2013). The other three models align more closely with traditional venture capital, since they assembly risk capital for entrepreneurial activities (Mollick 2013). Reward, lending and equity-crowdfunding models feature a tangible or monetary exchange. This creates contractual relationships and instruments between the entrepreneur and stakeholders comparable to those in traditional venture capital. (Ley and Weaven 2011; Agrawal, Catalini, and Goldfarb 2011). Crowdfunding also provides an ecosystem facilitating broader resource exchange between stakeholders (Lambert and

Schwienbacher 2010). This potentially facilitates the collective development of a business plan or other knowledge exchange not found in venture capital, which judges rather than co-creates the business plan. Crowdfunding participants may be able to use these ecosystems to increase market awareness and receive customer feedback.

Crowdfunding may be understood as a product pre-ordering model that enables price discrimination among early adopters (Belleflamme, Lambert, and Schwienbacher 2013). For example, reward-based crowdfunding projects commonly have pre-order mechanisms integrated into their reward structure (e.g. invest US$10 to a music project and receive the recorded music album once it is completed). This presents a zero-cost capital management technique to fuel organic growth in early business stages (Vanacker and Manigart 2010; McKelvie and Wiklund 2010).

Crowdfunding may also facilitate investment based on alternative investor utility factors, including social good or other non-fiduciary values (Lehner 2013). From this standpoint, legitimacy incorporates social *and* business goals in investors' evaluations. In this case, social and psychological factors may be equally or more important than strictly financial returns. This suggests that narrative may play a significant role in successful crowdfunding activities by establishing a convincing and compelling investment story distinct from the novel product or service attributes (Lounsbury and Glynn 2001).

Crowdfunding is an inherently distributed and socially embedded process. Equity- and lending-based crowdfunding activities may incorporate significantly more social and psychological processes than observed in traditional venture capital (Mollick 2014). Although equity crowdfunding is financially driven, investors might obtain utility from the excitement or sense of community associated with the process itself. This is supported by the characteristics of some equity-crowdfunding contracts, which are generally long-term and non-voting equity investment contracts (e.g. 10 years) without dividends.

### 3.2 Crowdfunding as social exchange

Social dynamics are fundamental features in the crowdfunding ecosystem, which is constructed around the relationships in heterogeneous social networks. Crowdfunding is intended to leverage the 'wisdom of the crowd' (Surowiecki 2004), but entrepreneurs must identify or create a suitable community accessible via the online platform (Belleflamme et al. 2013). Peer effects are important in these communities since membership and communications are publicly observable and likely to influence individual decisions and pitch outcomes as Ward and Ramachandran (2010) demonstrate. The development of social interactions surrounding a given project, and the nature of the development process itself, may be critical to the outcome of the crowdfunding effort (Burtch, Ghose, and Wattal 2011). The demonstrated interest and positive conversation about a given project may be drivers of project legitimacy – supporting some projects just enough but others not at all (Burtch, Ghose, and Wattal 2011; Zhang and Liu 2012)

Resource assembly through traditional venture capital tends to be geographically contingent (Rocha 2004; Harrison, Mason, and Robson 2010). By contrast, crowdfunding may facilitate resource assembly that is independent of geography. Although ICT reduces a variety of business barriers (Anderson 2004), there is some evidence that offline social relationships and perceptions of trust may not be easy to entirely virtualise. We cannot expect new business models or wider broadband to eradicate cultural and institutional boundaries and geographically de-structure investment clusters. We agree with Mollick (2014) and Agrawal, Catalini and Goldfarb (2011) who argue that space continue to matter and offline social relationships and perceptions of trust continue to shape patterns of crowdfunding interactivity: the potential of crowdfunding to overcome long-distance investment barriers is limited. Nor is crowdfunding likely to globalise attitudes towards risk-taking in science-based ventures, since crowdfunding investors bring to sites their inherited predilections and habituations. International patterning of technology-based firm investments is likely to persist for some time, despite the access opportunities crowdfunding sites create. Moreover, we expect urban clusters of particular technologies (software or games in San Francisco, apps in Bangalore) to continue providing new business pitches and investors from among offline communities with pre-understanding of the technology.

### 3.3   Crowdfunding as legitimacy building

Organisational legitimacy helps explain why some nascent entrepreneurial activities develop into successful firms and others do not (Suchman 1995). Indeed, Ahlstrom and Bruton (2002) found that organisational legitimacy may be understood as a resource, as well as a signal for resource assembly in entrepreneurial processes and activities. The lack of organisational legitimacy restricts access to prospective resource holders and hinders early stage development (Alvarez and Busenitz 2001; Tornikoski and Newbert 2007). Establishing legitimacy may facilitate faster and efficient capital acquisition (Lounsbury and Glynn 2001). Legitimacy and resource assembly are likely co-created during organisational development (Zimmerman and Zeitz 2002). Legitimacy gives ventures access to external stakeholders and is associated with inflow of exogenous resources (Mason and Harrison 2000; Chen, Yao, and Kotha 2009).

Organisational legitimacy is associated with a variety of individual and firm-level characteristics. These include founder education level and experience as well as the heterogeneity of the entrepreneurial team (Cohen and Dean 2005; Packalen 2007; Balboa and Marti 2007; Zimmerman 2008; Dalziel, Gentry, and Bowerman 2011). Firms may institutionalise entrepreneurial narrative into artefacts or market-facing documents to communicate internally generated legitimacy (Aldrich and Fiol 1994; Delmar and Shane 2004). Firms may seek conferral of legitimacy from external sources through certifications or authorisations (Rao 1994; Sorescu, Shankar, and Kushwaha 2007). Some ventures seek legitimisation by communicating projections of the firm's intended operational or commercial pathway (Baron and Markman 2003; Anderson 2005). Legitimacy may be primarily conferred through intangible and socially centred resources precisely because the firm has no financial history, operations or assets that may be rationally valued (Khaire 2010).

It is possible that online crowdfunding platforms play to the strengths of new venture legitimisation. The lack of assets or operations is not a hindrance to establishing a positive reputation in a fully virtualised context. Crowdfunding participants may have little or no expectation for physical demonstrations of venture viability, precisely because the media establishes a level playing field in which reputation may be the primary currency.

The evidence, however, suggests that legitimacy is not easily obtained during crowdfunding. Mollick's (2014) study reports that unsuccessful projects fail their funding target by large amounts while successful projects exceed their targets by small amounts. This suggests that project legitimacy is relatively difficult to achieve.

Projects that do achieve legitimacy do not generally benefit from a 'tipping point' model of broad acceptance.

### 3.4   The role of narrative in establishing crowdfunding legitimacy

Cultural entrepreneurship theory emphasises that the subjective perception of the firm to external agents, regardless of the objective value of the firm's resource stock, may be essential to legitimisation and ultimate resource assembly (Lounsbury and Glynn 2001). This contrasts with bounded rationality approaches to venture capital investment that rely on models of risk minimisation and management (Zimmerman and Zeitz 2002). When risks are not easily quantified at new ventures, 'stories can provide needed accounts that explain, rationalise, and promote a new venture to reduce the uncertainty typically associated with entrepreneurship' (Lounsbury and Glynn 2001, 546).

Research suggests that effective storytelling is essential to establishing firm legitimacy and acquiring capital (Roddick 2000; O'Connor 2004). By packaging the firm's intangible and tangible resources into a meaningful bundle, entrepreneurial narratives reduce the appearance of uncertainty to external stakeholders, encouraging investment at the margin (Shane and Cable 2002; Smith and Anderson 2004). Stories provide a link for shared sense-making between the entrepreneurs and the stakeholders (Martens, Jennings, and Jennings 2007). In this framework, the video pitch and text narrative provided by the entrepreneur would appear to be the primary tools for conveying a compelling narrative. Potential investors are attracted to projects that *appear likely to succeed* (Mollick 2014).

Crowdfunding enables entrepreneurs to facilitate organisational legitimacy primarily through cultural entrepreneurship activities rather than via demonstrated resource configurations. In contrast to the traditional venture capital market, crowdfunding leverages interactive ICT features to create a dynamic environment that could nurture and build organisational legitimacy.

Using crowdfunding mechanisms, entrepreneurs are able to construct storylines that communicate static information but also establish an interactive narrative through specific online-related features such as visual updates and synchronous and asynchronous textual communication. We anticipate verifying Reuber and Fischer's (2005) idea that active engagement facilitates ventures establishing organisational legitimacy with their customers, leveraging cultural dynamics inside online communities to support capital assembly.

## 4.   Research design and data

This study seeks to link specific features of reward-based crowdfunding platforms with organisational legitimacy creation and successful crowdfunding outcomes. We apply an explorative empirical research method. Research on crowdfunding is relatively new, so our focus is on identifying patterns and potential causal relationships to generate preliminary conclusions and advance further study (Cornelius, Landström, and Persson 2006; Blaikie 2011).

We analyse the dynamics and particular features in crowdfunding, contributing towards knowledge of entrepreneurial legitimacy creation in reward-based crowdfunding. While we present data that have been subject to statistical analysis, we use them not to validate a hypothesis, instead, given that this is an emergent area of research, we discuss the issues arising out of the data from an organisational legitimacy perspective triangulating with existing theory to develop new (Eisenhardt 1989).

Our exploratory analysis draws upon data-set derived from Kickstarter (2014), a successful crowdfunding platform established in 2009 that employs ICT features facilitating entrepreneurial organisational legitimacy construction and resource exchange and is the leading reward-based crowdfunding platform. According to Kickstarter's Statistics (2014) 136,000 projects were launched using Kickstarter since 2009, reporting an investment volume of US$1 billion and a community of $c$.5.7 million individual backers. In terms of crowdfunding success rate, Kickstarter reports that around 57,500 projects were successful (42.3%) in their financial capital assembly, capturing an investment volume of US$867 million (86.7% of the total investment volume). Approximately 74,500 projects (54.8%) were unsuccessfully funded with a total investment size of US$118 million, representing 11.8% of the total investment volume of Kickstarter (Kickstarter Statistics 2014).[1]

## 4.1 Data collection

We used a web data extraction method to capture detailed data from the Kickstarter website, similar to other crowdfunding studies (Mollick 2014). Web data extraction facilitates the collection of relatively large data-sets with high levels of data validity because the site is in active use and the data generated specifically for web-based transmission (Kosala and Blockeel 2000; Thelwall 2001; Chang et al. 2006).

We were able to capture activities on all projects listed on Kickstarter in New York between June and July 2012 having chosen New York since it originates 13.5% of all US Kickstarter crowdfunding and 11.9% of all global Kickstarter crowdfunding projects (Kickstarter 2014). This data-set allows us to explore Kickstarter's diversity and enables us to generalise our findings to the Kickstarter population. By collecting variables such as the project-funding target, number of backers, the reward-level structure and other project-related data we are able to provide a first attempt to study entrepreneurial practices in the development of organisational legitimacy and capital assembly in reward-based crowdfunding. The data sample represents 421 projects and captures an investment volume of US$3,514,125 provided by 44,578 backers.

## 4.2 Variables

Here we detail and justify the variables featuring in our study, which we chose as (1) projects required to provide information variables, and (2) they represent potential organisational legitimacy criteria as those variables are publicly observable and thus likely to influence crowdfunding efforts.

### 4.2.1 Funding target

Every crowdfunding project requires a funding target, which represents the amount of financial capital that project creators or entrepreneurs seek to assemble. On Kickstarter, entrepreneurs only receive the assembled financial capital when the funding target is achieved – the threshold crowdfunding model.

### 4.2.2 Final funding

The total amount of funds that the project collected between the starting date and the designated end date of the crowdfunding campaign. Reporting a final funding lower than the funding target means an unsuccessful effort. The final funding amount may be larger than the funding target, indicating that the respective crowdfunding project is over-funded.

### 4.2.3 Funding ratio

The funding ratio denotes the percentage of the funding target achieved at the end date of the crowdfunding campaign.

### 4.2.4 Backers

Individuals who financially support a project through Kickstarter represent the number of backers per project.

### 4.2.5 Funding per backer

Financial support per backer calculated as the final funding amount divided by the number of backers where high funding per backer indicates a project attracting less backers transacting a higher financial support. *Argumentum e contrario*, project creators were successful in communicating organisational legitimacy to stimulate backers to perform higher financial injections into the project.

### 4.2.6 Duration

The period of time (days) which projects can receive financial support from backers, which at Kickstarter is a maximum of 60 days.

### 4.2.7 Reward-level

The number of different reward-levels from which backers can select to financially support a project. Reward-levels are created and defined by project creators. Every project has a minimum of one reward-level with no maximum. Each reward-level will be given a predetermined price (maximum of US$10,000 on Kickstarter) and a specific configuration of intangible or tangible qualities.

### 4.2.8 Visual pitch

In addition to a textual pitch, projects can implement videos. This variable represents a dummy variable, where dummy $= 1$ if a crowdfunding project has a video.

### 4.2.9 Founding team composition

Crowdfunding projects provide additional information about the project creator in form of a user profile. This variable explores whether a project was created by an individual or by a team and categorises the number and composition of the founding team.

### 4.3 Descriptive statistics

Table 1 provides the descriptive statistics of the main variables.

From the total sample of 421 projects, 227 projects (54%) successfully achieved their funding target, 177 projects (42%) were unsuccessful and 17 projects (4%) were cancelled before they reached the official end date (see Table 1). Success rate in the

Table 1. Descriptive statistics.

| Variables | N | Min | p25 | Mean | p75 | Max | SD |
|---|---|---|---|---|---|---|---|
| | Successful | | | | | | |
| Funding Target ($) | 227 | 100.00 | 2500.00 | 9460.61 | 10,000.00 | 100,000.00 | 14,132.11 |
| Final Funding ($) | 227 | 100.00 | 3101.00 | 12,903.67 | 11,920.00 | 287,342.00 | 26,228.73 |
| Funding Ratio (%) | 227 | 100.00 | 103.76 | 133.31 | 133.89 | 953.50 | 79.85 |
| #Backers | 227 | 5 | 40 | 170 | 140 | 4242 | 374 |
| Funding/Backer ($) | 227 | 15 | 49 | 88 | 98 | 729 | 73 |
| #Duration | 227 | 8 | 30 | 33 | 36 | 60 | 11 |
| #Video | | | | | | | |
| No | 21 | | | | | | |
| Yes | 206 | | | | | | |
| #Reward-Levels | 227 | 2 | 7 | 9 | 10 | 32 | 4 |
| | Failed | | | | | | |
| Funding Target ($) | 177 | 57.00 | 5000.00 | 31,840.86 | 30,000.00 | 1,000,000.00 | 82,803.79 |
| Final Funding ($) | 177 | 0.00 | 45.00 | 3244.36 | 2631.00 | 53,422.00 | 8082.12 |
| FundingRatio (%) | 177 | 0.00 | 0.46 | 12.04 | 17.00 | 82.57 | 17.02 |
| #Backers | 177 | 0 | 1 | 33 | 29 | 515 | 72 |
| Funding/Backer ($) | 177 | 0 | 23 | 74 | 97 | 1007 | 104 |
| #Duration | 177 | 10 | 30 | 37 | 45 | 60 | 13 |
| #Video | | | | | | | |
| No | 33 | | | | | | |
| Yes | 144 | | | | | | |
| #Reward-Levels | 177 | 1 | 6 | 9 | 10 | 33 | 5 |
| | Cancelled | | | | | | |
| Funding Target ($) | 17 | 1500.00 | 5000.00 | 28,794.12 | 50,000.00 | 124,000.00 | 36,920.97 |
| Final Funding ($) | 17 | 0.00 | 100.00 | 631.82 | 775.00 | 4550.00 | 1083.96 |
| Funding Ratio (%) | 17 | 0.00 | 0.88 | 5.84 | 3.86 | 56.88 | 13.51 |
| #Backers | 17 | 0 | 2 | 9 | 14 | 37 | 9 |
| Funding/Backer ($) | 17 | 0 | 24 | 61 | 89 | 228 | 60 |
| #Duration | 17 | 21 | 30 | 37 | 41 | 60 | 11 |
| #Video | | | | | | | |
| No | 2 | | | | | | |
| Yes | 15 | | | | | | |
| #Reward-Levels | 17 | 1 | 7 | 9 | 11 | 16 | 4 |
| | Total | | | | | | |
| Funding Target ($) | 421 | 57.00 | 3000.00 | 19,650.57 | 15,000.00 | 1,000,000.00 | 56,166.83 |
| Final Funding ($) | 421 | 0.00 | 360.00 | 8347.09 | 7647.00 | 287,342.00 | 20,547.55 |
| Funding Ratio (%) | 421 | 0.00 | 4.50 | 77.18 | 112.49 | 953.50 | 85.19 |
| #Backers | 421 | 0 | 7 | 106 | 96 | 4242 | 287 |
| Funding/Backer ($) | 421 | 0 | 38 | 81 | 97 | 1007 | 87 |
| #Duration | 421 | 8 | 30 | 35 | 40 | 60 | 12 |
| #Video | | | | | | | |
| No | 56 | | | | | | |
| Yes | 365 | | | | | | |
| #Reward-Levels | 421 | 1 | 6 | 9 | 10 | 33 | 4 |

sample is about 10% higher than the official Kickstarter statistics (Kickstarter Statistics 2014). The sample exhibits a strong deviation in terms of project's funding target in reward-based crowdfunding, with a minimum funding target in our sample of US$57, and the maximum funding target of US$1,000,000. The average funding target for our sample size is US$19,650. The average final funding is US$8347. The largest project achieved a final funding of US$287,342. The average number of backers for projects is 106 individual backers. The largest backer number for a crowdfunding project is 4242. The samples average funding per backer is US$81.27.

## 5. Findings

### 5.1 *Funding target and final funding*

Successful projects tend to have a much lower funding target (US$9,415) in comparison to unsuccessful (US$32,002) and cancelled (US$30,281) projects (see Table 1). However, the mean final funding for successful projects is US$12,807, hence, successful projects tend to get over-funded by 32.6% on average. Figure 1 illustrates the distribution of the sample plotted against projects funding target and funding ratio, showing that the density of projects lie in the funding area between 100% and 150% for successful projects and between 0% and 25% for unsuccessful projects. The mean funding ratio value for successful projects is 133.31%, while for unsuccessful and cancelled projects the funding ratio illustrates that projects fail by large margin, with mean values of 12.04% and 5.84%, respectively.

Figure 2 exemplifies the frequency of successful, unsuccessful and cancelled projects for each category group and demonstrates that projects from the Music and Theatre category expose by far more successful than unsuccessful crowdfunding efforts. The data reveal that most reward-based crowdfunding projects come from the Film (117), Music (66), Theatre (66), Publishing (46) and Art (37) categories and demonstrate that reward-based crowdfunding platforms such as Kickstarter are exploited by entrepreneurs that are aiming to explore 'new ways to raise funds for creative projects'

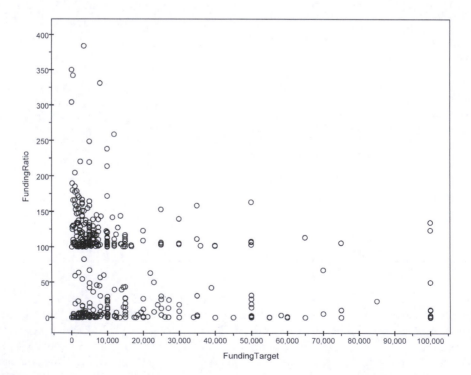

Figure 1.   Scatter plot – funding target and funding ratio.

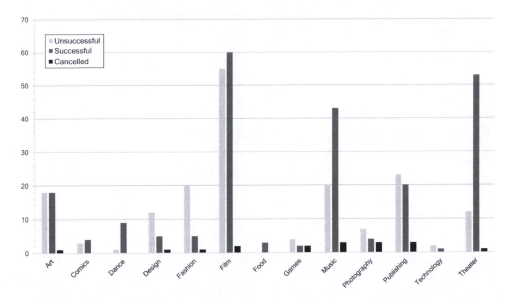

Figure 2.   Histogram – Funding outcome per project categories.

(Kickstarter 2014). In fact, the total investment for projects from the two categories Film (US$1,425,480) and Publishing (US$492,010) count for 54.6% of the samples investment volume.

## 5.2   Funding period

Surprisingly we find no significant difference between successful and unsuccessful crowdfunding projects fund-raising duration (see Table 1) with an average campaign days for unsuccessful projects at 37 and for successful projects 33 days.

We assumed that projects with a higher funding target have a higher chance to successfully assemble the required capital through a longer funding period. However, our data suggest that the combination of a high funding target and a long funding period (which is understood as any funding period above the mean value) is associated with less successful crowdfunding efforts. Vice versa, our explorative data suggest that shorter campaign periods seem to be related to a higher success rate. Yet, Figure 3 illustrates a low degree of correlation between the project duration and the funding ratio.

Kickstarter suggests campaign durations of 30 days: 'Statistically, projects lasting 30 days or less have our highest success rate' (Kickstarter School 2014). Comparing the project duration among the various categories, we do not observe significant differences among them (see the Appendix). However, the mean values of the project duration are distributed around the suggested 30 days project period.

## 5.3   Reward-level structure

It is not possible to draw clear conclusions causally linking reward-level to success. While we observe that the average number of reward-levels seem to be relatively similar for successful and unsuccessful projects, we deduced that creatively oriented projects

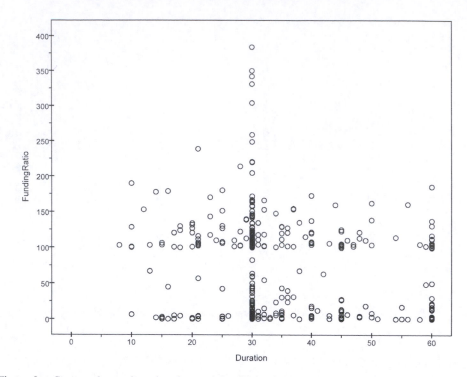

Figure 3.   Scatter plot project duration and funding ratio.

(e.g. Art, Design and Publishing) have a higher number of reward-levels (Figure 4 and the Appendix).

### 5.4   Visual pitch

In additional to a textual presentation, often a business plan, crowdfunding platforms allow project initiators to include visual presentation. Most crowdfunding platforms facilitate the use of a video recorded pitch. In our data-set, 365 projects, representing 86.7% of the sample, incorporated a visual pitch in their crowdfunding campaign

(Table 1 and the Appendix). A total of 206 of these projects were successfully funded (56%). Kickstarter encourages the project initiator to use video: '[...] a video is by far the best way to get a feel for the emotions, motivations, and character of a project. It's a demonstration of effort and a good predictor of success' (Kickstarter School 2014).

Our data suggest the fact that a visual pitch is far from being a guarantee of success. Of the 227 successful projects, 206 projects (90.75%) had a visual pitch; 81.26% of failed projects also had a visual presentation (144 of 177 failing projects). A visual pitch has thus become standard, challenging the idea that using visual pitches predicts success.

### 5.5   Founding team composition

Table 2 summarises data on the founding team composition of the crowdfunding projects showing that 320 projects (76%) were created by individual entrepreneurs and only 36

CROWDFUNDING AND ENTREPRENEURIAL FINANCE

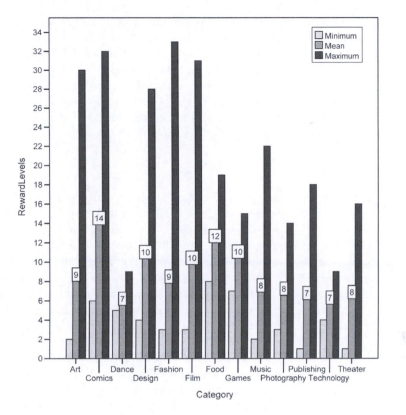

Figure 4.  Histogram of reward-levels for project categories.

Table 2.  Summary statistics – founding team composition.

| Composition | All | | Successful | | Failed | |
|---|---|---|---|---|---|---|
| | # | % | # | % | # | % |
| Single | | | | | | |
| Female | 93 | 22.1 | 64 | 68.8 | 29 | 31.2 |
| Male | 227 | 53.9 | 104 | 45.8 | 123 | 54.2 |
| Pair | | | | | | |
| Female | 9 | 2.1 | 7 | 70.0 | 2 | 30.0 |
| Male | 13 | 3.1 | 9 | 69.2 | 4 | 30.8 |
| Mix | 10 | 2.4 | 5 | 50.0 | 5 | 50.0 |
| Three | | | | | | |
| Female | 1 | 0.2 | 1 | 100.0 | 0 | 0.0 |
| Male | – | – | – | – | – | – |
| Mix | 1 | 0.2 | 1 | 100.0 | 0 | 0.0 |
| Four | | | | | | |
| Female | – | – | – | – | – | – |
| Male | 1 | 0.2 | 1 | 100.0 | 0 | 0.0 |
| Mix | 1 | 0.2 | 1 | 100.0 | 0 | 0.0 |
| Organisation | 65 | 15.4 | 34 | 52.3 | 31 | 47.7 |
| Total | 421 | 100 | 227 | 53.9 | 194 | 46.1 |

crowdfunding projects (8.55%) had an entrepreneurial team, with established organisations creating 65 funding projects (15.44%).

The numbers are too small to draw firm conclusions; however, in traditional venture capital a balanced team (technical, financial, sales, operational expertise) is a clear predictor of success: none of the projects with teams failed (4 in number) and those with pairs of entrepreneurs (numbering 32) succeeded more than those with individuals (320). This suggests that in addition to evaluating the business idea, investors do look at the capability of the entrepreneur(s) to deliver the plan.

## 6.  Discussion

Crowdfunding is of increasing significance to policy-makers and venturesome businesses caught in the funding gap facing many small and high-risk start-ups. How far the crowdfunding model will grow and internationalise is as yet unclear. Also unclear is the extent to which the model might disrupt traditional venture capital. Reward-based crowdfunding provides investors with the opportunity to invest relative small amounts in businesses to which they have subjective attachment in addition to gaining reward; they also have the opportunity to participate in online communities, which may shape the nature of proposed business propositions. For entrepreneurs, crowdfunding is a new way of marshalling capital resources, learning from the wisdom of crowds and/or creating a market for a nascent business.

We have explored the reward-based crowdfunding mechanism from a cultural entrepreneurship perspective providing tentative explanations of how particular features of crowdfunding process influence organisational legitimacy and success and failure in reward-based crowdfunding. The data reveal findings linking project characteristics to legitimacy and success.

### 6.1  Funding target and final funding

Our data suggest that the funding targets are associated with the creation of organisational legitimacy creation: a high funding target implies more effort is required by the project creator or entrepreneur to legitimate the requested funding. Accordingly, it seems important for project initiators to be transparent and persuasive about the funding goal. We support Achleitner, Engel, Reiner's (2013) and Sievers, Mokwa and Keienburg's (2013) conclusion that crowdfunding and traditional venture capital both require detailed, internally consistent and market-referencing business plans to achieve legitimacy, though high funding targets decrease organisational legitimacy without a convincing justification of source and use of funds.

We agree with Reuber and Fischer (2011) and Zhang and Liu (2012) that herding behaviour is influential in online communities' supporting pitches, since the openness of interactivity on crowdfunding platforms allows others note comments and feedback and to follow the herd. Crowdfunding platforms may reinforce this behaviour by introducing popularity data, shortlisting of projects and staff-picks, all of which serve herding by narrowing choices. Ward and Ramachandran's (2010) finding reveals a positive correlation between the listing on a popularity list and successful achievement of the funding target exists. The funding ratio values in our data illustrate that crowdfunding projects succeed by relatively small margins but fail by large margin, suggesting a dynamic that success amplifies success analogous to Mollick's (2014) findings. Interestingly, this finding is quite different from traditional venture capital processes where successful entrepreneurial resource assembly is usually realised by large margins and profitable ventures or projects tend to be heavily over-funded. One reason for that is that sophisticated investors have the knowledge and managerial skills to exploit good investment opportunities. In contrast, potential investors in communities such as crowdfunding appear to rely more on group dynamics and interactive entrepreneurial narrative activities in terms of investment choices, which lead to narrowed choices.

However, Burtch, Ghose and Wattal (2011, 11) highlight how community-driven popularity indicators might negatively influence the overall funding outcome, as 'higher contribution frequencies are associated with lower subsequent contribution amounts, as are lower contribution densities.' Although, Brynjolfsson, Hu and Simester (2011) illustrate that the long-tail hypothesis (Anderson 2004) is valid in product sales through digital environments, it seems that the implemented popularity indicators on crowdfunding platforms do diminish the effect of the long-tail phenomenon in online crowdfunding platforms, distributing financial capital into more likely succeeding projects. As a result successful projects tend to be over-funded as such mechanism seem to influence the organisational legitimacy creation. Community behaviour, therefore, might be a stronger indicator for organisational legitimacy rather than narrative legitimacy factors such as the funding target variable.

## 6.2 Crowdfunding duration

Our data illustrate that projects with higher funding targets tend to have longer funding durations. However, the data suggest that longer fund-raising periods lead to lower funding ratio values. Based from an organisational legitimacy perspective, we can assume that a longer fund-raising period might expose an uncertain narrative for the project, resulting in decreasing support for the project.

An explanation for that result can be deduced from the importance of project momentum for organisational legitimacy creation within reward-based crowdfunding platforms. Ward and Ramachandran (2010) illustrate that entrepreneurs have increased difficulties to effectively maintain and gather momentum for their projects the longer the fundraising period is. In highly heterogeneous and dynamic communities such as crowdfunding platforms, attention for specific projects seems to diminish with time. Apparently it is more efficient to implement a shorter funding period as projects seem to go relatively quickly out of support with the crowdfunding community (Ward and Ramachandran 2010). Kickstarter states that 'shorter projects set a tone of confidence and help motivate your backers to join the party. Longer durations incite less urgency, encourage procrastination, and tend to fizzle out' (Kickstarter School 2014).

## 6.3 Reward-level structure

While the data did not provide clear implications of the relationship of the reward-level structure and successful crowdfunding efforts, we identified that creative projects tend to incorporate a higher number of reward-levels. Projects from creative categories seem to have a better ability to implement mixed intangible/tangible rewards. This allows project initiators to incorporate additional reward-levels in order to include supplementary social-psychological investment incentives. The possibility to create rewards in any kind of tangible or intangible form establishes a key feature of reward-based crowdfunding. Therefore, rewards create a key driver for activities within the community and create strong narrative legitimacy factors. We argue that the reward-levels demonstrate an important factor that makes a project compelling to the audience. Burtch, Ghose and Wattal (2011) suggest that projects that are positioned with their product or service in trending and popular content of the broader Internet are more likely to receive higher contribution from the community. Kickstarter (2014) highlights the influence of the right rewards for successful crowdfunding efforts and states that 'the importance of creative, tangible, and fairly priced rewards cannot be overstated. Projects whose rewards are overpriced or uninspired struggle to find support'. Therefore, it seems those projects that are able to offer additional social-psychological reward-levels are more successful to motivate the community for financial support.

## 6.4   Visual pitch

The large majority of projects in our data included a visual pitch in their crowdfunding campaign. Unlike previous studies, which understand visual pitches in crowdfunding projects as quality signals, we argue that visual elements in crowdfunding pitches appeared to developed into a crowdfunding standard and therefore weakened its controlling character to predict success in reward-based crowdfunding. While the measurement of visual pitches is not adequate to predict success, we however understand visual pitches from the cultural entrepreneurship perspective as a powerful entrepreneurial narrative instrument.

Clarke (2011) highlights the importance of visual communication and the use of visual symbols to increase organisational legitimacy and develop support for nascent ventures. Visual pitches support entrepreneurs to attain support and funding for their projects and allow entrepreneurs to actively create and manage emotions of stakeholders (Clarke 2011). As more projects utilise the power of visual pitches to persuade the community to financially support the project, the findings emphasise a more social-psychological rather than rational business oriented organisational legitimacy creation process in reward-based crowdfunding.

## 6.5   Founding' team composition

The composition and characteristics of the founding team in entrepreneurial ventures play an important role for organisational legitimacy and resource assembly processes (Kotha and George 2012; Zhao, Song, and Storm 2013). Shepherd and Zacharakis (2003) illustrate that organisational legitimacy can be built by providing additional information of the organisation and management team of the entrepreneurial venture. Research has illustrated that information about the founding team represents a critical factor of traditional venture capital investment decision-making processes (Zimmerman and Zeitz 2002; Baum und Silverman 2004). It appears that investors in reward-based crowdfunding look at the team composition as well in evaluating the business idea. The data show that the majority of the sample projects were created by individual entrepreneurs (76%), followed by organisations (15.4%), pairs (7.6%) and teams (0.5%). Projects with pairs and teams demonstrate much higher success rates than projects with individuals. Most interestingly, however, is that projects created by females experienced a higher success rate than males.

## 7.   Conclusions

In this paper we have contributed to crowdfunding literature referencing the results of an empirical study that is explorative and descriptive in nature. This study illustrates that cultural entrepreneurship activities play a significant role in creating online organisational legitimacy and links specific features to successful crowdfunding efforts. While this study offers additional understanding of some dynamics that take place in crowdfunding and can be associated with organisational legitimacy, research on crowdfunding is still limited and further research is required.

The possibilities for entrepreneurs to facilitate the collective development of a business idea establish an interesting research issue linked to co-creation. It appears that a distinctive feature of reward-based crowdfunding is the joint effort to develop and promote a business idea rather than primarily evaluating a business plan. It is important that future research focuses on the co-creation possibilities and its impact on the organisational legitimacy and resource assembly process. Further, our data-set revealed that women experience a higher success rate than males. This presents a fascinating area for future study, given the high male-to-female ratio generally present in both entrepreneur and investor populations.

Overall, further crowdfunding research is necessary as current studies are outcome oriented and utilise quantitative methods to explain specific patterns in crowdfunding. Current knowledge lacks understanding of the business processes that are associated with crowdfunding outcome. It is important to move crowdfunding research into more qualitative research methods to provide deeper understanding of specific entrepreneurial activities and processes. Moreover, qualitative research would enable to capture a broader picture of the crowdfunding phenomena and allow to link offline activities with online processes. It is important to disclose offline activities to understand online crowdfunding processes and outcomes as our current understanding is built on knowledge that originates from activities on online crowdfunding platforms. While this paper focuses on specific variables that are captured by crowdfunding projects, further work is required to analyse more qualitative features of crowdfunding project pitches such as textual and visual pitches. Such future studies will allow us to extend knowledge about the organisational legitimacy creation of crowdfunding projects in terms of entrepreneurial narrative.

## Note

1. The provided percentages do not equal 100% as numbers were rounded.

## References

Achleitner, A.-K., N. Engel, and U. Reiner. 2013. "The Performance of Venture Capital Investments: Do Investors Overreact?" *Review of Financial Economics* 22 (1): 20–35.

Agrawal, A. K., C. Catalini, and A. Goldfarb. 2011. "The Geography of Crowdfunding." NBER Working Paper No. 16820. http://www.nber.org/papers/w16820

Ahlstrom, D., and G. D. Bruton. 2002. "An Institutional Perspective on the Role of Culture in Shaping Strategic Actions by Technology-Focused Entrepreneurial Firms in China." *Entrepreneurship Theory and Practice* 26 (4): 53–70.

Aldrich, H., and C. Fiol. 1994. "Fools Rush in? The Institutional Context of Industry Creation." *The Academy of Management Review* 19 (4): 645–670.

Alvarez, S., and L. W. Busenitz. 2001. "The Entrepreneurship of Resource-Based Theory." *Journal of Management* 27 (6): 755–775.

Anderson, C. 2004, October. "The Long Tail." *Wired Magazine*, http://www.wired.com/wired/archive/12.10/tail.html

Anderson, A. 2005. "Enacted Metaphor: The Theatricality of the Entrepreneurial Process." *International Small Business Journal* 23 (6): 587–603.

Balboa, M., and J. Marti. 2007. "Factors That Determine the Reputation of Private Equity Managers in Developing Markets." *Journal of Business Venturing* 22 (4): 453–480.

Baron, R. A., and G. D. Markman. 2003. "Beyond Social Capital: The Role of Entrepreneurs' Social Competence in Their Financial Success." *Journal of Business Venturing* 18 (1): 41–60.

Baum, J., and B. Silverman. 2004. "Picking Winners or Building Them? Alliance, Intellectual, and Human Capital as Selection Criteria in Venture Financing and Performance of Biotechnology Startups." *Journal of Business Venturing* 19 (3): 411–436.

Belleflamme, P., T. Lambert, and A. Schwienbacher. 2013. "Crowdfunding: Tapping the Right Crowd." *Forthcoming at Journal of Business Venturing.* doi:10.1016/j.jbusvent.2013.07.003.

Blaikie, N. W. H. 2011. *Designing Social Research.* Cambridge: Polity Press.

Bremner, R. H. 1996. *Giving: Charity and Philanthropy in History.* New Brunswick, NJ: Transaction.

Brynjolfsson, E., Y. Hu, and D. Simester. 2011. "Goodbye Pareto Principle, Hello Long Tail: The Effect of Search Costs on the Concentration of Product Sales." *Management Science* 57 (8): 1373–1386.

Burtch, G., A. Ghose, and S. Wattal. 2011. "An Empirical Examination of the Antecedents and Consequences of Investment Patterns in Crowdfunded Markets.", Paper presented at the International Conference on Information Systems (ICIS), Shanghai, December 4–7.

Chang, C., M. Kayed, M. Girgis, and K. Shaalan. 2006. "A Survey of Web Information Extraction Systems." *IEEE Transactions on Knowledge and Data Engineering* 18 (10): 1411–1428.

Chen, X., X. Yao, and S. Kotha. 2009. "Entrepreneur Passion and Preparedness in Business Plan Presentations: A Persuasion Analysis of Venture Capitalists' Funding Decision." *Academy of Management Journal* 52 (1): 199–214.

Ciabuschi, F., A. Perna, and I. Snehota. 2012. "Assembling Resources when Forming a New Business." *Journal of Business Research* 65 (2): 220–229.

Clarke, J. 2011. "Revitalizing Entrepreneurship: How Visual Symbols Are Used in Entrepreneurial Performances." *Journal of Management Studies* 48 (6): 1365–1391.

Cohen, B. D., and T. J. Dean. 2005. "Information Asymmetry and Investor Valuation of IPOs: Top Management Team Legitimacy as a Capital Market Signal." *Strategic Management Journal* 26 (7): 683–690.

Cornelius, B., H. Landström, and O. Persson. 2006. "Entrepreneurial Studies: The Dynamic Research Front of a Developing Social Science." *Entrepreneurship Theory and Practice* 30 (3): 375–398.

Dalziel, T., R. J. Gentry, and M. Bowerman. 2011. "An Integrated Agency-Resource Dependence View of the Influence of Directors' Human and Relational Capital on Firms' R&D Spending." *Journal of Management Studies* 48 (6): 1217–1242.

Delmar, F., and S. Shane. 2004. "Legitimating First: Organizing Activities and the Survival of New Ventures." *Journal of Business Venturing* 19 (3): 385–410.

Eisenhardt, K. M. 1989. "Building Theories from Case Study Approach." *Academy of Management Review* 14 (4): 532–550.

Harrison, R. 2013. "Crowdfunding and the Revitalisation of the Early Stage Risk Capital Market: Catalyst or Chimera?" *Venture Capital: An International Journal of Entrepreneurial Finance* 15 (4): 283–287.

Harrison, R., C. Mason, and R. Robson. 2010. "Determinants of Long-Distance Investing by Business Angels in the UK." *Entrepreneurship and Regional Development* 22 (2): 113–137.

Hitt, M. A., R. D. Ireland, D. G. Sirmon, and C. A. Trahms. 2011. "Strategic Entrepreneurship: Creating Value for Individuals, Organizations, and Society." *Academy of Management Perspectives* 25 (2): 57–75.

Ingenhoff, D., and A. M. Koelling. 2009. "The Potential of Web Sites as a Relationship Building Tool for Charitable Fundraising NPOs." *Public Relations Review* 35 (1): 66–73.

Ingram, C., R. Teigland, and E. Vaast. 2013. "Solving the Puzzle of Crowdfunding: Where Technology Affordances and Institutional Entrepreneurship Collide." SSRN Working Paper Series. http://www.ssrn.com/abstract=2285426

Khaire, M. 2010. "Young and No Money? Never Mind: The Material Impact of Social Resources on New Venture Growth." *Organization Science* 21 (1): 168–185.

Kickstarter. http://www.kickstarter.com. 2014.

Kickstarter School. 2014. "Kickstarter School." https://www.kickstarter.com/help/school?ref= footer#defining_your_project

Kickstarter Statistics. 2014. "Kickstarter Stats." http://www.kickstarter.com/help/stats?ref=footer

Kosala, R., and H. Blockeel. 2000. "Web Mining Research: A Survey." *ACM SIGKDD Explorations Newsletter* 2 (1): 1–15.

Kotha, R., and G. George. 2012. "Friends, Family, or Fools: Entrepreneur Experience and its Implications for Equity Distribution and Resource Mobilization." *Journal of Business Venturing* 27 (5): 525–543.

Lambert, T., and A. Schwienbacher. 2010. "An Empirical Analysis of Crowdfunding." *Crowdsourcing.org*, [online]. Accessed November 22, 2011. http://www.crowdsourcing.org/document/an-empirical-analysis-of-crowdfunding-/2458

Lane, F. C. 1944. "Family Partnerships and Joint Ventures in the Venetian Republic." *The Journal of Economic History* 4 (2): 178–196.

Lehner, O. M. 2013. "Crowdfunding Social Ventures: A Model and Research Agenda." *Venture Capital: An International Journal of Entrepreneurial Finance* 15 (4): 289–311.

Ley, A., and S. Weaven. 2011. "Exploring Agency Dynamics of Crowdfunding in Start-up Capital Financing." *Academy of Entrepreneurship Journal* 17 (1): 85–111.

Lounsbury, M., and M. A. Glynn. 2001. "Cultural Entrepreneurship: Stories, Legitimacy, and the Acquisition of Resources." *Strategic Management Journal* 22 (6–7): 545–564.

Martens, M. L., J. E. Jennings, and P. D. Jennings. 2007. "Do the Stories They Tell Get Them the Money They Need? The Role of Entrepreneurial Narratives in Resource Acquisition." *Academy of Management Journal* 50 (5): 1107–1132.

Mason, C. M., and R. T. Harrison. 2000. "The Size of the Informal Venture Capital Market in the United Kingdom." *Small Business Economics* 15 (2): 137–148.

Massolution. 2013. *2013CF – The Crowdfunding Industry Report*. Massolution. http://research.crowdsourcing.org/2013cf-crowdfunding-industry-report

McKelvie, A., and J. Wiklund. 2010. "Advancing Firm Growth Research: A Focus on Growth Mode Instead of Growth Rate." *Entrepreneurship Theory and Practice* 34 (2): 261–288.

Mollick, E. 2013. "Swept Away by the Crowd? Crowdfunding, Venture Capital, and the Selection of Entrepreneurs.", SSRN Working Paper Series. http://papers.ssrn.com/sol3/papers.cfm?abstract_id=2239204

Mollick, E. 2014. "The Dynamics of Crowdfunding: An Explorative Study." *Journal of Business Venturing* 29 (1): 1–16.

Morduch, J. 1999. "The Microfinance Promise." *Journal of Economic Literature* 37 (4): 1569–1614.

O'Connor, E. 2004. "Storytelling to be Real: Narrative, Legitimacy Building and Venturing." In *Narrative and Discursive Approaches in Entrepreneurship*, edited by D. Hjorth and C. Steyaert, 105–124. Northampton: Edward Elgar.

Packalen, K. A. 2007. "Complementing Capital: The Role of Status, Demographic Features and Social Capital in Founding Teams' Abilities to Obtain Resources." *Entrepreneurship Theory and Practice* 31 (6): 873–891.

Rao, H. 1994. "The Social Construction of Reputation: Certification Contests, Legitimation and the Survival of Organization in the American Automobile Industry: 1895–1912." *Strategic Management Journal* 15 (S1): 29–44.

Reuber, A. R., and E. Fischer. 2005. "The Company You Keep: How Young Firms in Different Competitive Contexts Signal Reputation through Their Customers." *Entrepreneurship Theory and Practice* 29 (1): 57–78.

Reuber, A. R., and E. Fischer. 2011. "International Entrepreneurship in Internet-Enabled Markets." *Journal of Business Venturing* 26 (6): 660–679.

Rocha, H. 2004. "Entrepreneurship and Development: The Role of Clusters." *Small Business Economics* 23 (5): 363–400.

Roddick, A. 2000. *Business as Unusual*. London: Thorsons.

Shane, S., and D. Cable. 2002. "Network Ties." *Reputation, and the Financing of New Ventures. Management Science* 48 (3): 364–381.

Shepherd, D. A., and A. Zacharakis. 2003. "A New Venture's Cognitive Legitimacy: An Assessment by Customers." *Journal of Small Business Management* 41 (2): 148–167.

Sievers, S., C. F. Mokwa, and G. Keienburg. 2013. "The Relevance of Financial versus Non-Financial Information for the Valuation of Venture Capital-backed Firms." *European Accounting Review* 22 (3): 467–511.

Smith, R., and A. R. Anderson. 2004. "The Devil is in the E-Tale: Forms and Structures in the Entrepreneurial Narratives." In *Narrative and Discursive Approaches in Entrepreneurship*, edited by D. Hjorth and C. Steyaert, 125–143. Northampton: Edward Elgar.

Sorescu, A., V. Shankar, and T. Kushwaha. 2007. "New Product Preannouncements and Shareholder Value: Don't Make Promises You Can't Keep." *Journal of Marketing Research* 44 (3): 468–489.

Stinchcombe, A. L. 1965. "Social Structure and Organization." In *Handbook of Organizations*, edited by J. G. March, 142–193. Chicago, IL: Rand-McNally.

Suchman, M. C. 1995. "Managing Legitimacy: Strategic and Institutional Approaches." *The Academy of Management Review* 20 (3): 571–610.

Surowiecki, J. 2004. *The Wisdom of Crowds: Why the Many Are Smarter Than the Few and How Collective Wisdom Shapes Business, Economies, Societies, and Nations*. New York: Doubleday.

Thelwall, M. 2001. "A Web Crawler Design for Data Mining." *Journal of Information Science* 27 (5): 319–325.

Tornikoski, E. T., and S. L. Newbert. 2007. "Exploring the Determinants of Organizational Emergence: A Legitimacy Perspective." *Journal of Business Venturing* 22 (2): 311–335.

Vanacker, T. R., and S. Manigart. 2010. "Pecking Order and Debt Capacity Considerations for High-Growth Companies Seeking Financing." *Small Business Economics* 35 (1): 53–69.

Ward, C., and V. Ramachandran. 2010. "Crowdfunding the Next Hit: Microfunding Online Experience Goods." http://www.cs.umass.edu/~wallach/workshops/nips2010css/papers/ward.pdf

Zhang, J., and P. Liu. 2012. "Rational Herding in Microloan Markets." *Management Science* 58 (2): 892–912.

Zhao, Y. L., M. Song, and G. L. Storm. 2013. "Founding Team Capabilities and New Venture Performance: The Mediating Role of Strategic Positional Advantages." *Entrepreneurship Theory and Practice* 37 (4): 789–814.

Zimmerman, M. A. 2008. "The Influence of Top Management Team Heterogeneity on the Capital Raised through Initial Public Offering." *Entrepreneurship Theory and Practice* 32 (3): 391–414.

Zimmerman, M. A., and G. J. Zeitz. 2002. "Beyond Survival: Achieving New Venture Growth by Building Legitimacy." *Academy of Management Review* 27 (3): 414–431.

**Appendix A. Descriptive statistics on project categories.**

| | Variables | Total | | | Successful | | Failed | | Cancelled | |
|---|---|---|---|---|---|---|---|---|---|---|
| | | Min | Mean | Max | N | Mean | N | Mean | N | Mean |
| Art | Funding Target ($) | 57.00 | 40,799.65 | 1000,000.00 | 18 | 6485.00 | 18 | 77,186.50 | 1 | 3500.00 |
| (N = 37) | Final Funding ($) | 0.00 | 7034.27 | 53,422.00 | 18 | 7782.33 | 18 | 6662.00 | 1 | 270.00 |
| | Funding Ratio (%) | 0.00 | 67.83 | 171.70 | 18 | 122.58 | 18 | 16.42 | 1 | 7.71 |
| | #Backers | 0.00 | 69.32 | 317.00 | 18 | 102.11 | 18 | 40.28 | 1 | 2.00 |
| | Funding/Backer ($) | 0.00 | 89.43 | 250.00 | 18 | 78.89 | 18 | 97.44 | 1 | 135.00 |
| | Duration | 10.00 | 31.73 | 60.00 | 18 | 29.33 | 18 | 34.22 | 1 | 30.00 |
| | #Reward-Levels | 2.00 | 9.41 | 30.00 | 18 | 9.17 | 18 | 9.61 | 1 | 10.00 |
| | #Video | | | | | | | | | |
| | No | | | | 1 | | 5 | | 0 | |
| | Yes | | | | 17 | | 13 | | 1 | |
| Comics | Funding Target ($) | 3000.00 | 10,142.86 | 27,000.00 | 4 | 6125.00 | 3 | 15,500.00 | 0 | – |
| (N = 7) | Final Funding ($) | 0.00 | 6048.71 | 21,372.00 | 4 | 9659.50 | 3 | 1234.33 | 0 | – |
| | Funding Ratio (%) | 0.00 | 84.06 | 213.72 | 4 | 143.42 | 3 | 4.92 | 0 | – |
| | #Backers | 0.00 | 207.14 | 962.00 | 4 | 351.75 | 3 | 14.33 | 0 | – |
| | Funding/Backer ($) | 0.00 | 37.46 | 90.08 | 4 | 34.71 | 3 | 41.14 | 0 | – |
| | Duration | 20.00 | 33.86 | 45.00 | 4 | 35.50 | 3 | 31.67 | 0 | – |
| | #Reward-Levels | 6.00 | 13.86 | 32.00 | 4 | 16.25 | 3 | 10.67 | 0 | – |
| | #Video | | | | | | | | | |
| | No | | | | 0 | | 1 | | 0 | |
| | Yes | | | | 4 | | 2 | | 0 | |
| Dance | Funding Target ($) | 2000.00 | 6750.00 | 16,700.00 | 9 | 7166.67 | 1 | 3000.00 | 0 | – |
| (N = 10) | Final Funding ($) | 511.00 | 8585.70 | 31,028.00 | 9 | 9482.89 | 1 | 511.00 | 0 | – |
| | Funding Ratio (%) | 17.03 | 111.14 | 258.57 | 9 | 121.59 | 1 | 17.03 | 0 | – |
| | #Backers | 9.00 | 63.70 | 153.00 | 9 | 69.78 | 1 | 9.00 | 0 | – |
| | Funding/Backer ($) | 40.69 | 121.84 | 294.12 | 9 | 129.07 | 1 | 56.78 | 0 | – |
| | Duration | 13.00 | 31.00 | 55.00 | 9 | 28.33 | 1 | 55.00 | 0 | – |
| | #Reward-Levels | 5.00 | 6.90 | 9.00 | 9 | 7.00 | 1 | 6.00 | 0 | – |
| | #Video | | | | | | | | | |
| | No | | | | 1 | | 0 | | 0 | |
| | Yes | | | | 8 | | 1 | | 0 | |
| Design | Funding Target ($) | 300.00 | 51,945.56 | 275,000.00 | 5 | 26,360.00 | 12 | 62,768.33 | 1 | 50,000.00 |
| (N = 18) | Final Funding ($) | 375.00 | 18,432.78 | 135,002.00 | 5 | 35,346.40 | 12 | 12,843.58 | 1 | 935.00 |
| | Funding Ratio (%) | 1.87 | 53.67 | 158.26 | 5 | 134.85 | 12 | 24.16 | 1 | 1.87 |
| | #Backers | 7.00 | 286.61 | 2279.00 | 5 | 645.40 | 12 | 159.67 | 1 | 16.00 |
| | Funding/Backer ($) | 30.57 | 80.58 | 200.69 | 5 | 49.30 | 12 | 95.46 | 1 | 58.44 |
| | Duration | 30.00 | 37.00 | 60.00 | 5 | 39.40 | 12 | 36.17 | 1 | 35.00 |
| | #Reward-Levels | 4.00 | 10.33 | 28.00 | 5 | 7.60 | 12 | 11.58 | 1 | 9.00 |
| | #Video | | | | | | | | | |
| | No | | | | 1 | | 2 | | 0 | |
| | Yes | | | | 4 | | 10 | | 1 | |
| Fashion | Funding Target ($) | 1000.00 | 10,365.38 | 100,000.00 | 5 | 6600.00 | 20 | 11,325.00 | 1 | 10,000.00 |
| (N = 26) | Final Funding ($) | 0.00 | 6961.77 | 128,722.00 | 5 | 31,932.80 | 20 | 1062.10 | 1 | 100.00 |
| | Funding Ratio (%) | 0.00 | 69.36 | 953.50 | 5 | 332.12 | 20 | 7.09 | 1 | 1.00 |
| | #Backers | 0.00 | 93.46 | 1181.00 | 5 | 419.20 | 20 | 16.65 | 1 | 1.00 |
| | Funding/Backer ($) | 0.00 | 76.17 | 500.00 | 5 | 63.54 | 20 | 78.13 | 1 | 100.00 |
| | Duration | 15.00 | 31.73 | 50.00 | 5 | 31.00 | 20 | 32.00 | 1 | 30.00 |
| | #Reward-Levels | 3.00 | 9.19 | 33.00 | 5 | 10.20 | 20 | 9.20 | 1 | 4.00 |
| | #Video | | | | | | | | | |
| | No | | | | 1 | | 7 | | 0 | |
| | Yes | | | | 4 | | 13 | | 1 | |

*(Continued)*

**Appendix A** – *continued*

| | Variables | Total | | | Successful | | Failed | | Cancelled | |
|---|---|---|---|---|---|---|---|---|---|---|
| | | Min | Mean | Max | N | Mean | N | Mean | N | Mean |
| Film | Funding Target ($) | 100.00 | 28,230.16 | 200,000.00 | 60 | 17,741.77 | 55 | 38,353.15 | 2 | 64,500.00 |
| (N = 117) | Final Funding ($) | 0.00 | 12,183.59 | 124,114.00 | 60 | 20,577.03 | 55 | 3461.24 | 2 | 245.00 |
| | Funding Ratio (%) | 0.00 | 67.58 | 350.00 | 60 | 120.77 | 55 | 11.94 | 2 | 1.96 |
| | #Backers | 0.00 | 125.81 | 1976.00 | 60 | 216.18 | 55 | 31.42 | 2 | 10.50 |
| | Funding/Backer ($) | 0.00 | 99.73 | 1006.62 | 60 | 113.01 | 55 | 87.95 | 2 | 25.49 |
| | Duration | 10.00 | 37.36 | 60.00 | 60 | 34.60 | 55 | 40.25 | 2 | 40.50 |
| | #Reward-Levels | 3.00 | 9.74 | 31.00 | 60 | 10.22 | 55 | 9.15 | 2 | 12.00 |
| | #Video | | | | | | | | | |
| | No | | | | 2 | | 2 | | 0 | |
| | Yes | | | | 58 | | 53 | | 2 | |
| Food | Funding Target ($) | 5000.00 | 10,666.67 | 20,000.00 | 3 | 10,666.67 | 0 | – | 0 | – |
| (N = 3) | Final Funding ($) | 8212.00 | 13,379.67 | 21,777.00 | 3 | 13,379.67 | 0 | – | 0 | – |
| | Funding Ratio (%) | 108.89 | 139.38 | 164.24 | 3 | 139.38 | 0 | – | 0 | – |
| | #Backers | 75.00 | 193.67 | 272.00 | 3 | 193.67 | 0 | – | 0 | – |
| | Funding/Backer ($) | 30.19 | 86.19 | 135.33 | 3 | 86.19 | 0 | – | 0 | – |
| | Duration | 30.00 | 30.00 | 30.00 | 3 | 30.00 | 0 | – | 0 | – |
| | #Reward-Levels | 8.00 | 12.00 | 19.00 | 3 | 12.00 | 0 | – | 0 | – |
| | #Video | | | | | | | | | |
| | No | | | | 0 | | 0 | | 0 | |
| | Yes | | | | 3 | | 0 | | 0 | |
| Games | Funding Target ($) | 600.00 | 30,889.00 | 100,000.00 | 2 | 14,750.00 | 4 | 50,653.00 | 2 | 7500.00 |
| (N = 8) | Final Funding ($) | 1.00 | 5202.63 | 15,081.00 | 2 | 14,826.00 | 4 | 2669.25 | 2 | 646.00 |
| | Funding Ratio (%) | 0.16 | 28.84 | 100.54 | 2 | 100.52 | 4 | 3.94 | 2 | 6.95 |
| | #Backers | 1.00 | 102.88 | 435.00 | 2 | 286.00 | 4 | 52.50 | 2 | 20.50 |
| | Funding/Backer ($) | 1.00 | 39.70 | 106.36 | 2 | 70.52 | 4 | 30.00 | 2 | 28.28 |
| | Duration | 30.00 | 33.63 | 41.00 | 2 | 32.00 | 4 | 33.50 | 2 | 35.50 |
| | #Reward-Levels | 7.00 | 10.38 | 15.00 | 2 | 10.00 | 4 | 10.25 | 2 | 11.00 |
| | #Video | | | | | | | | | |
| | No | | | | 0 | | 0 | | 0 | |
| | Yes | | | | 2 | | 4 | | 2 | |
| Music | Funding Target ($) | 500.00 | 7552.95 | 100,000.00 | 43 | 4652.19 | 20 | 13,147.55 | 3 | 11,833.33 |
| (N = 66) | Final Funding ($) | 0.00 | 3710.74 | 13,327.00 | 43 | 5339.63 | 20 | 739.45 | 3 | 172.00 |
| | Funding Ratio (%) | 0.00 | 83.69 | 342.00 | 43 | 123.61 | 20 | 10.06 | 3 | 2.34 |
| | #Backers | 0.00 | 48.68 | 221.00 | 43 | 70.33 | 20 | 8.70 | 3 | 5.00 |
| | Funding/Backer ($) | 0.00 | 71.40 | 270.27 | 43 | 84.43 | 20 | 48.69 | 3 | 36.17 |
| | Duration | 8.00 | 36.03 | 60.00 | 43 | 34.84 | 20 | 38.10 | 3 | 39.33 |
| | #Reward-Levels | 2.00 | 8.27 | 22.00 | 43 | 8.23 | 20 | 8.10 | 3 | 10.00 |
| | #Video | | | | | | | | | |
| | No | | | | 5 | | 9 | | 0 | |
| | Yes | | | | 38 | | 11 | | 3 | |
| Photography | Funding Target ($) | 500.00 | 11,971.43 | 55,000.00 | 4 | 9150.00 | 7 | 7714.29 | 3 | 25,666.67 |
| (N = 14) | Final Funding ($) | 0.00 | 3665.21 | 16,935.00 | 4 | 10,784.50 | 7 | 1062.14 | 3 | 246.67 |
| | Funding Ratio (%) | 0.00 | 41.66 | 172.72 | 4 | 132.91 | 7 | 6.72 | 3 | 1.52 |
| | #Backers | 0.00 | 44.21 | 223.00 | 4 | 122.75 | 7 | 17.00 | 3 | 3.00 |
| | Funding/Backer ($) | 0.00 | 52.80 | 145.99 | 4 | 87.17 | 7 | 39.46 | 3 | 38.13 |
| | Duration | 25.00 | 36.57 | 60.00 | 4 | 40.00 | 7 | 32.43 | 3 | 41.67 |
| | #Reward-Levels | 3.00 | 7.93 | 14.00 | 4 | 10.00 | 7 | 6.29 | 3 | 9.00 |
| | #Video | | | | | | | | | |
| | No | | | | 0 | | 0 | | 1 | |
| | Yes | | | | 4 | | 7 | | 2 | |
| Publishing | Funding Target ($) | 120.00 | 14,771.63 | 100,000.00 | 20 | 7821.25 | 23 | 15,437.83 | 3 | 56,000.00 |
| (N = 46) | Final Funding ($) | 0.00 | 10,695.87 | 287,342.00 | 20 | 22,721.50 | 23 | 1355.74 | 3 | 2132.67 |
| | Funding Ratio (%) | 0.00 | 78.15 | 718.36 | 20 | 167.74 | 23 | 7.86 | 3 | 19.75 |
| | #Backers | 0.00 | 174.72 | 4242.00 | 20 | 380.20 | 23 | 17.00 | 3 | 14.00 |
| | Funding/Backer ($) | 0.00 | 67.75 | 416.44 | 20 | 80.70 | 23 | 47.20 | 3 | 139.00 |
| | Duration | 10.00 | 33.33 | 60.00 | 20 | 33.20 | 23 | 34.26 | 3 | 27.00 |
| | #Reward-Levels | 1.00 | 7.48 | 18.00 | 20 | 8.55 | 23 | 6.26 | 3 | 9.67 |
| | #Video | | | | | | | | | |
| | No | | | | 4 | | 7 | | 1 | |
| | Yes | | | | 16 | | 16 | | 2 | |

*(Continued)*

**Appendix A** – *continued*

| | Variables | Total | | | Successful | | Failed | | Cancelled | |
|---|---|---|---|---|---|---|---|---|---|---|
| | | Min | Mean | Max | N | Mean | N | Mean | N | Mean |
| Technology | Funding Target ($) | 2000.00 | 7333.33 | 10,000.00 | 1 | 9999.99 | 2 | 6000.00 | 0 | – |
| (N = 3) | Final Funding ($) | 30.00 | 3358.33 | 10,000.00 | 1 | 10,000.00 | 2 | 37.50 | 0 | – |
| | Funding Ratio (%) | 0.45 | 33.98 | 100.00 | 1 | 100.00 | 2 | 0.98 | 0 | – |
| | #Backers | 1.00 | 78.67 | 233.00 | 1 | 233.00 | 2 | 1.50 | 0 | – |
| | Funding/Backer ($) | 22.50 | 31.81 | 42.92 | 1 | 42.92 | 2 | 26.25 | 0 | – |
| | Duration | 15.00 | 31.67 | 45.00 | 1 | 45.00 | 2 | 25.00 | 0 | – |
| | #Reward-Levels | 4.00 | 7.00 | 9.00 | 1 | 9.00 | 2 | 6.00 | 0 | – |
| | #Video | | | | | | | | | |
| | No | | | | 0 | | 0 | | 0 | |
| | Yes | | | | 1 | | 2 | | 0 | |
| Theatre | Funding Target ($) | 100.00 | 7131.11 | 100,000.00 | 53 | 4678.36 | 12 | 18,433.33 | 1 | 1500.00 |
| (N = 66) | Final Funding ($) | 0.00 | 4656.30 | 40,903.00 | 53 | 5416.72 | 12 | 1685.83 | 1 | 0.00 |
| | Funding Ratio (%) | 0.00 | 108.39 | 304.00 | 53 | 129.92 | 12 | 22.33 | 1 | 0.00 |
| | #Backers | 0.00 | 62.24 | 269.00 | 53 | 72.40 | 12 | 22.58 | 1 | 0.00 |
| | Funding/Backer ($) | 0.00 | 77.08 | 410.00 | 53 | 73.96 | 12 | 97.30 | 1 | 0.00 |
| | Duration | 12.00 | 33.29 | 60.00 | 53 | 31.06 | 12 | 41.42 | 1 | 54.00 |
| | #Reward-Levels | 1.00 | 7.58 | 16.00 | 53 | 7.55 | 12 | 8.25 | 1 | 1.00 |
| | #Video | | | | | | | | | |
| | No | | | | 6 | | 0 | | 0 | |
| | Yes | | | | 47 | | 12 | | 1 | |

# Social finance and crowdfunding for social enterprises: a public–private case study providing legitimacy and leverage

Othmar M. Lehner and Alex Nicholls

*SAID Business School, University of Oxford, Oxford, UK*

The authors work closely with academia and governmental organizations in the UK and abroad to develop new, innovative schemes for social impact investing. Such schemes include considerations for public–private collaborations, legislative actions, and especially in this case, for the leveraged use of public and philanthropic funds in Crowdfunding (CF). The relatively new phenomenon of CF can not only provide necessary funds for the social enterprises, it may also lead to a higher legitimacy of these through early societal interaction and participation. This legitimacy can be understood as a strong positive signal for further investors. Governmental tax-reliefs and guarantees from venture-philanthropic funds provide additional incentives for investment and endorse future scaling by leveraging additional debt-finance from specialized social banks. This case study identifies idiosyncratic hurdles to why an efficient social finance market has yet to be created and examines a schema as a case of how individual players' strengths and weaknesses can be balanced out by a concerted action. The paper discusses the necessary actions, benefits and implications for the involved actors from the public, private and third sector.

## Introduction

Over the last few years, sociological as well as economic developments have combined to raise the level of activities and policy interest in various forms of social entrepreneurial activities and investments (Kerlin 2010; Dorado and Ventresca 2013; Gawell 2012; Moore, Westley, and Nicholls 2012). New institutions and actors have been exploring hybrid logics, mechanisms and rationales for investment that combine social, economic and environmental components of value, together with personal values and the disciplined pursuit of financial returns (Moore, Westley, and Nicholls 2012; Geobey, Westley, and Weber 2012). Such activities often take place despite the lack of suitable metrics and instruments for building portfolios of social investments (Manetti 2012; Nicholls 2009; Geobey, Westley, and Weber 2012). Moreover, public and private philanthropic finance has been explored in the literature and more so in practice as a means to encourage and empower innovative private social activities, aiming to deliver social value through market-based activities (Daly 2008, 2011; Wirgau, Farley, and Jensen 2010). However, at the present stage of development, there seems to be no rational, efficient global market; more a loose network of supply and demand with diverse intermediary groups linking capital and projects (Moore, Westley, and Nicholls 2012; Mendell and Barbosa 2013).

Especially, the interplay between (a) traditional funding sources such as (social) banks, (b) new governmental impact activities and (c) individuals and organizations looking for alternative, more 'ethical' investment initiatives seems to hold a special promise for the further development of social enterprises (SEs) – yet this very collaboration only starts to be examined from an academic and theory-building perspective (Moore, Westley, and Nicholls 2012; Geobey, Westley, and Weber 2012).

The addressed market participants display an array of different concerns, needs and motivations – ranging from financial returns to creating social impact and acting non-discriminating in the selection of beneficiaries in the case of public bodies (Geobey, Westley, and Weber 2012). Achleitner, Spiess-Knafl, and Volk (2014) examine empirical evidence that SEs have a rather concentrated financing structure. They track the reasons and see that a diversified financing structure in the SE sphere would often result in conflicts, which either originate from the capital providers' divergent return requirements (between social and financial) or the very design of financing instruments, which might be incompatible with SE structures. To reduce these conflicts stemming from a diversified financing structure, SEs often concentrate on the most suitable financing sources only and thus leave out potential for expansion and scaling. This diversity of needs and wants poses serious hurdles in the creation of a social finance market place, and thus solutions combining the strengths and motivations of the individual players whilst addressing each other's idiosyncratic concerns may well leverage additional funding sources for SEs.

This paper thus sets out to look at the motivations of the individual players in the field of social finance by looking at a case of a public–private partnership scheme to leverage the 'power of the many' through a careful interplay between the public, private and third sectors using Crowdfunding (CF), tax-reliefs and public–private consortia guarantees.

## SEs, (venture) philanthropy and impact investing

SEs are a widely discussed, contested and diverse, yet very practical concept to look at the different non-governmental players active in the delivery of social services. SEs are broadly defined by their, at least, partial use of market-based approaches to address broader 'social' issues, in combination with a sustainable commercial source of revenue (Kerlin 2010; McKay et al. 2014). Many efforts have been made to define an ideal type of such an enterprise (Young and Lecy 2013), including a spectrum approach looking at the trade-off between profit-making and social impact (Weerawardena and Mort 2006) and the conceptualization of hybrid organizations (Jäger and Schröer 2013). Others look more at the Schumpeterian perspective of 'disruptive' social innovations (Moore, Westley, and Nicholls 2012; Light 2009; Nicholls and Murdock 2012), and yet others examine social entrepreneurship as a pre-paradigmatic field and accept that there is no clear definition of the concept and that the very contest is necessary and fruitful for its further development (Lehner and Kansikas 2013; Moore, Westley, and Nicholls 2012; Nicholls 2010c).

Kerlin (2010) draws on social origins theory and finds that the various concepts of a SE can be understood by looking at historical and institutional roots within the different social welfare regimes. Along with Kerlin's social origins approach, Henriksen, Smith, and Zimmer (2011) find an on-going 'convergence' in the dimension of ideas, regulation, providers and revenue-mixes within the existing different traditional welfare regimes, which leads to similar approaches of adapting market solutions to public problems.

Some scholars even go so far and bring up the metaphor of a 'SE zoo', in which many different 'animals' combine social and market goals in substantially different ways

(Young and Lecy 2013). As Doherty, Haugh, and Lyon (2014) examine: 'scholarly interest in social enterprise (SE) has progressed beyond the early focus on definitions and context to investigate their management and performance'.

The related funding and financing of such SEs is yet another complex area in practice and research; scholars see the need to bridge the conceptual frameworks of social innovation and social finance practices (Moore, Westley, and Nicholls 2012; Shockley 2013) in order to understand the conditions and constraints creating social impact and scale. Several idiosyncratic hurdles for SEs to the access of traditional financial means have been identified in the literature (Moore, Westley, and Nicholls 2012; Fedele and Miniaci 2010; Ridley-Duff 2009; Brown and Murphy 2003), among others:

- Ambiguous and sometimes dichotomous aims of SEs (Dacin, Dacin, and Matear 2010) – SEs torn between the social and commercial (Lehner and Kansikas 2013; Moss et al. 2011)
- Alien corporate-governance, legal and organizational structures in SEs with complex reporting duties that are difficult to understand for traditional investors and lenders (Lehner 2014; Nicholls 2010b)
- Cultural and cognitive distance-related barriers between for-profit investors and SEs lacking the managerial terminology and valuation metrics that hinder communication (Brown and Murphy 2003; Moore, Westley, and Brodhead 2012).

Yet, out of a growing need and perhaps lately a greater understanding of the concept, several specialized solutions and agents have emerged (Moore, Westley, and Brodhead 2012; Geobey, Westley, and Weber 2012), creating a supporting spectrum ranging from micro-financing organizations (Estapé-Dubreuil and Torreguitart-Mirada 2013), 'social banks' (Nakagawa and Laratta 2010) to venture philanthropy (Daly 2008, 2011), impact investing (Mendell and Barbosa 2013) and public–private collaborations (Van Slyke 2006; Warner and Hefetz 2008). However, many of these efforts remain yet to be 'institutionalised' or replicable, and often still fail to be fully understood in their individual and combined impacts. Daly (2011), for example, examines philanthropy as an essentially contested concept with a greater promise despite its conceptual ambiguity; yet other scholars take a more critical perspective on the potential downside of the diverse income and funding sources and their impact on the actual mission achievement (Thompson and Williams 2014). In addition, the implications of a 'marketized philanthropy', leading to more business-oriented models for bringing about social change, are yet to be examined for their legitimacy and value proposition (Wirgau, Farley, and Jensen 2010).

Along with these new funding and financing opportunities, new investment logics have emerged; most emphasizing the evaluation and accountability of 'hybrid' ventures while looking at commercial and social returns (Manetti 2012; Nicholls 2009; Barman 2007). Especially, the social return on investment (SROI) has been investigated as a decision-making and rationalizing principle (Rotheroe and Richards 2007; Flockhart 2005), albeit within a certain scholarly stream only, and on the other hand, the very nature and legitimacy of measuring and accounting in SEs are currently put under scrutiny in some length (Wirgau, Farley, and Jensen 2010; Manetti 2012; Luke, Barraket, and Eversole 2013; Arvidson et al. 2013). An important stream deals with the logic of impact investing (Bugg-Levine and Emerson 2011). Impact investors seek to place capital in businesses and funds that generate social or environmental value, and at the same time ask for a nominal interest payment (Geobey, Westley, and Weber 2012).

Impact investments are 'intended to create positive impact beyond financial return' (O'Donohoe et al. 2010), yet impact investors carry high reputational risks besides the more obvious financial risks, and the social impact market seems to be still in its infancy (O'Donohoe et al. 2010; Geobey, Westley, and Weber 2012).

The interplay between these players and investment logics so far remains very limited in practice; yet the displayed varying individual promises, strengths but also constraints, would call for a more concerted action and collaboration between the actors to improve the SE funding and financing situation (Moore, Westley, and Nicholls 2012; Moore, Westley, and Brodhead 2012).

Geobey, Westley, and Weber (2012) come up with first attempts and suggest links between the seemingly distinct players to overcome structural challenges and maximize their impact at different stages of the innovation process in a complex socio-ecological system. In addition, they examine the so-far under-conceptualized concept of 'risk' in the SE sphere and propose a possible portfolio strategy. The authors identify another important, yet still somewhat abstract player in the field that has so far not been truly activated when it comes to investments in SEs – the crowd.

## CF for SEs

On the very basis, CF means tapping a large, dispersed audience dubbed as 'the crowd', for small pledges that can sum up to incredible amounts due to the sheer numbers of participants. While the idea itself has been successfully employed in donation marketing for a long time, nowadays CF is typically empowered by the social media communication over the Internet and includes a distinct reward and investment logic (Belleflamme, Lambert, and Schwienbacher 2013b). CF has been addressed in the literature so far mostly in the context of creative industries, for example for funding of Indie music records or retro software games (Mollick 2014; Belleflamme, Lambert, and Schwienbacher 2013a; Schwienbacher and Larralde 2010). The context of SEs has remained largely unexplored in the literature so far, despite several promising activities in the field, with the exception of Lehner (2013), creating a model of CF for social ventures.

Improving our knowledge of CF seems especially important for SEs, as traditional means of finance have proven as sub-par or sometimes even inadequate, and the market for donations and public grants has become more and more competed for and seems to slowly dry out due to changes in policy (Fedele and Miniaci 2010; Moore, Westley, and Nicholls 2012; Okten and Weisbrod 2000).

Idiosyncratic hurdles in SEs as identified in the previous paragraph (such as hybrid aims) additionally aggravate the already difficult financing situation that many start-ups find themselves in (Cosh, Cumming, and Hughes 2009). Recent developments such as the financial crisis also contribute to the problematic situation and increase pressure to find alternative means of finance, as the public sector has reduced some forms of spending to cope with the perceivably high, accumulated governmental debts throughout the European Union (Bielefeld 2009; Ferrera, Hemerijck, and Rhodes 2004; Lehner 2011).

Finding alternative, tailored methods of funding and financing by innovatively combining existing potentates and building upon everyday people's values and opinions, social media platforms and alternative reward systems thus seems a consistent step for SEs, and fits well to the newly identified 'emancipation' of the global crowd (Drury and Stott 2011). As Lehner (2013) examines, CF may offer one especially suited answer to the financing needs of social ventures, as 'typically "crowd-investors" do not look much at collaterals or business plans, but at the ideas and core values of the opportunity, and thus at its legitimacy'.

Crowd-based processes may bring the additional benefit of being perceived as per se democratic (Drury and Stott 2011), and more and more governments are becoming aware of the untapped potential and are trying to reduce legal barriers for CF, especially in the UK and the USA (Parrino and Romeo 2012).

Despite this potential for social entrepreneurs, few academic articles exist so far that address CF in this context (Clarkin 2014; Lehner 2013; Frydrich, Bock, and Kinder 2014) – apart from a small stream focusing on donations (Firth 2012; Muller and Kräussl 2011).

CF in a social entrepreneurship perspective may provide additional 'legitimacy' to the venture, as the crowd will select and support the social needs it deems worthy (Drury and Stott 2011; Frydrich, Bock, and Kinder 2014) and thus create a strong investment signal to other players in the field. Such legitimacy and strong signals are of high value for SEs because of their dealing between the market, civil society and public (Kerlin 2010; Lehner 2014).

## Collaborations between the sectors

Looking at collaborations between players from the various sectors, the authors identify several research streams. One distinct avenue examines the link between purely commercial companies and non-profit organizations, often combined through activities stemming from the corporate social responsibility sphere (Aguinis and Glavas 2012; Ljubownikow 2012; Austin and Reficco 2009; Cornelius et al. 2008; Baron 2007). Concerning new partnerships and financial sources, Bingham and Walters (2013) for example see that the recent change in political leadership in the UK has created financial uncertainty and instability for many third-sector organizations. They even go so far to state that an over-reliance on government funding is supposed to be a risky strategy and that there is a growing need to diversify and seek out alternative sources of revenue. Seitanidi and Crane (2009) examine the deeper-level micro-processes in the selection, design and institutionalization of such partnerships and provide valuable insights. Suárez and Hwang (2012) look at institutional and resource dependence effects in non-profit interactions with businesses and find that rationalized non-profits are more likely to attract business donations while those with earned income are less likely. Overall, they see that a funding diversity has a salient positive effect on the non-profits. Taking a more critical standpoint, Thompson and Williams (2014) see that SEs with a distinct income from trading activities show a negative link with the achievement of their social objectives.

A closely related research stream considers (venture) philanthropists and their supporting activities (Pepin 2005; Hafenmayer 2013; Van Slyke and Newman 2006) in the financing and development of SEs. This leads to the logic of 'impact investing' which seems to be of especially high relevance in the UK and the USA (Wood, Thornley, and Grace 2013) and is more and more embraced in governmental agendas (Jackson 2013b; Guo 2007). Closely related to these developments are newly developed sources and instruments, such as the 'Big Society Capital' (Rodger 2013; Lister 2014; Grint and Holt 2013), a kind of public fund for social impact, and 'Social Impact Bonds' (SIBs) (Eames et al. 2014; Warner 2013; Jackson 2013a), a form of repayable debt for SEs in which the interest rate depends on the actually achieved social impact.

However, these instruments are not without their critics. McHugh et al. (2013) for example warn about unintended consequences for the social outcomes and see SIBs as just 'the latest manifestation of the ideological shift which the UK third sector is undergoing'. Another stream looks at public–private partnerships and sees these as a good way to provide important civil services that would deliver only sub-par financial returns and are not addressed through direct public spending (Eames et al. 2014; Koppenjan and Enserink 2009; Martimort and Pouyet 2008; Maskin and Tirole 2008).

Few academic inquiries, however, exist examining the value and possible role of the combined potential of small individual 'investors' for the funding of SEs, apart from the traditional turn on donations (Firth 2012; Dart 2004). While commercial capital markets have successfully tapped this potential, the 'social-capital market' so far has not been very popular and attractive, despite some early efforts such as the social stock exchange in London or Ethex in Oxford and the well-demonstrated fundamental willingness of people to contribute to social causes in the case of volunteering. Practice and early research thus sees a tremendous, yet largely unexploited financial potential for SEs, based on the investment-power of the many, when highly legitimate investment opportunities are offered to the public in combination with regulatory governmental action (Clarkin 2014; Lehner 2013).

## The case

### *Relevance and involved agents*

The case study was taken from recent work and discussions of the author with the UK cabinet on the future of the UK social finance market and CF.

Along the lines of the previous paragraphs, the examined scheme seeks to combine strengths and weaknesses of different parties to come up with an integrated solution in order to provide new means of funding for SEs. It does so by first identifying the individual characteristics of the various actors and subsequently trying to leverage the strengths of some to alleviate the weaknesses of the others.

Pintelon et al. (2013) see that 'welfare states have evolved towards a "social investment" model of welfare' which is characterized by a focus on equality of opportunity and upward social mobility, along with a greater emphasis on individual responsibility. Therefore, any governmental action needs to ensure a non-discrimination policy concerning the treatment of other (regulated) agents, in this case fund-seeking SEs, venture philanthropic funds and financial-intermediaries. In addition, governmental managerial actions need to be based on a rationalized decision-making process aiming to serve the political will and at the same time optimize risk and return in order to fulfil their fiduciary duties to the taxpayers (Lecy, Schmitz, and Swedlund 2011; Guo 2007; Van Slyke 2006).

The question raised was how to come up with an economical solution leveraging governmental potential (financial and regulatory), when rational decision-making instruments are either yet underdeveloped (e.g. focusing too much on the financial side) or are not entirely suitable for portfolio building as in the case of SROI (Manetti 2012).

CF, as introduced earlier, may provide a solution to this selection process. When many people deem a social idea worthy, it can be seen as a basic democratic selection process and as such, crowd-endorsement may create the necessary signals for investments (Lehner 2013; Ahlers et al. 2012) (Table 1).

The crowd on the other side often remains reluctant to actually invest in SEs (apart from donations, which are completely different in their logic). The reasons behind could

Table 1.  Relevant actors and their wants and needs.

| Who | Wants and needs |
| --- | --- |
| Government | • Non-discrimination in the selection process<br>• Economical, efficient approach, limiting administrational costs<br>• Fulfilment of political will<br>• Active and engaged society in the delivery of social services<br>• Responsibility and fiduciary duties to taxpayers – rationalized decisions and optimized financial risk/returns |
| Private (venture) philanthropists | • Fulfilment of mission and vision of founders<br>• High leverage of invested funds<br>• Fiduciary duties to the shareholders – rationalized decisions and optimized financial risk/returns |
| Social banks | • Fulfilment of mission<br>• Optimize risk and return<br>• Careful portfolio building to avoid risk-clusters |
| Individuals in the crowd | • Interesting opportunities to invest<br>• Enough information to decide upon 'social' criteria<br>• Emancipation through participation in society<br>• Some form of financial return |
| SEs | • Fulfilment of their mission and vision of founders<br>• Participation of stakeholders<br>• Start-up funding<br>• Easy processes to apply for funding<br>• Low interest rates<br>• Capital for scaling |

be that the perceived financial, risk-adjusted returns (e.g. interest rates) may be too small to outweigh the positive social return. Another explanation might find that many members of the crowd are not even aware of social investment opportunities. Governmental action could change this to a win–win situation. Providing a tax relief on small crowd-investments in SEs might create the necessary financial return without putting too much strain on the administration. This relief could either directly reduce the tax basis, or work alongside the existing (from April 2014 on) social investment tax relief at the current rate of 30%, which would need to be improved to overcome the current GBP 150.000 hurdle for enterprises, and comprise more suitable instruments. It seems important that the eligible investment sums should be limited per person (not per enterprise), to keep the individual risk-taking at level and at the same time make room for a larger crowd to participate and have a large combined impact. This return in form of a tax relief will still be below par concerning risk, but as research indicates, investors in SEs do add the social return to the financial (Arvidson et al. 2013; Nicholls 2010a) in their logic.

One example for clarification – if the individuals in the crowd lend money for 5 years at a zero interest rate to an eligible SE, a tax relief would provide (on the average) 25% tax reduction, so the average annual compounded interest would be 4.56%, which is more than most savings account would provide (however of course at a higher risk). Besides the main crowd motivation of investing in a valid social cause, this may well provide an additional stimulus to invest (Figure 1).

This tax relief could be limited to certain legal forms, such as charities, but also include community interest companies limited by guarantee or shares, which have to have a dividend cap in their articles. Regulated but privately run platforms as

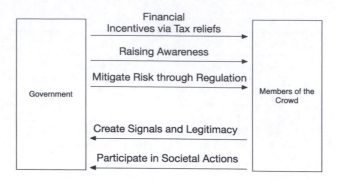

Figure 1. Collaboration between government and members of the crowd.

intermediaries would provide information and investment opportunities to the crowd and help with the forms. Governmental endorsement through media and events will be necessary to raise the awareness-levels of these opportunities and the related tax reliefs.

While there are ideas of additionally backing the crowd-investments by a direct public guarantee, the authors do not see that individuals investing small sums, typically around 100–500 GBPs on the average, are overly concerned because of the low value at risk. They are well aware that they may risk a complete loss. On the contrary, a public guarantee might provide the wrong incentives to the wrong people and disable important mechanisms of screening. Crowd members, for example, would not carefully inform themselves about the opportunity and the people behind, but rather see these investments as a simple chance to get a 'free lunch'. Ultimately, we might even see SEs being created just to draw money from the crowd without ever delivering their social promise. In order to keep the 'wisdom of the crowd' sharp and alive, a public guarantee for crowd-funded investments would be detrimental. Such guarantees, even from private partners, for example venture philanthropic funds, may also overtax the administrative capacity of these organizations (Figure 2).

However, a public–private consortium provided guarantee as an additional, subsequent security instrument could leverage the crowd supplied money even further. Taking only subordinate risk, it would also be an excellent opportunity to make leveraged use of the market power of big social funds. Given that a SE has successfully

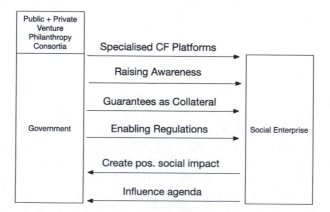

Figure 2. Collaboration between government and SEs.

completed a round of CF, the achieved amount could be matched by a guarantee from public–private consortia. This guarantee could be used for up to two years after the original CF campaign as a security, not for the crowd investment, but to allow the SE get an additional bank loan running from 5 to 7 years from specialised social banks or other impact investors at a discounted interest rate. To give an example, a crowd-investment of 70k would be matched by a public–private consortium with a guarantee instrument as security of another 70k. As banks typically lend money in a 1:2 or even 1:3 ratio, provided the cash flow planning has been approved, this may provide additional funds of 140–210k, while public funds are only taking subordinate risk of 70k. The total amount available for the SE would be around $70 + 140 = 210k$. In addition, the organizations providing it would act non-discriminating, as they provide the guarantee instrument to those enterprises deemed worthy by the people, and ultimately the financing decision would still be made by social banks or other social finance providers (Figure 3).

This would also provide a strong leverage on the market power of public–private consortia funds, as they only take subordinate risk in form of a guarantee instrument and thus can make use of the 'law of large numbers' to create leveraged risk optimized portfolios while fulfilling their statutory or political agenda.

## A diagram of the scheme (Figure 4)

### *The process*

SEs thus can turn to the new source 'crowd' for investments under this scheme using special dedicated platforms. The individual members of the crowd can invest small sums of money typically for 5 + years, up to a certain limit per investor into those SEs, which they deem legitimate. This money is invested as a loan or a special form of equity and will need to be repaid in full after 5 years at a zero interest level. However, the proposed scheme allows for a tax-relief for this kind of investment. Thus, given an average tax relief of 25%, the annual nominal interest over 5 years would be 5% (compounded interest at 4.56%), which is higher than the current savings rate. Of course, the risk of default is also much higher, therefore the limit is imposed to reduce the individual exposure. In any case, the individual crowd-investors are typically more motivated by the social cause than the financial return; otherwise, they would use different opportunities in the first place (Arvidson et al. 2013; Nicholls 2010a). However, to

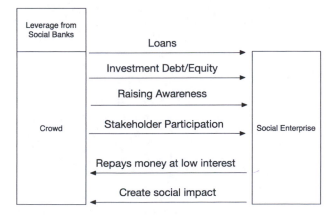

Figure 3.   Collaboration between crowd and SEs.

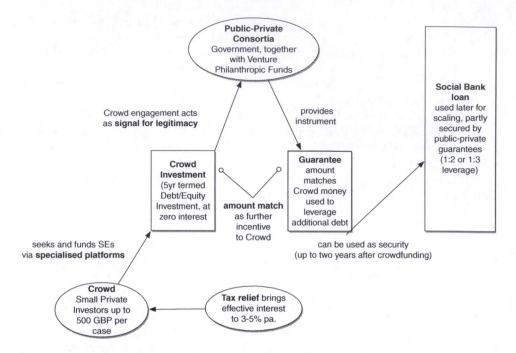

Figure 4.   An illustration of the scheme. *Source*: authors.

mitigate fraudulent risk, the platforms such as financial-intermediaries need to be specially regulated, though privately run, perhaps as SEs themselves, and should provide information and basic screening about the projects.

Another rule to reduce risk would be the introduction of a so-called threshold funding (Mollick 2014). Only if the total amount of the crowd-pledges has reached the self-reported funding goal within the funding period, the investments will actually be transferred to the SE; otherwise, all investors have their money returned. This reduces the risk of an *individual* adverse selection through collective crowd-intelligence. Additional schemes for more established SEs may yet be put in place later to fulfil on-going financial needs without a specific threshold or funding period.

As an optional, subsequent step in this scheme, public–private consortia may match the crowd-funded sum with a 7- to 10-year termed guarantee instrument that can be used up to two years later to secure a further loan by a social bank or an other social finance provider. At a leverage of 1:2 or even 1:3, such a move would provide additional funds for a possible later expansion at a modest interest rate, while consortia funds would only take subordinate risk and thus can use probability functions for even higher impact and leverage. An example for this: if the risk of actual default for a large number of SEs can be safely estimated at 10%, then 1M GBP could in theory be used for guarantees up to 10M GBP. Provided the inflow of new funds into the consortia would be sustainable and cover actual defaults, 1M GBP could therefore, at a ratio of 1:2, unlock 20M GBP of funds for SEs (Figure 5).

## *The benefits*

First, a democratic choice through the participation of the many (again the individual limit helps to ensure a great number of stakeholders) would screen select the SEs eligible

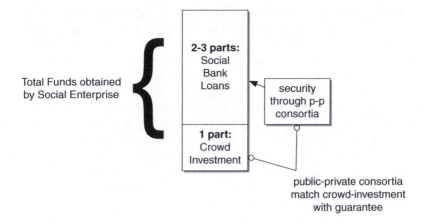

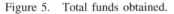

Figure 5.    Total funds obtained.


Table 2.    The benefits of the scheme for the individual players.

| Who for? | Benefits | Engagement through |
|---|---|---|
| Government | • Public – basic democratic decision-making<br>• Rationalized and transparent criteria<br>• High efficiency and inclusion of other funding sources for impact<br>• Low value at risk because of subordinate guarantee<br>• Attracting new investors<br>• Raising awareness and create opportunities for participation | • Offering tax reliefs<br>• Creating regulation for platform intermediaries<br>• Providing guarantee instruments for leveraged use in social bank loans<br>• Taking subordinate risk<br>• Using public outlets to create awareness |
| Private (venture) philanthropists | • Fulfil their mission/vision<br>• Optimize risk/return due to public–private partnerships | • Being part of the consortia providing guarantees<br>• Taking subordinate risk<br>• Helping in setting up platforms and supporting SEs in their CF activities |
| Social banks | • Fulfil their mission<br>• Having a pre-selection through CF lowers risk | • Providing loans as follow-up finance<br>• Due diligence<br>• Taking primary risk |
| Individuals in the crowd | • Supporting a worthy social cause<br>• Creating some form of financial return<br>• Feeling empowered through participation | • Take individual high risk, yet mitigated by thresholds and limits on investment<br>• Provide the 'wisdom of the crowd' through interaction and web 2.0 |
| SEs | • Tap a new type of investors for investment funds<br>• Reduce dependency of traditional investors and financiers<br>• Gain visibility and CF supports marketing activities<br>• Fulfil their mission/vision | • Take entrepreneurial risk<br>• Create organizational forms<br>• Communication with Crowd via platforms |

for this scheme. A successful CF campaign has been identified in the literature as a strong signal of legitimacy (Lehner 2013; Stemler 2013). The crowd is incentivized by a tax relief while SEs can borrow at a zero interest rate. Information about regulated platforms for SEs as intermediaries can be dispersed using official channels, thus awareness levels and subsequently engagement would rise. (Table 2)

Second, while it is optional for the SEs to accept the additional offered guarantee, it would be available as an instrument in later stages and can be used by all qualified social banks and other social funds providers. The ultimate decision of providing loans, however, would be up to these sources (taking the primary risk), but the security incentivizes and reduces interest rates, while public–private consortia funds are only at subordinate risk and thus their capital can be highly leveraged for portfolios of social causes. The two-year time span to decide on taking the guarantee allows the SEs to build their business models on the crowd-funded money first, and use the additional loans to scale up later. This again reduces the risk for social banks and public–private funds, as there would be more data available for a credit rating.

## Conclusion and implications

This paper sets out to explore the needs and wants of the individual players in the field of social finance. It identifies idiosyncratic hurdles to why an efficient social finance market has yet to be created and looks at an exemplary case study of a scheme of how individual players' strengths and weaknesses can be balanced out by a concerted action.

Ultimately, it is up to the policy-makers to provide further attractive *schemes of participation* in the creation of a social impact market, along with rules to protect the legitimate interests of people and organizations. Future research will need to look into these concepts from many viewpoints, assisting in the fine-tuning, proliferation and evaluation but also taking a critical viewpoint in addressing possible discrimination through the collaboration of powerful players. From a more practical perspective, this scheme, if put into action, has the potential to unleash the power of the many small, ethically concerned investors in the UK – who are already looking for more sustainable alternatives – for the benefit of SEs.

## References

Achleitner, A. K., W. Spiess-Knafl, and S. Volk. 2014. "The Financing Structure of Social Enterprises: Conflicts and Implications." *International Journal of Entrepreneurial Venturing* 6 (1): 85–99.

Aguinis, H., and A. Glavas. 2012. "What We Know and Don't Know About Corporate Social Responsibility: A Review and Research Agenda." *Journal of Management* 38 (4): 932–968. doi:10.1177/0149206311436079.

Ahlers, G. K., D. Cumming, C. Günther, and D. Schweizer. 2012. "Signaling in Equity Crowdfunding." SSRN Working Paper Series 2161587.

Arvidson, M., F. Lyon, S. McKay, and D. Moro. 2013. "Valuing the Social? The Nature and Controversies of Measuring Social Return on Investment (SROI)." *Voluntary Sector Review* 4 (1): 3–18.

Austin, J., and E. Reficco. 2009. "Corporate Social Entrepreneurship." Working Paper Series No. 09-101, Harvard Business School.

Barman, E. 2007. "What is the Bottom Line for Nonprofit Organizations? A History of Measurement in the British Voluntary Sector." *VOLUNTAS: International Journal of Voluntary and Nonprofit Organizations* 18 (2): 101–115. doi:10.1007/s11266-007-9039-3.

Baron, D. P. 2007. "Corporate Social Responsibility and Social Entrepreneurship." *Journal of Economics & Management Strategy* 16 (3): 683–717.

Belleflamme, P., T. Lambert, and A. Schwienbacher. 2013a. "Crowdfunding: Tapping the Right Crowd." *Journal of Business Venturing*. doi:10.1016/j.jbusvent.2013.07.003.

Belleflamme, P., T. Lambert, and A. Schwienbacher. 2013b. "Individual Crowdfunding Practices." *Venture Capital* 15 (4): 313–333. doi:10.1080/13691066.2013.785151.

Bielefeld, W. 2009. "Issues in Social Enterprise and Social Entrepreneurship." *Journal of Public Affairs Education* 15 (1): 69–86.

Bingham, T., and G. Walters. 2013. "Financial Sustainability Within UK Charities: Community Sport Trusts and Corporate Social Responsibility Partnerships." *VOLUNTAS: International Journal of Voluntary and Nonprofit Organizations* 24 (3): 606–629.

Brown, H., and E. Murphy. 2003. "The Financing of Social Enterprises: A Special Report by the Bank of England." London: Bank of England.

Bugg-Levine, A., and J. Emerson. 2011. "Impact Investing: Transforming How We Make Money While Making a Difference." *Innovations* 6 (3): 9–18.

Clarkin, J. E. 2014. "Crowdfunding, Foundations, and Impact Investors as Sources of Financial Capital for Social Entrepreneurs." In *Theory and Empirical Research in Social Entrepreneurship*, edited by P. P. Phan, S. Bacq, and M. Nordqvist, 191–219. Cheltenham: Edward Elgar.

Cornelius, N., M. Todres, S. Janjuha-Jivraj, A. Woods, and J. Wallace. 2008. "Corporate Social Responsibility and the Social Enterprise." *Journal of Business Ethics* 81 (2): 355–370. doi:10.1007/s10551-007-9500-7.

Cosh, A., D. Cumming, and A. Hughes. 2009. "Outside Enterpreneurial Capital." *The Economic Journal* 119 (540): 1494–1533.

Dacin, P. A., M. T. Dacin, and M. Matear. 2010. "Social Entrepreneurship: Why We Don't Need a New Theory and How We Move Forward From Here." *The Academy of Management Perspectives* 24 (3): 37–57.

Daly, S. 2008. "Institutional Innovation in Philanthropy: Community Foundations in the UK." *VOLUNTAS: International Journal of Voluntary and Nonprofit Organizations* 19 (3): 219. doi:10.1007/s11266-008-9067-7.

Daly, S. 2011. "Philanthropy as an Essentially Contested Concept." *VOLUNTAS: International Journal of Voluntary and Nonprofit Organizations* 23 (3): 535–557. doi:10.1007/s11266-011-9213-5.

Dart, R. 2004. "The Legitimacy of Social Enterprise." *Nonprofit Management and Leadership* 14 (4): 411–424.

Doherty, B., H. Haugh, and F. Lyon. 2014. "Social Enterprises as Hybrid Organizations: A Review and Research Agenda." *International Journal of Management Reviews*.

Dorado, S., and M. J. Ventresca. 2013. "Crescive Entrepreneurship in Complex Social Problems: Institutional Conditions for Entrepreneurial Engagement." *Journal of Business Venturing* 28 (1): 69–82. doi:10.1016/j.jbusvent.2012.02.002.

Drury, J., and C. Stott. 2011. "Contextualising the Crowd in Contemporary Social Science." *Contemporary Social Science* 6 (3): 275–288.

Eames, S., V. Terranova, L. Battaglia, I. Nelson, C. Riesenberg, and L. Rosales. 2014. "A Review of Social Impact Bonds: Financing Social Service Programs through Public–Private Partnerships." Working Paper No. 02/2014, University of Texas at Austin.

Estapé-Dubreuil, G., and C. Torreguitart-Mirada. 2013. "The Public Sector and the Development of Microfinance in Spain." *International Journal of Social Economics* 40 (10): 866–884. doi:10.1108/ijse-2011-0078.

Fedele, A., and R. Miniaci. 2010. "Do Social Enterprises Finance Their Investments Differently from For-Profit Firms? The Case of Social Residential Services in Italy." *Journal of Social Entrepreneurship* 1 (2): 174–189. doi:10.1080/19420676.2010.511812.

Ferrera, M., A. Hemerijck, and M. Rhodes. 2004. *The Future of European Welfare States: Recasting Welfare for a New Century*. Oxford: Oxford University Press.

Firth, N. 2012. "Crowdfunding Successes Show Value of Small Donations." *The New Scientist* 213 (2858): 22.

Flockhart, A. 2005. "Raising the Profile of Social Enterprises: The Use of Social Return on Investment (SROI) and Investment Ready Tools (IRT) to Bridge the Financial Credibility Gap." *Social Enterprise Journal* 1 (1): 29–42.

Frydrich, D., A. J. Bock, and T. Kinder. 2014. "Exploring Entrepreneurial Legitimacy in Reward-Based Crowdfunding." *Venture Capital* 16 (3).

Gawell, M. 2012. "Social Entrepreneurship: Action Grounded in Needs, Opportunities and/or Perceived Necessities?" *VOLUNTAS: International Journal of Voluntary and Nonprofit Organizations* 24 (4): 1071–1090. doi:10.1007/s11266-012-9301-1.

Geobey, S., F. R. Westley, and O. Weber. 2012. "Enabling Social Innovation through Developmental Social Finance." *Journal of Social Entrepreneurship* 3 (2): 151–165. doi:10. 1080/19420676.2012.726006

Grint, K., and C. Holt. 2013. "5. Public value and localism in the UK." *Managing Social Issues: A Public Values Perspective* 71.

Guo, C. 2007. "When Government Becomes the Principal Philanthropist: The Effects of Public Funding on Patterns of Nonprofit Governance." *Public Administration Review* 67 (3): 458–473.

Hafenmayer, W. 2013. "Venture Philanthropy: Approach, Features, and Challenges." *Trusts & Trustees* 19 (6): 535–541.

Henriksen, L. S., S. R. Smith, and A. Zimmer. 2011. "At the Eve of Convergence? Transformations of Social Service Provision in Denmark, Germany, and the United States." *VOLUNTAS: International Journal of Voluntary and Nonprofit Organizations* 23 (2): 458–501. doi:10.1007/s11266-011-9221-5.

Jackson, E. T. 2013a. "Evaluating Social Impact Bonds: Questions, Challenges, Innovations, and Possibilities in Measuring Outcomes in Impact Investing." *Community Development* 44 (5): 608–616.

Jackson, E. T. 2013b. "Interrogating the Theory of Change: Evaluating Impact Investing Where It Matters Most." *Journal of Sustainable Finance & Investment* 3 (2): 95–110.

Jäger, U. P., and A. Schröer. 2013. "Integrated Organizational Identity: A Definition of Hybrid Organizations and a Research Agenda." *VOLUNTAS: International Journal of Voluntary and Nonprofit Organizations* 1–26.

Kerlin, J. 2010. "A Comparative Analysis of the Global Emergence of Social Enterprise." *VOLUNTAS: International Journal of Voluntary and Nonprofit Organizations* 21 (2): 162–179. doi:10.1007/s11266-010-9126-8.

Koppenjan, J. F. M., and B. Enserink. 2009. "Public–Private Partnerships in Urban Infrastructures: Reconciling Private Sector Participation and Sustainability." *Public Administration Review* 69 (2): 284–296.

Lecy, J. D., H. P. Schmitz, and H. Swedlund. 2011. "Non-Governmental and Not-for-Profit Organizational Effectiveness: A Modern Synthesis." *VOLUNTAS: International Journal of Voluntary and Nonprofit Organizations* 23 (2): 434–457. doi:10.1007/s11266-011-9204-6.

Lehner, O. M. 2011. "Social Entrepreneurship Perspectives: Triangulated Approaches to Hybridity." In *Studies in Business and Economics*, edited by Takala Tuomo. Vol. 111. Jyväskylä: JSBE.

Lehner, O. M. 2013. "Crowdfunding Social Ventures: A Model and Research Agenda." *Venture Capital* 15 (4): 289–311. doi:10.1080/13691066.2013.782624.

Lehner, O. M. 2014. "The Formation and Interplay of Social Capital in Crowd Funded Social Ventures." *Entrepreneurship and Regional Development.* 26 (5–6). doi:10.1080/08985626. 2014.922623.

Lehner, O. M., and J. Kansikas. 2013. "Pre-Paradigmatic Status of Social Entrepreneurship Research: A Systematic Literature Review." *Journal of Social Entrepreneurship* 1–22. doi:10. 1080/19420676.2013.777360.

Light, P. 2009. "Social Entrepreneurship Revisited: Not Just Anyone, Anywhere, in Any Organization Can Make Breakthrough Change." *Social Innovation Review* 7 (3): 21–22.

Lister, M. 2014. "Citizens, Doing It for Themselves? The Big Society and Government Through Community." *Parliamentary Affairs.* doi:10.1093/pa/gst025.

Ljubownikow, S. 2012. "Lester M. Salamon: Rethinking Corporate Social Engagement: Lessons from Latin America." *VOLUNTAS: International Journal of Voluntary and Nonprofit Organizations* 23 (1): 285–286.

Luke, B., J. Barraket, and R. Eversole. 2013. "Measurement as Legitimacy Versus Legitimacy of Measures: Performance Evaluation of Social Enterprise." *Qualitative Research in Accounting & Management* 10 (3): 234–258. doi:10.1108/qram-08-2012-0034.

Manetti, G. 2012. "The Role of Blended Value Accounting in the Evaluation of Socio-Economic Impact of Social Enterprises." *VOLUNTAS: International Journal of Voluntary and Nonprofit Organizations* 25 (2): 443–464. doi:10.1007/s11266-012-9346-1.

Martimort, D., and J. Pouyet. 2008. "To Build or Not to Build: Normative and Positive Theories of Public–Private Partnerships." *International Journal of Industrial Organization* 26 (2): 393–411.

Maskin, E., and J. Tirole. 2008. "Public–private Partnerships and Government Spending Limits." *International Journal of Industrial Organization* 26 (2): 412–420.

McHugh, N., S. Sinclair, M. Roy, L. Huckfield, and C. Donaldson. 2013. "Social Impact Bonds: A Wolf in Sheep's Clothing?" *Journal of Poverty & Social Justice* 21 (3).

McKay, S., D. Moro, S. Teasdale, and D. Clifford. 2014. "The Marketisation of Charities in England and Wales." *VOLUNTAS: International Journal of Voluntary and Nonprofit Organizations*. doi:10.1007/s11266-013-9417-y.

Mendell, M., and E. Barbosa. 2013. "Impact Investing: A Preliminary Analysis of Emergent Primary and Secondary Exchange Platforms." *Journal of Sustainable Finance & Investment* 3 (2): 111–123. doi:10.1080/20430795.2013.776258.

Mollick, E. 2014. "The Dynamics of Crowdfunding: An Exploratory Study." *Journal of Business Venturing* 29 (1): 1–16. doi:10.1016/j.jbusvent.2013.06.005.

Moore, M.-L., F. R. Westley, and T. Brodhead. 2012. "Social Finance Intermediaries and Social Innovation." *Journal of Social Entrepreneurship* 3 (2): 184–205. doi:10.1080/19420676.2012.726020.

Moore, M.-L., F. R. Westley, and A. Nicholls. 2012. "The Social Finance and Social Innovation Nexus." *Journal of Social Entrepreneurship* 3 (2): 115–132. doi:10.1080/19420676.2012.725824.

Moss, T. W., J. C. Short, G. T. Payne, and G. Lumpkin. 2011. "Dual Identities in Social Ventures: An Exploratory Study." *Entrepreneurship Theory and Practice* 35 (4): 805–830.

Muller, A., and R. Kräussl. 2011. "Doing Good Deeds in Times of Need: A Strategic Perspective on Corporate Disaster Donations." *Strategic Management Journal* 32 (9): 911–929. doi:10.1002/smj.917.

Nakagawa, S., and R. Laratta. 2010. "How Can Co-Operative Banks Spread the Spirit of Co-Operation in Deprived Communities?" *Social Enterprise Journal* 6 (2): 162–180. doi:10.1108/17508611011069284.

Nicholls, A. 2009. "'We Do Good Things, Don't We?': 'Blended Value Accounting' in Social Entrepreneurship." *Accounting, Organizations and Society* 34 (6-7): 755–769. doi:10.1016/j.aos.2009.04.008.

Nicholls, A. 2010a. "The Institutionalization of Social Investment: The Interplay of Investment Logics and Investor Rationalities." *Journal of Social Entrepreneurship* 1 (1): 70–100.

Nicholls, A. 2010b. "Institutionalizing Social Entrepreneurship in Regulatory Space: Reporting and Disclosure by Community Interest Companies." *Accounting, Organizations and Society* 35 (4): 394–415. doi:10.1016/j.aos.2009.08.001.

Nicholls, A. 2010c. "The Legitimacy of Social Entrepreneurship: Reflexive Isomorphism in a Pre-Paradigmatic Field." *Entrepreneurship Theory and Practice* 34 (4): 611–633.

Nicholls, A., and A. Murdock, eds. 2012. "The Nature of Social Innovation." In *Social innovation*, 1–30. Basingstoke: Palgrave Macmillan.

O'Donohoe, N., C. Leijonhufvud, Y. Saltuk, A. Bugg-Levine, and M. Brandenburg. 2010. "Impact Investments: An Emerging Asset Class." *JP Morgan* 6.

Okten, C., and B. A. Weisbrod. 2000. "Determinants of Donations in Private Nonprofit Markets." *Journal of Public Economics* 75 (2): 255–272.

Parrino, R. J., and P. J. Romeo. 2012. "JOBS Act Eases Securities-Law Regulation of Smaller Companies." *Journal of Investment Compliance* 13 (3): 27–35.

Pepin, J. 2005. "Venture Capitalists and Entrepreneurs Become Venture Philanthropists." *International Journal of Nonprofit and Voluntary Sector Marketing* 10 (3): 165–173.

Pintelon, O., B. Cantillon, K. Van den Bosch, and C. T. Whelan. 2013. "The Social Stratification of Social Risks: The Relevance of Class for Social Investment Strategies." *Journal of European social policy* 23 (1): 52–67.

Ridley-Duff, R. 2009. "Co-Operative Social Enterprises: Company Rules, Access to Finance and Management Practice." *Social Enterprise Journal* 5 (1): 50–68.

Rodger, J. J. 2013. "'New Capitalism', Colonisation and the Neo-Philanthropic Turn in Social Policy: Applying Luhmann's Systems Theory to the Big Society Project." *International Journal of Sociology and Social Policy* 33 (11/12): 6.

Rotheroe, N. C., and A. Richards. 2007. "Social Return on Investment and Social Enterprise: Transparent Accountability for Sustainable Development." *Social Enterprise Journal* 3 (1): 31–48.

Schwienbacher, A., and B. Larralde. 2010. "Crowdfunding of Small Entrepreneurial Ventures." In *The Oxford Handbook of Entrepreneurial Finance*, 369–392. Oxford: Oxford University Press.

Seitanidi, M. M., and A. Crane. 2009. "Implementing CSR Through Partnerships: Understanding the Selection, Design and Institutionalisation of Nonprofit-Business Partnerships." *Journal of Business Ethics* 85 (2): 413–429.

Shockley, G. E. 2013. "Alex Nicholls, Alex Murdock (eds.): Social Innovation: Blurring Boundaries to Reconfigure Markets." *VOLUNTAS: International Journal of Voluntary and Nonprofit Organizations* 24 (4): 1209–1211.

Stemler, A. R. 2013. "The JOBS Act and Crowdfunding: Harnessing the Power – and Money – of the Masses." *Business Horizons* 56 (3): 271–275. doi:10.1016/j.bushor.2013.01.007.

Suárez, D. F., and H. Hwang. 2012. "Resource Constraints or Cultural Conformity? Nonprofit Relationships With Businesses." *VOLUNTAS: International Journal of Voluntary and Nonprofit Organizations* 24 (3): 581–605. doi:10.1007/s11266-012-9267-z.

Thompson, P., and R. Williams. 2014. "Taking Your Eyes Off the Objective: The Relationship Between Income Sources and Satisfaction with Achieving Objectives in the UK Third Sector." *VOLUNTAS: International Journal of Voluntary and Nonprofit Organizations* 25 (1): 109–137.

Van Slyke, D. M. 2006. "Agents or Stewards: Using Theory to Understand the Government-Nonprofit Social Service Contracting Relationship." *Journal of Public Administration Research and Theory* 17 (2): 157–187. doi:10.1093/jopart/mul012.

Van Slyke, D. M., and H. K. Newman. 2006. "Venture Philanthropy and Social Entrepreneurship in Community Redevelopment." *Nonprofit Management and Leadership* 16 (3): 345–368.

Warner, M. E. 2013. "Private Finance for Public Goods: Social Impact Bonds." *Journal of Economic Policy Reform* 16 (4).

Warner, M. E., and A. Hefetz. 2008. "Managing Markets for Public Service: The Role of Mixed Public–Private Delivery of City Services." *Public Administration Review* 68 (1): 155–166.

Weerawardena, J., and G. Mort. 2006. "Investigating Social Entrepreneurship: A Multidimensional Model." *Journal of World Business* 41 (1): 21–35.

Wirgau, J. S., K. W. Farley, and C. Jensen. 2010. "Is Business Discourse Colonizing Philanthropy? A Critical Discourse Analysis of (PRODUCT) RED." *VOLUNTAS: International Journal of Voluntary and Nonprofit Organizations* 21 (4): 611–630. doi:10.1007/s11266-010-9122-z.

Wood, D., B. Thornley, and K. Grace. 2013. "Institutional Impact Investing: Practice and Policy." *Journal of Sustainable Finance & Investment* 3 (2): 75–94.

Young, D. R., and J. D. Lecy. 2013. "Defining the Universe of Social Enterprise: Competing Metaphors." *VOLUNTAS: International Journal of Voluntary and Nonprofit Organizations*. doi:10.1007/s11266-013-9396-z.

# Demand-driven securities regulation: evidence from crowdfunding

Douglas Cumming[a] and Sofia Johan[a,b]

[a]*Schulich School of Business, York University, Toronto, Canada;* [b]*Tilburg Law and Economics Centre (TILEC), University of Tilburg, LE Tilburg, The Netherlands*

We study the law production race-to-the-bottom/race-to-the-top debate in a unique context of crowdfunding in which potential agency problems are extreme. Our empirical setting is based on survey data from Canada in 2013 Q1 when equity crowdfunding was not permitted but was openly contemplated by regulators. The data show some tension towards a race to the bottom insofar as start-ups prefer fewer restrictions on their ability to crowdfund, and portals prefer fewer disclosure requirements and fewer restrictions on free trading of crowdfunded shares. However, this evidence is tempered by the fact that investors demand more disclosure, limits on amounts entrepreneurs can raise, and lower thresholds for audited financial statements, among other things. Based on the ease with which the Internet facilitates cross-jurisdictional investment, we infer from the data that investor demands will give rise to a race to the top in the crowdfunding space.

Ontario examines ways to loosen crowdfunding rules.

(*The Globe and Mail,* November 29, 2012)

Regulators struggle with crowdfunding model ... Ontario looked upon as key to setting pace ... Using our existing regulatory framework to deal with something like equity crowdfunding is like trying to jam a round peg into a square hole.

(*Lawyers' Weekly,* April 19, 2013, issue)

## 1. Introduction

In select OECD countries around the world, such as Australia, the UK, Ireland, France, the Netherlands, and Switzerland, it is possible for entrepreneurs to raise capital by selling equity stakes in their business through crowdfunding or open calls to investors over Internet portals. Other types of crowdfunding platforms include donations, rewards based, and lending (for a description, see Agrawal, Catalini, and Goldfarb 2011; Ahlers et al. 2012; Belleflamme, Lambert, and Schwienbacher 2010, 2013; Bradford 2012; Burtch, Ghose, and Wattal 2012; Griffin 2012; Mollick 2012; Schwienbacher and Larralde 2013). In total across all types of crowdfunding models worldwide, there were 39 equity crowdfunding platforms which comprised 7.3% of the 452 platforms, and there was a total of US$ 88 million raised in

2011 from equity crowdfunding and a total of US$ 1441 million raised among all platforms and all crowdfunding models (Ahlers et al. 2012; Crowdfunding Industry Report 2012). Countries which currently (as at 2013) do not permit equity crowdfunding are contemplating enabling crowdfunding through legislative changes, for example, see the JOBS (Jumpstart Our Business Startups) Act in the USA.

In Canada, the Ontario Securities Commission is currently contemplating legislation to permit crowdfunding, largely in response to demand pressure from entrepreneurs and other stakeholders. Empirical evidence is consistent with the view that the adaptability of a country's legal system facilitates access to finance (e.g., Beck, Demirgüç-Kunt, and Levine 2005; Cumming and Johan 2008). But whether securities laws should be adaptable to demand pressures to permit crowdfunding is unclear.

Potential benefits associated with equity crowdfunding are highly pronounced. Entrepreneurs may obtain needed capital that would facilitate the existence of their business that would not have been available from other sources, such as banks, angel investors, or venture capital. Indeed, some companies may not exist without having had the option of raising money through crowdfunding. Famous examples of crowdfunding include the pebble watch[1] and the Statue of Liberty.[2] Potential risks associated with equity crowdfunding are likewise very pronounced. For instance, an entrepreneur may squander the proceeds, or raise equity capital through crowdfunding and then subsequently issue more shares to himself/herself, thereby diluting the equity stake held by the crowd investors. Entrepreneurs may simply pay themselves more and not invest in appropriate projects with the money raised. Nevertheless, it is possible to mitigate such risks through conditions imposed on entrepreneurs, portals, and investors, as discussed below.

In view of the pronounced benefits and severe risks with equity crowdfunding, along with the evolving regulatory landscape around the world, the crowdfunding setting provides a fascinating new environment in which to re-examine an old question: is the competitive model of law production one that gives rise to a race to the top or a race to the bottom? The corporate law framework in the USA has been a forum for much debate on the advantages and disadvantages of competitive models of legal production (Bebchuk 1992; Cumming and MacIntosh 2000, 2002; Daines 2001, 2002; Daines and Klausner 2001; Roe 2003; Romano 1985, 1987, 1993), but has not previously been examined in the crowdfunding context. In view of legislative developments in Canada, the USA, and other countries around the world where new crowdfunding models and legislative reforms are being contemplated in 2012 and 2013 and frequently discussed in the media, it is timely and worthwhile to examine the race-to-the-top/race-to-the-bottom debate in the context of crowdfunding.

In this paper we present three alternative hypotheses pertaining to regulation of equity crowdfunding. First, the race-to-the-bottom view posits that portals, entrepreneurs, and investors prefer jurisdictions which offer the least stringent regulation in order to maximize capital that entrepreneurs are able to raise. Second, the neutrality or uniformity view posits that portals, entrepreneurs, and investors are indifferent to the substantive crowdfunding laws. If so, regulators are likely to exhibit a preference for uniformity across jurisdictions or simply adopt models that replicate that of other jurisdictions in order to minimize the cost of law production. Third, the race-to-the-top view posits that portals, entrepreneurs, and investors want strict regulation and mechanisms that mitigate risk.

We test these three competing hypotheses by using crowdfunding survey data gathered by the National Crowdfunding Association of Canada (NCFA) in 2013 Q1. As detailed herein, the data were collected to ascertain whether, first, there were differences in the views about how to mitigate risk in crowdfunding across portals, investors (accredited and otherwise), and start-up entrepreneurs, and, second, the intended reasons for seeking crowdfunding participation. The data gathered were Canada-wide. The data show some tension towards a race to the bottom insofar as start-ups prefer fewer restrictions on their ability to crowdfund, and portals prefer fewer disclosure requirements and fewer restrictions on free trading of crowdfunded shares. However, this evidence is tempered by the fact that investors demand more disclosure, limits on amounts entrepreneurs can raise, and lower thresholds for audited financial statements, among other things. Based on the ease with which the Internet facilitates cross-jurisdictional investment, we infer from the data that investor demands will give rise to a race to the top in the crowdfunding space.[3]

This paper is organized as follows. Section 2 presents our main testable hypotheses in the context of prior research and the unique crowdfunding institutional setting. The data and summary statistics are presented in Section 3. Section 4 presents our multivariate empirical tests. The last section concludes, provides suggestions for further research, and discusses policy implications.

## 2. Institutional setting and hypotheses

Equity crowdfunding is the antithesis to traditional models in which entrepreneurs raise capital by preparing a formal prospectus. The costs of preparing a prospectus are large, and can reach tens or hundreds of thousands of dollars in terms of legal and accounting fees; for initial public offerings (IPOs) on stock exchanges, prospectus costs can be in the millions (Ritter 1987). Exemptions from the prospectus requirement are very stringent in most jurisdictions around the world. Exemptions in principle can include limits on the number of solicited investors, limits on the number of actual investors, and limits on the minimum wealth of the investors.

Without a prospectus, investors are arguably not as well-informed. Because the costs of preparing a prospectus may outweigh the benefits, and hence discourage or prevent entrepreneurs from raising external capital, many jurisdictions have permitted equity crowdfunding (such as Australia and select countries in Europe; see the Crowdfunding Industry Report 2012) and others are contemplating equity crowdfunding, including Canada and the USA. Under equity crowdfunding, an Internet portal is used to inform and solicit investment from a wide range of investors who typically do not fit within the traditional wealth levels that would enable a prospectus exemption. Moreover, the number of investors solicited is far beyond the maximum allowable for a prospectus exemption. Hence, some jurisdictions contemplating equity crowdfunding are doing so by introducing a new crowdfunding exemption.

This paper tests three alternative hypotheses pertaining to regulation of equity crowdfunding. The first view is that entrepreneurs, portals, and their investors prefer less stringent regulation. Securities regulators work to further public interest by supporting investor protection and facilitating market integrity. However, it is noted that securities regulations are not insurance policies against investor losses, and they are not designed to protect all investors from losing their money in all circumstances (Heminway and Hoffman 2011). Securities regulators may simply work to offer the regulators sought by lobbyists on behalf of entrepreneurs who seek greater flexibility in ways to raise capital, as suggested by Cary (1974) and Bebchuk (1992). Under this view, entrepreneurs do not want limits on the amount of capital that they can raise. Portals want minimum restrictions on the background and due diligence checks they are required to carry out.

Investors want to be able to invest in more projects and not face limits on their ability to invest for they may miss out on profitable opportunities.

*Hypothesis 1*:    Race to the bottom: portals, entrepreneurs, and investors prefer jurisdictions which offer the least stringent regulation

From a policy perspective, of course, we worry that such a view is short-lived. A major fraud or scandal would lead to a change in preferences, but not without a major cost or externality imposed on the public taxpayer. Therefore, to test for the presence of such a view, it is worthwhile to examine a jurisdiction in which equity crowdfunding has not yet happened.

The second hypothesis posits that entrepreneurs, portals, and investors have little preference one way or the other for the substantive law governing crowdfunding. If so, regulators drafting such laws can do so and meet stakeholder interests by minimizing the cost of legal production by replicating a legislative framework already in place in another jurisdiction. Evidence of the neutrality/uniformity view was found in empirical studies of the Canadian incorporation market by Cumming and MacIntosh (2000, 2002), for example. Corporate codes in different Canadian provinces are near perfect copies of one another, and resemble the federal incorporation code in Canada.

*Hypothesis 2*:    Neutrality or uniformity: there is little or no demand for substantive law, and hence the supply of law is likely to reflect a least-cost replication of regulations from other jurisdictions

The third hypothesis is that the market can figure out on its own what is the best model for governing itself. If regulations are inefficient, in terms of being either too onerous or not onerous enough, the entrepreneurs, portals, and investors will migrate to a different jurisdiction that better meets their needs. Similarly, there is evidence (Daines 2002; Romano 1985, 1987) that US corporate laws have evolved out of a competitive model of corporate law production in a way that has led to a race to the top.

*Hypothesis 3*:    Race to the top: portals, entrepreneurs, and investors want strict regulation and mechanisms that most effectively mitigate risk while still enabling capital raising

In support of the race-to-the-top view, there is evidence from other jurisdictions such as Australia that disclosure is something that investors pay close attention to in the crowdfunding context. For instance, Ahlers et al. (2012) find evidence that disclosure of firms' financial roadmaps (e.g., preplanned exit strategies such as IPOs or acquisitions), internal governance (such as board structure), and risk factors (such as amount of equity offered and the presence of disclaimers) affect fund-raising success. Firms that disclose financing plans and have sound boards of directors with professional curriculum vitae are more likely to raise more money and do it more quickly. Firms that seek to give too much equity end up doing much worse, consistent with theoretical models of selling equity stakes (Myers and Majluf 1984; see also Leland and Pyle 1977). By contrast, Ahlers et al. (2012) find evidence that external certification (awards, government grants, and patents) has much less relevance for fund-raising success, which can be explained by the fact that if firms had such certification from external bodies and it was valuable, then the firm would not have to resort to the crowdfunding market to raise external equity.

In further support of the race-to-the-top view, there is evidence from other sources of entrepreneurial finance that reputation matters a great deal to the eventual success of the venture (Nahata 2008; see also Nahata, Hazarika, and Tandon 2012;

Schwienbacher 2008). As such, we would expect portals that adhere to higher due diligence standards to attract more investors and, in turn, attract higher quality entrepreneurial ventures.

## 3. Data

Survey data were gathered by the NCFA in order to ascertain perceptions of crowdfunding and possible ways to mitigate risks. A copy of the survey is available from the NCFA and also available online.[4]

Surveys were completed online and distributed across Canada to potential investors (accredited and otherwise), investees (start-up entrepreneurs), portals, and service providers in 2013 Q1. A total of 144 surveys were completed.

The data are summarized in Table 1. The dependent variables used in our empirical models in Section 4 are first presented at the top of Table 1. The dependent variables included the following:

- What measures, if any, would be the most effective at reducing investor risks and the potential for fraud?
- Education for issuers and investors.
- Limits on the total amount raised by an issuer and on individual investment size.
- Ongoing continuous disclosure requirements.
- Prohibiting advertising or sales solicitation except by an authorized portal and issuer's website.
- Portals required to do background checks of each officer, director, and significant shareholders of issuers selling securities on its portal.
- Purchasers are provided with a rescission/redemption right within a certain number of days.

As indicated in Table 1, these six variables were measured on a ranking basis (1−5 scale, where 1 = strongly disagree, 2 = disagree, 3 = undecided, 4 = agree, and 5 = strongly agree). The highest ranked measure was Education, which received an average ranking of 3.931, and the lowest ranked variable was the prohibition on advertising, which received a ranking of 3.382.

In addition, the survey asked the question:

Should any crowdfunding exemption in Canada be approved on a trial or limited basis at first?

For this variable, a response of 'yes' was assigned the value 2, 'undecided' was assigned the value 1, and 'no' was assigned the value '0'. The average response was 1.375, and the median response was 2.

Similarly, the survey asked these two related questions:

- Should crowdfunding securities be free-trading securities after a period of time?
- And when should they be eligible for secondary market trading?

For the first part of the question, a response of 'yes' was assigned the value 2, 'undecided' was assigned the value 1, and 'no' was assigned the value '0'. The average response was 1.208, and the median response was 1. For the second part of the question, the average number of months was 21.792, the median was 24 months, the minimum was 12 months, and the maximum was 36 months.

Table 1. Variable definitions.

| Variable name | Definition | Mean | Median | SD | Minimum | Maximum |
|---|---|---|---|---|---|---|
| Dependent variables | | | | | | |
| q14education | 14. What measures, if any, would be the most effective at reducing investor risks and the potential for fraud? Education for issuers and investors | 3.931 | 4 | 0.882 | 1 | 5 |
| q14limits | 14. What measures, if any, would be the most effective at reducing investor risks and the potential for fraud? Limits on the total amount raised by an issuer and on individual investment size | 3.535 | 3 | 0.996 | 1 | 5 |
| q14disclosure | 14. What measures, if any, would be the most effective at reducing investor risks and the potential for fraud? Ongoing continuous disclosure requirements | 3.792 | 4 | 0.852 | 2 | 5 |
| q14advertise | 14. What measures, if any, would be the most effective at reducing investor risks and the potential for fraud? Prohibiting advertising or sales solicitation except by an authorized portal and issuer's website | 3.382 | 3 | 1.134 | 1 | 5 |
| q14portals | 14. What measures, if any, would be the most effective at reducing investor risks and the potential for fraud? Portals required to do background checks of each officer, director, and significant shareholders of issuers selling securities on its portal | 3.708 | 4 | 1.044 | 1 | 5 |
| q14redemption | 14. What measures, if any, would be the most effective at reducing investor risks and the potential for fraud? Purchasers are provided with a rescission/redemption right within a certain number of days | 3.625 | 4 | 0.938 | 1 | 5 |
| q11atrial | 11. (A) Should any crowdfunding exemption in Canada be approved on a trial or limited basis at first? (2 = yes, 1 = undecided, 0 = no) | 1.375 | 2 | 0.810 | 0 | 2 |
| q17freetrade | 17. (A) Should crowdfunding securities be free trading after a period of time? (2 = yes, 1 = undecided, 0 = no) | 1.208 | 1 | 0.827 | 0 | 2 |
| q17freetradetime | 17. (B) When should they be eligible for secondary market trading? | 21.792 | 24 | 7.015 | 12 | 36 |

Table 1 – *continued*

| Variable name | Definition | Mean | Median | SD | Minimum | Maximum |
|---|---|---|---|---|---|---|
| q12b | 12. (B) What is the maximum amount of capital an investor should be able to invest in any 12-month period? | $12,729 | $1250 | $6601 | $1000 | $20,000 |
| q15limit | 15. What is the aggregate amount of capital that an issuer should be able to raise in any 12-month period? | $2,607,639 | $1,750,000 | $1,732,972 | $250,000 | $5,000,000 |
| q16bthresholdaudited | 19. (B) Please select an appropriate capital threshold where audited financial statements should be required? | $1,226,389 | $1,000,000 | $685,411 | $100,000 | $5,000,000 |
| *Explanatory variables* | | | | | | |
| q99financial | 9. What do you believe would motivate an investor to make an investment through crowdfunding? Financial incentives | 3.813 | 4 | 0.869 | 1 | 5 |
| q99nonfinancial | 9. What do you believe would motivate an investor to make an investment through crowdfunding? Non-financial incentives | 3.611 | 4 | 0.862 | 1 | 5 |
| q99diversify | 9. What do you believe would motivate an investor to make an investment through crowdfunding? Diversification of portfolio | 3.583 | 4 | 0.873 | 1 | 5 |
| q99direct | 9. What do you believe would motivate an investor to make an investment through crowdfunding? Gain a direct channel to entrepreneurs and owners and in a transparent way | 3.938 | 4 | 0.813 | 2 | 5 |
| q99network | 9. What do you believe would motivate an investor to make an investment through crowdfunding? Networking opportunities within the start-up and the SME community | 3.771 | 4 | 0.867 | 2 | 5 |
| q99support | 9. What do you believe would motivate an investor to make an investment through crowdfunding? Support entrepreneurism and the development of innovative products/services | 4.167 | 4 | 0.845 | 2 | 5 |
| q5familiar | 5. Are you familiar with the term crowdfunding? | 3.021 | 3 | 1.387 | 1 | 5 |
| startup | 4. Please select a stakeholder category that best represents your survey responses: start-up | 0.340 | 0 | 0.475 | 0 | 1 |
| sme | 4. Please select a stakeholder category that best represents your survey responses: SME | 0.410 | 0 | 0.493 | 0 | 1 |
| serviceprovider | 4. Please select a stakeholder category that best represents your survey responses: potential service provider | 0.264 | 0 | 0.442 | 0 | 1 |
| portal | 4. Please select a stakeholder category that best represents your survey responses: potential portal | 0.174 | 0 | 0.380 | 0 | 1 |

*(Continued on next page)*

Table 1 – *continued*

| Variable name | Definition | Mean | Median | SD | Minimum | Maximum |
|---|---|---|---|---|---|---|
| nonaccreditedinvestor | 4. Please select a stakeholder category that best represents your survey responses: non-accredited investor | 0.382 | 0 | 0.488 | 0 | 1 |
| accreditedindividual | 4. Please select a stakeholder category that best represents your survey responses: accredited investor | 0.139 | 0 | 0.347 | 0 | 1 |
| accreditedinstitutional | 4. Please select a stakeholder category that best represents your survey responses: accredited institutional investor | 0.007 | 0 | 0.083 | 0 | 1 |
| investmentdealer | 4. Please select a stakeholder category that best represents your survey responses: investment dealer | 0.014 | 0 | 0.117 | 0 | 1 |
| portfoliomanager | 4. Please select a stakeholder category that best represents your survey responses: portfolio manager | 0.028 | 0 | 0.165 | 0 | 1 |
| exemptmarketdealer | 4. Please select a stakeholder category that best represents your survey responses: exempt market dealer | 0.042 | 0 | 0.201 | 0 | 1 |
| alberta | Please | 0.111 | 0 | 0.315 | 0 | 1 |
| ontario | Please | 0.472 | 0 | 0.501 | 0 | 1 |
| bc | Please | 0.181 | 0 | 0.386 | 0 | 1 |
| quebec | Please | 0.076 | 0 | 0.267 | 0 | 1 |

Note: This table presents definitions and summary statistics for the main variables in the dataset. Unless otherwise indicated, ranking variables range on a 1–5 scale, where 1 = strongly disagree, 2 = disagree, 3 = undecided, 4 = agree, and 5 = strongly agree. Variable names, such as 'q14 . . .' for example, refer to the question numbers used from the NCFA survey.

The following three questions are examined as dependent variables:

- What is the maximum amount of capital an investor should be able to invest in any 12-month period?
- What is the aggregate amount of capital that an issuer should be able to raise in any 12-month period?
- What is the appropriate capital threshold where audited financial statements should be required?

For the maximum amount of capital investors should be allowed to invest in a 12-month period, the average reply was $12,729, where the median was $1250, and the range was $1000–$20,000. For the aggregate amount of capital an issuer should be allowed to raise in a 12-month period, the average was $2.608 million, while the average was $1.750 million, and the range was $250,000–$5 million. For the capital-raising threshold for which audited financial statements should be required, the average reply was $1.226 million, and the median was $1 million.

In our analyses below, we make use of the following explanatory variables that are summarized in Table 1. First, we consider this question:

- What do you believe would motivate an investor to make an investment through crowdfunding?
- Financial Incentives
- Non-Financial Incentives
- Diversification of Portfolio
- Gain a direct channel to entrepreneurs and owners and in a transparent way
- Networking opportunities within the start-up and the small and medium-sized enterprise (SME) community
- Support entrepreneurism and the development of innovative products/services

This question is a ranking question with the same ranking scale as the other variables (1–5 scale, where 1 = strongly disagree, 2 = disagree, 3 = undecided, 4 = agree, and 5 = strongly agree). Table 1 indicates that the highest ranked variable was 'support entrepreneurialism' which received an average ranking of 4.167, and the lowest ranking was 'diversification of the portfolio' which received an average ranking of 3.583.

Second, we use this question to address the respondent's belief of their expertise with crowdfunding:

- Are you familiar with the term crowdfunding?

We note that the survey was prefaced with an explanation of the term crowdfunding so that respondents would be aware of what they were being asked about. The average ranking for this variable was 3.021 out of 5, and the median ranking was 3, and the full range of 1–5 is observed in the data. As such, we believe the respondents do not represent an overly biased set of people who are crowdfunding experts, but rather they provide an appropriate mix of different levels of experience and understanding of the term crowdfunding.

Finally, we make use of survey data that asked the respondents to select a stakeholder category that best represents themselves as one of the following and to select the region in which they are primarily located:

- potential portal
- non-accredited investor

- accredited investor
- accredited institutional investor
- investment dealer
- portfolio manager
- exempt market dealer
- Please select a province/territory – Alberta, Ontario, British Columbia, Quebec, etc.

Based on the data included in Table 1, we are able to show that 34% of the respondents were start-ups, 41% were SMEs, 26.4% were potential service providers, 17.4% were potential portals, 38.2% were non-accredited investors, 13.9% were accredited investors, 0.7% were accredited institutional investors, 1.4% were investment dealers, and 2.8% were portfolio managers. We note that it is possible for overlap across these categories, as respondents may be both SMEs and non-accredited investors, for example. The potential overlap has no significant implication on our data analyses and interpretations.

Most respondents were from the provinces of Ontario (68), followed by British Columbia (26), Alberta (16), and Quebec (11). There were 23 respondents from the rest of Canada. As the population of Ontario, British Columbia, Alberta, Quebec, and the rest of Canada is 13.5 million, 4.4 million, 3.6 million, 8.1 million, and 4.9 million, respectively, the surveys are equally representative of the population in the different regions with the sole exception of Quebec which is underrepresented in our sample. The likely explanation for this lower response rate in Quebec is the language and political/cultural differences between Quebec and the rest of Canada. Nevertheless, our empirical findings in the regressions are robust to the inclusion/exclusion of Quebec. These regressions are discussed below in the next section.

## 4. Multivariate regressions

The next section discusses the empirical findings pertinent to the multivariate tests of H1, H2, and H3 as summarized in Section 2. Our first set of regressions is presented in Table 2. In Table 2 we examine ordered logit models of the ranking of the importance of different risk reduction measures for Education (Model 1), Limits on Amounts Raised (Model 2), Continuous Disclosure (Model 3), Advertising (Model 4), Portal Due Diligence (Model 5), and Redemption Rights (Model 6). These six different ranking variables are explained as a function of the following variables:

- Perceived reasons for crowdfunders' investment: Financial, Non-Financial, Diversification, Networking, Support Entrepreneurialism
- Characteristics of the survey respondent: Familiarity with crowdfunding, Start-up, SME, Service Provider, Portal, Non-Accredited Investor, Accredited Individual Investor, Accredited Institutional Investor, Investment Dealer, Portfolio Manager, Exempt Market Dealer
- Province: Alberta, British Columbia, Ontario, Quebec, other provinces.

The regressions in Table 2 show that risk reduction is closely related to the perceived reasons for the crowdfunders' reasons for investment. First, note that Financial Reasons for Investment are significantly related to Education as a risk reduction measure at the 10% level of significance, Investment Limits at the 1% level, Continuous Disclosure at the 1% level, and Redemption at the 10% level. In terms of the economic significance, a 1-point increase in the ranking for Financial Reasons for Investment is associated with

Table 2. Regression analyses of risk reduction measures.

| | Model 1: q14education | | Model 2: q14limits | | Model 3: q14disclosure | | Model 4: q14advertise | | Model 5: q14portals | | Model 6: q14redemption | |
|---|---|---|---|---|---|---|---|---|---|---|---|---|
| | Coefficient | t-statistic | Coefficient | t-statistic | Coefficient | t-statistic | Coefficient | t-statistic | Coefficient | t-statistic | Coefficient | t-statistic |
| Perceived reasons for crowdfunders' investment | | | | | | | | | | | | |
| q99financial | 0.397 | 1.67* | 0.618 | 2.63*** | 0.840 | 3.19*** | 0.230 | 0.98 | 0.086 | 0.37 | 0.447 | 1.80* |
| q99nonfinancial | 0.271 | 1.10 | −0.701 | −2.84*** | −0.448 | −1.75* | 0.021 | 0.09 | −0.151 | −0.59 | 0.182 | 0.72 |
| q99diversify | 0.150 | 0.60 | −0.032 | −0.13 | −0.218 | −0.89 | 0.099 | 0.41 | 0.632 | 2.43** | 0.157 | 0.64 |
| q99direct | 0.182 | 0.58 | −0.140 | −0.44 | 0.331 | 1.03 | −0.533 | −1.71* | 0.416 | 1.34 | 0.486 | 1.58 |
| q99network | 0.553 | 1.86* | −0.068 | −0.23 | 0.039 | 0.14 | 0.387 | 1.39 | −0.619 | −2.16** | −0.097 | −0.36 |
| q99support | 0.389 | 1.24 | 0.579 | 1.82* | 0.763 | 2.39** | 0.582 | 1.91* | 0.645 | 2.12** | 0.052 | 0.16 |
| Characteristics of survey respondent | | | | | | | | | | | | |
| q5familiar | 0.193 | 1.16 | 0.170 | 1.07 | 0.117 | 0.70 | −0.163 | −1.04 | 0.084 | 0.53 | 0.047 | 0.29 |
| startup | 0.090 | 0.17 | −0.925 | −1.83* | 0.024 | 0.05 | 0.780 | 1.62 | 0.052 | 0.11 | 0.301 | 0.6 |
| sme | 0.068 | 0.14 | −0.639 | −1.38 | −0.109 | −0.22 | 0.972 | 2.09** | 0.670 | 1.43 | 0.662 | 1.31 |
| serviceprovider | −0.407 | −0.84 | 0.098 | 0.22 | −0.453 | −1.00 | 0.294 | 0.66 | −0.160 | −0.36 | 0.405 | 0.84 |
| portal | 0.426 | 0.87 | −0.176 | −0.37 | −0.812 | −1.65* | −0.226 | −0.48 | −0.216 | −0.47 | 0.675 | 1.47 |
| nonaccreditedinvestor | −0.005 | −0.01 | 0.483 | 1.22 | 0.962 | 2.37** | −0.621 | −1.64 | −0.282 | −0.73 | 0.304 | 0.75 |
| accreditedindividual | 0.382 | 0.59 | 0.988 | 1.49 | 1.838 | 2.74*** | −0.047 | −0.07 | −0.115 | −0.18 | 0.145 | 0.22 |
| accreditedinstitutional | 34.306 | 0.00 | 0.438 | 0.19 | −0.893 | −0.36 | 0.655 | 0.3 | −3.638 | −1.64 | 2.246 | 0.99 |
| investmentdealer | 0.015 | 0.01 | −1.963 | −1.23 | −0.555 | −0.36 | −0.817 | −0.44 | −1.062 | −0.42 | 0.235 | 0.18 |
| portfoliomanager | 1.201 | 0.86 | −0.100 | −0.08 | 2.763 | 1.86* | −0.079 | −0.07 | 0.828 | 0.68 | −2.550 | −2.10** |
| exemptmarketdealer | 1.066 | 0.97 | 0.071 | 0.08 | −1.156 | −1.22 | −1.614 | −1.69* | 1.229 | 1.29 | 0.730 | 0.72 |
| Alberta | 0.181 | 0.26 | 0.351 | 0.53 | −1.009 | −1.39 | −0.839 | −1.36 | −0.263 | −0.42 | 1.479 | 2.25** |
| Ontario | −0.261 | −0.53 | −0.512 | −1.11 | −0.178 | −0.37 | 0.064 | 0.15 | 0.156 | 0.35 | −0.034 | −0.07 |
| British Columbia | −0.478 | −0.82 | −0.924 | −1.70* | −1.540 | −2.56** | −1.085 | −1.95* | −0.627 | −1.12 | −0.675 | −1.16 |
| Quebec | 0.662 | 0.80 | 0.450 | 0.57 | 1.184 | 1.57 | −0.278 | −0.37 | 0.572 | 0.76 | −0.126 | −0.15 |
| Pseudo R² | 0.186 | | 0.071 | | 0.182 | | 0.082 | | 0.088 | | 0.120 | |

Note: This table presents ordered logit estimates of the determinants of perceived benefits for risk reduction to investors. Ordered logit cut-off parameters are not presented for conciseness. Variables are as defined in Table 1.
* Significant at the 10% level of significance; ** significant at the 5% level of significance; *** significant at the 1% level of significance.

an 8.1% increase in the probability of a top rank for Education, a 9.1% increase in probability of the top rank for Investment Limits, an 11.3% increase in the probability of a top rank for Continuous Disclosure, and a 1.5% increase in the probability of a top rank for Redemption.[5] By contrast, Non-Financial Reasons for Investment is negatively associated with higher ranks for Limits on Investment Limits and Continuous Disclosure, and these effects are significant at the 1% and 10% levels, respectively. In terms of the economic significance, a 1-point increase in Non-Financial Reasons is associated with a 10.3% reduction in the probability of a top rank for Investment Limits, and a 6.0% reduction in the probability of a top rank for Continuous Disclosure. Taken together, these findings pertinent to financial versus non-financial reasons for investment show that the would-be market participants in Canada are sensitive to the needs for protecting investor interests to a greater degree, where such investors are investing for profit, which supports the race-to-the-top hypothesis (H3).

The regressions indicate that Diversification Reasons for Investment are statistically associated with higher rankings for Portal Due Diligence, and this effect is significant at the 5% level in Model 5. The economic significance is such that a 1-point increase in Diversification is associated with an 11.0% increase in the probability of a top ranking for Portal Due Diligence. Again, this result is intuitive since diversified investors are spread over a large number of investments, by definition, and time constraints require that due diligence be outsourced to a greater degree. In this case, by requiring portals to undertake a higher responsibility for due diligence, investors are better able to diversify their investments across a greater number of crowdfunded projects. As such, this result provides further support for the race-to-the-top hypothesis (H3).

Direct Access Reasons for Investment is statistically negatively associated with Advertising Restrictions, and this effect is significant at the 10% level in Model 4. The economic significance is such that a 1-point increase in Direct Access gives rise to a 6.7% reduction in the probability of a top rank for Advertising Restrictions. This finding further supports the race-to-the-top view (H3) since advertising facilitates the flow of information from entrepreneurs to would-be investors, thereby enabling investors to connect with entrepreneurs.

Networking Reasons for Investment is positively associated with Education, and negatively associated with Portal Due Diligence, and these effects are significant at the 10% and 5% levels, respectively. The economic significance is such that a 1-point increase in Networking is associated with an 11.3% increase in the probability of a top rank for Education and a 10.8% reduction in the probability of a top rank for Portal Due Diligence. These findings are intuitive and consistent with the race-to-the-top view since networking is facilitated by educational forums, and investors who network are ones that seek their own information and are thereby able to better and more efficiently carry out their own due diligence.

Support Entrepreneurialism Reasons for Investment is positively associated with Limits on Investment, Continuous Disclosure, Advertising, and Portal Due Diligence, and these effects are significant at the 10%, 5%, 10%, and 5% levels, respectively. The economic significance is such that a 1-point increase in Support Entrepreneurialism gives rise to an 8.5% increase in the probability of a top rank for Limits on Investment, a 10.2% increase in the probability of a top rank for Continuous Disclosure, a 7.3% increase in the probability of a top rank for Advertising, and a 11.3% increase in the probability of a top rank for Portal Due Diligence. Since investors who want to support entrepreneurialism generally may be prone to over-investment without adequate information, be heavily influenced by advertising, and not carry out effective and proper due diligence on their own, these findings support the race-to-the-top view (H3).

Overall, the data on reasons for investment are very consistent with effective risk-mitigation strategies tailored to those reasons for investment. In other words, the data indicate that the market would work rather efficiently if different jurisdictions attracted different types of investors and different entrepreneurs and portals. All of the findings can be interpreted as consistent with the race-to-the-top view (H3).

Our second set of results in Table 2 pertains to the characteristics of the market participants. On one hand, four findings pertinent to market participant characteristics are consistent with the race-to-the-top view (H3). First, SMEs are 13.0% more likely to have top rank for Advertising Restrictions, and this effect is significant at the 5% level. Second, non-accredited investors are 14.0% more likely to have top rank for Continuous Disclosure, and this effect is significant at the 5% level. Third, accredited individual investors are 35.2% more likely to have top rank for Continuous Disclosure, and this effect is significant at the 1% level. Fourth, portfolio managers are 58.6% more likely to have top rank for Continuous Disclosure, and this effect is significant at the 10% level.

On the other hand, four findings are consistent with the race-to-the-bottom view (H1). First, the data indicate that start-ups are $-12.4\%$ less likely to have top rank for Limits on Capital Raising, and this effect is significant at the 10% level of significance. Second, portals are 9.1% less likely to have top rank for Continuous Disclosure, and this effect is marginally significant at the 10% level. Third, portfolio managers are 17.3% less likely to have top rank for redemption, and this effect is significant at the 5% level. Fourth, exempt market dealers are 12.0% less likely to have top rank for Advertising Restrictions, and this effect is significant at the 10% level. These four findings could be viewed as market participants behaving in their own self-interest in a way that is detrimental to investor's interest, consistent with H1. But taken in conjunction with the other findings pertinent to investor characteristics and interests discussed above, it is unlikely that markets that mainly serve the interests of start-ups and portals are likely to attract significant retail investor presence, and as such the supply of capital would be significantly reduced in such markets that narrowly served the interests of select market participants.

Our third set of results in Table 2 pertains to regional differences. The data indicate some differences across provinces. Respondents from Alberta show they are 4.3% more likely to have top rank for Redemption, while respondents from British Columbia are 11.2% less likely to have top rank for Limits on Capital Raising, 15.0% less likely to have top rank for Continuous Disclosure, and 10.7% less likely to have top rank for Advertising. These differences are suggestive that there is not a preference for uniformity across provinces, counter to H2. Based on the other evidence above, there is no apparent reason to not let the provinces compete in a way that is consistent with the market for corporate charters in the USA (Romano 1985, 1993).

The second set of regressions is presented in Table 3. Table 3 shows two ordered logit models in Models 7 and 8 for Offering Crowdfunding on a Trial Basis (Model 7) and Freely Traded Shares (Model 8). Table 3 also presents ordinary least squares (OLS) models of when shares should be freely trading (Model 9), the maximum amount of capital allowed to invest (Model 10), the maximum amount of capital allowed to raise (Model 11), and the capital-raising threshold for which audited financial statements should be required (Model 12). Consistent with the regressions in Table 2, these variables are regressed on the following explanatory variables:

- Perceived reasons for crowdfunders' investment: Financial, Non-Financial, Diversification, Networking, Support Entrepreneurialism

Table 3. Regression analyses of trial periods, freely tradable shares, and limits on investing, capital raising, and audited financials.

| | Model 7: q11atrial | | Model 8: q17freetrade | | Model 9: q17freetradetime | | Model 10: q12b | | Model 11: q15limit | | Model 12: q16thresholdaudited | |
|---|---|---|---|---|---|---|---|---|---|---|---|---|
| | Coefficient | t-statistic | Coefficient | t-statistic | Coefficient | t-statistic | Coefficient | t-statistic | Coefficient | t-statistic | Coefficient | t-statistic |
| Perceived reasons for crowdfunders' investment | | | | | | | | | | | | |
| q99financial | -0.336 | -1.07 | -0.341 | -1.30 | -0.935 | -1.18 | 749.43 | 1.08 | 66658.64 | 0.35 | 13017.24 | 0.17 |
| q99nonfinancial | -0.425 | -1.25 | -0.023 | -0.09 | 0.948 | 1.13 | -468.38 | -0.64 | 92659.79 | 0.46 | -74454.07 | -0.89 |
| q99diversify | -0.333 | -1.01 | 0.255 | 0.95 | -1.979 | -2.36** | 1645.94 | 2.25** | -40641.75 | -0.20 | -55650.72 | -0.67 |
| q99direct | 1.221 | 3.00*** | 0.785 | 2.31** | -0.897 | -0.84 | 1535.50 | 1.65* | 527293.80 | 2.05** | -190267.70 | -1.80* |
| q99network | 0.028 | 0.08 | 0.002 | 0.01 | -0.362 | -0.38 | -1248.04 | -1.50 | 150521.40 | 0.66 | -31698.40 | -0.34 |
| q99support | 0.520 | 1.40 | -0.202 | -0.59 | 0.954 | 0.90 | 2852.59 | 3.07*** | 272700.30 | 1.06 | 220510.70 | 2.09** |
| Characteristics of survey respondent | | | | | | | | | | | | |
| q5familiar | 0.001 | 0.00 | 0.189 | 1.11 | -0.448 | -0.79 | -466.75 | -0.94 | -50943.95 | -0.37 | -75938.07 | -1.35 |
| startup | -1.017 | -1.81* | 0.156 | 0.30 | 0.105 | 0.06 | -1470.11 | -0.98 | -25662.46 | -0.06 | -7665.40 | -0.04 |
| sme | -0.415 | -0.81 | 0.495 | 1.01 | 0.385 | 0.23 | -1461.72 | -0.98 | 413606.40 | 1.00 | -260118.00 | -1.53 |
| serviceprovider | -0.187 | -0.37 | 0.534 | 1.12 | 1.685 | 1.05 | 1758.51 | 1.26 | -481479.10 | -1.24 | 151703.00 | 0.95 |
| portal | -0.259 | -0.47 | 1.337 | 2.37** | -1.552 | -0.95 | 2094.09 | 1.46 | -241496.60 | -0.61 | 19459.75 | 0.12 |
| nonaccreditedinvestor | 0.814 | 1.78* | -0.003 | -0.01 | -0.416 | -0.31 | 314.55 | 0.26 | 560317.50 | 1.70* | -339324.90 | -2.50** |
| accreditedindividual | 1.251 | 1.58 | -1.307 | -1.93* | -0.723 | -0.32 | 741.54 | 0.38 | -156153.50 | -0.29 | -279290.00 | -1.25 |
| accreditedinstitutional | 35.405 | 0.00 | 31.013 | 0.00 | -12.516 | -1.44 | 1801.74 | 0.24 | 425415.80 | 0.20 | -1477569.00 | -1.70 |
| investmentdealer | 33.388 | 0.00 | -0.480 | -0.31 | 5.688 | 1.11 | 2575.43 | 0.57 | 2539446.00 | 2.04** | -752687.40 | -1.47 |
| portfoliomanager | -0.915 | -0.74 | -1.239 | -1.02 | -0.521 | -0.12 | -1634.18 | -0.44 | 1832786.00 | 1.79* | 858917.00 | 2.04** |
| exemptmarketdealer | -1.672 | -1.51 | -0.121 | -0.12 | 0.207 | 0.06 | -320.66 | -0.11 | 1514151.00 | 1.90* | -85318.66 | -0.26 |
| Alberta | -0.106 | -0.14 | 1.021 | 1.34 | 0.649 | 0.28 | 494.32 | 0.25 | -794031.70 | -1.43 | -328314.20 | -1.43 |
| Ontario | -0.693 | -1.33 | -0.353 | -0.74 | 4.076 | 2.44** | -561.45 | -0.38 | -483354.90 | -1.20 | -243407.20 | -1.46 |
| British Columbia | -0.635 | -0.99 | 0.379 | 0.65 | 3.391 | 1.69* | -16.74 | -0.01 | -592746.90 | -1.22 | -20341.25 | -0.10 |
| Quebec | 0.855 | 0.89 | -0.009 | -0.01 | -0.506 | -0.20 | 2682.19 | 1.18 | -775120.70 | -1.24 | -103707.70 | -0.40 |
| Constant | | | | | 28.635 | 6.86 | -6083.12 | -1.66* | -1315221.00 | -1.30 | 2221942.00 | 5.34*** |
| Pseudo R² (Models 7–10), adjusted R² (Models 10–12) | 0.151 | | 0.1205 | | 0.1152 | | 0.21 | | 0.12 | | 0.05 | |

Note: This table presents ordered logit estimates of the determinants of perceived benefits for a trial period for crowdfunding (Model 7), whether crowdfunded shares should be freely tradable (Model 8), and OLS estimates of free tradable after a limited period of time in terms of the number of months (Model 9). Ordered logit cut-off parameters are not presented for conciseness. Model 10 presents OLS estimates of the determinants of the aggregated amount of capital an investor should be able to invest during a 12-month period. Model 11 presents OLS estimates of the determinants of the aggregate amount of capital an issuer should be able to raise during a 12-month period. Model 12 presents OLS estimates of the determinants of capital threshold limits for audited financial statements. Variables are as defined in Table 1.
* Significant at the 10% level of significance; ** significant at the 5% and level of significance; *** significant at the 1% level of significance.

- Characteristics of the survey respondent: Familiarity with crowdfunding, Start-up, SME, Service Provider, Portal, Non-Accredited Investor, Accredited Individual Investor, Accredited Institutional Investor, Investment Dealer, Portfolio Manager, Exempt Market Dealer
- Province: Alberta, British Columbia, Ontario, Quebec, other provinces.

Models 9 and 10 in Table 3 indicate that a 1-point increase in Diversification Reasons for Investment is associated with two fewer months until shares should be freely tradable and $1646 extra capital-raising restrictions in a 12-month period, and these effects are both significant at the 5% level of significance. These findings are consistent with H3 insofar as diversification is facilitated by less onerous resale restrictions and less idiosyncratic risk associated with a single issuer.

Table 3 further shows that Direct Access Reasons for Investment is associated with a 20.0% increase in the probability of freely tradable shares (Model 8, significant at the 5% level), $1536 extra capital allowed for investment in 12-month period (Model 10, significant at the 10% level), $527,294 extra amount raised in a 12-month period (Model 11, significant at the 5% level), and a $190,268 lower threshold for audited financial statements (Model 12, significant at the 10% level). To the extent that investors who seek direct access are more sophisticated investors akin to angel investors who seek to add value to their investees, these findings can be interpreted as consistent with the race-to-the-top H3 view. Also, investors who seek direct access are likewise associated with a 21.5% increase in the probability of a Trial Period for Crowdfunding (Model 7, significant at the 1% level), which further supports H3.

Models 10 and 12 in Table 3 indicate that a 1-point increase in Support Entrepreneurialism Reasons for Investment is associated with $2853 extra capital invested in a 12-month period (significant at the 1% level) and a $220,511 higher threshold for audited financial statements (significant at the 5% level). As indicated in conjunction with the findings in Table 2, Support Entrepreneurialism as a reason for investment has the potential to become prone to over-investment without adequate due diligence, and hence the first finding pertaining to extra capital invested is consistent with the race-to-the-bottom view (H1), while the second findings is consistent with the race-to-the-top view (H3).

A number of the investor characteristic variables are significant in Table 3. Start-ups are 19.4% less likely to be interested in a trial period for crowdfunding (significant at the 10% level), portals are 30.0% more likely to be interested in freely tradable shares (significant at the 5% level), and portfolio managers seek $1,832,786 more capital raised and $858,917 higher threshold for audited financial statements. Each of these findings may be interpreted as consistent with the race to the bottom, since they serve their own interests potentially at investors' expense. However, non-accredited investors are 13.6% more likely to be interested in a trial period for crowdfunding (significant at the 10% level), while accredited individual investors are 30.1% less likely to seek freely tradable shares (significant at the 10% level), suggesting that investors' interest temper the ability of other market participants to act in ways that serve only their own self-interests. Moreover, non-accredited investors prefer on average $560,318 higher thresholds for amounts of capital that can be raised (significant at the 10% level), which is consistent with the preference of portfolio managers. Further, non-accredited investors prefer on average a $339,325 lower threshold for audited financial statements (significant at the 5% level). Consistent with the evidence in Table 2, the data suggest that investor capital will flow to markets with regulations that are not self-serving to entrepreneurs and portals.

Finally, as in Table 2, there is some (albeit not much) evidence of regional differences across Canada. Respondents from Alberta preferred on average 4.1 months longer until shares should be freely tradable (significant at the 5% level), while respondents in British Columbia on average preferred 3.4 months longer until shares should be freely tradable (significant at the 10% level). There were no other evident differences across the regions.

The main findings from the regression evidence are summarized in Table 4. Overall, there is more support for H3 (race to the top) than H1 (race to the bottom). Also, there is some evidence that is inconsistent with uniformity. The data are consistent with the view that investor demands will give rise to a race to the top in crowdfunding markets.

## 5. Conclusions

This paper presented evidence on crowdfunding from a Canadian nationwide survey of potential investors, portals, entrepreneurs, service providers, and other market participants in 2013 Q1, prior to any legalized equity crowdfunding in Canada. The data provide insights into the ways in which market participants would allocate capital and jurisdiction shop in the event of any regional differences in the ways in which crowdfunding markets are regulated.

Some of the evidence is consistent with the race-to-the-bottom view insofar as start-ups want fewer limits on the amount of capital they are able to raise each year, and portals want less onerous continuous disclosure requirements and freely tradable shares without time restrictions. However, investors seek more heavily regulated markets, particularly where there are financial reasons for investment and for investors whose incentives are to support the entrepreneurial community. Such investors seek greater limits on the amount entrepreneurs can raise, and lower thresholds for audited financial statements, more education, greater portal due diligence, and other protections to mitigate risks. In effect, as both sides of the market must come together, the data are, on balance, consistent with the view that capital will flow to better regulated markets that appropriately protect investors and enable entrepreneurs to operate in an environment which facilitates capital raising.

We noted that there were some apparent regional differences in the data, and in conjunction with the other evidence on the race to the top, no apparent reason to not let the provinces compete in terms of offering the best set of regulations and attract both entrepreneurs and investors. Along these lines, in 2013 Q1, the Province of Ontario in Canada was contemplating the introduction of crowdfunding rules. As a first step, this legislative review began with an exhaustive review of current and proposed crowdfunding models around the world by senior staff members at the Ontario Securities Commission. A review document was prepared, and comments were solicited from a wide array of stakeholders in industry. This type of proactive securities regulatory strategy is consistent with the view that regulators are doing their best to serve the interests of all market participants, and pushing forward the regulatory landscape to make the Province of Ontario a leading jurisdiction. The data herein are consistent with the view that more successful jurisdictions will attract more investors who feel safe, and hence attract entrepreneurs who can more efficiently and effectively raise capital, thereby facilitating a race to the top. But further research from other jurisdictions that are contemplating the introduction of crowdfunding legislation is warranted. As the Canadian survey evidence herein shows, one does not need to have crowdfunding put in place in order to empirically study the potential outcomes from

Table 4. Summary of main findings pertinent to the race-to-the-bottom, neutrality, and race-to-the-top hypotheses.

| | H1: Race to the bottom | H2: Uniformity | H3: Race to the top |
|---|---|---|---|
| Model 1: q14education | | | Yes – financial and network reasons for investment |
| Model 2: q14limits | Yes – start-ups | No – British Columbia | Yes – financial, non-financial and support entrepreneurialism reasons for investment |
| Model 3: q14disclosure | Yes – portals | No – British Columbia | Yes – financial, non-financial and support entrepreneurialism reasons for investment, as well as non-accredited investors and portfolio managers |
| Model 4: q14advertise | Yes – exempt market dealers | | Yes – direct access and support entrepreneurialism reasons for investment, as well as SMEs |
| Model 5: q14portals | | | Yes – diversify, networking, and support entrepreneurialism reasons for investment |
| Model 6: q14redemption | Yes – portfolio managers | No – Alberta | Yes – financial reasons for investment |
| Model 7: q11atrial | Yes – start-ups | | Yes – direct access reasons for investment, as well as non-accredited investors |
| Model 8: q17freetrade | Yes – portals | | Yes – direct access reasons for investment |
| Model 9: q17freetradetime | | | Yes – diversification reasons for investment |
| Model 10: q12b | Yes – support entrepreneurialism reasons for investment | No – Ontario, British Columbia | Yes - diversification and direct access reasons for investment |
| Model 11: q15limit | Yes – portfolio managers | | Yes – direct access reasons for investment, as well as non-accredited investors |
| Model 12: q16thresholdaudited | Yes – support entrepreneurialism reasons for investment as well as portfolio managers | | Yes – direct access reasons for investment, as well as non-accredited investors |

Note: This table summarizes the main findings from the regression evidence in Tables 2 and 3. Variables are as defined in Table 1.

crowdfunding. Likewise, further research as the fascinating crowdfunding regulatory landscape changes over time and across jurisdictions could provide much insight into securities regulation more generally.

## Acknowledgements

We owe a special thanks to Richard Harrison for very helpful and timely comments on this paper. Also, we are indebted to the National Crowdfunding Association of Canada, in particular Craig Asano and Sunny Shao, for sharing data and providing helpful comments and suggestions. The Social Sciences and Humanities Research Council of Canada provided financial support. We thank Jo-Anne Mataer, Elizabeth Topp, and James Turner from the Ontario Securities Commission, and Brian Koscak from the Exempt Market Dealers Association for helpful comments and suggestions. Also, we thank the seminar participants at Kobe University, Old Dominion University, the Ontario Securities Commission, and York University. A version of this paper was presented at the Canadian Law and Economics Association Meeting September 2013 and the 13th FRAP – Finance, Risk and Accounting Perspectives Conference, University of Cambridge, November 2013.

## Notes

1. www.kickstarter.com/projects/597507018/pebble-e-paper-watch-for-iphone-and-android
2. http://dailycrowdsource.com/20-resources/projects/169-pulitzer-crowdfunded-the-statue-of-liberty
3. This inference is consistent with recent commentary from the Angel Capital Association in the USA regarding certain provisions in the JOBS Act. See http://venturebeat.com/2013/07/28/why-angels-are-making-a-big-deal-about-the-secs-new-rules-on-advertising-investment-opportunities/
4. http://www.ncfacanada.org/. The survey was designed and created by Craig Asano and Brian Koscak of the Exempt Markets Dealers Association. The authors of this paper were unaware of the survey at the time it was created, and did not influence the questions asked and to whom it was distributed. Likewise, Craig Asano and Brian Koscak did not direct or influence the experimental design or results from this paper, but did offer constructive comments for the purpose of providing helpful feedback on the paper. The findings herein are in no way driven by industry interests for pushing crowdfunding and the like, but instead are completely independent and impartial.
5. Marginal effects are presented for the top rankings only to highlight the size of the effects. Technically, we could present the marginal effects for each of the five rankings, but those added details do not provide much additional insight and such details would detract from the overall insights (in other words, five times the number of marginal effects would give rise to not seeing the forest through the trees, so to speak).

## References

Agrawal, A., C. Catalini, and A. Goldfarb. 2011. "The Geography of Crowdfunding." Available at SSRN: http://ssrn.com/abstract=1692661
Ahlers, G. K. C., D. J. Cumming, C. Guenther, and D. Schweitzer. 2012. "Signaling in Equity Crowdfunding." Available at SSRN: http://ssrn.com/abstract=2161587
Bebchuk, L. A. 1992. "Federalism and the Corporation: The Desirable Limits on State Competition in Corporate Law." *Harvard Law Review* 105: 1435–1510.
Beck, T., A. Demirgüç-Kunt, and R. Levine. 2005. "Law and Firm's Access to Finance." *American Law and Economics Review* 7: 211–252.
Belleflamme, P., T. Lambert, and A. Schwienbacher. 2010. "Crowdfunding: An Industrial Organization." Working Paper, Louvain School of Management, Universite catholique de Louvain.
Belleflamme, P., T. Lambert, and A. Schwienbacher. 2013. "Individual Crowdfunding Practices." *Venture Capital: An International Journal of Entrepreneurial Finance* (this issue).
Bradford, S. C. 2012. "Crowdfunding and the Federal Securities Laws." *Columbia Business Law Review* 1: 3–148.

Burtch, G., A. Ghose, and S. Wattal. 2012. "An Empirical Examination of the Antecedents and Consequences of Investment Patterns in Crowd-Funded Markets." *Information Systems Research*, forthcoming.

Cary, W. 1974. "Federalism and Corporate Law: Reflections upon Delaware." *Yale Law Journal* 83: 663–705.

Crowdfunding Industry Report. 2012. *Crowdfunding Industry Report: Market Trends, Composition and Crowdfunding Platforms*. New York: Crowdsourcing.org.

Cumming, D. J., and S. Johan. 2008. "Global Market Surveillance." *American Law and Economics Review* 10: 454–506.

Cumming, D. J., and J. MacIntosh. 2000. "The Role of Interjurisdictional Competition in Shaping Canadian Corporate Law." *International Review of Law and Economics* 20 (2): 141–186.

Cumming, D. J., and J. MacIntosh. 2002. "The Rationales Underlying Reincorporation and Implications for Canadian Corporations." *International Review of Law and Economics* 22 (3): 277–330.

Daines, R. 2002. "The Incorporation Choices of IPO Firms." *New York University Law Review* 77: 1559–1611.

Daines, R. M. 2001. "Does Delaware Law Improve Firm Value?" *Journal of Financial Economics* 62: 525–558.

Daines, R. M., and M. Klausner. 2001. "Do IPO Charters Maximize Firm Value? Antitakeover Protection in IPOs." *Journal of Law, Economics, and Organization* 17: 83–120.

Griffin, Z. J. 2012. "Crowdfunding: Fleecing the American Masses." *Case Western Reserve Journal of Law, Technology & the Internet*, forthcoming.

Heminway, J. M., and S. R. Hoffman. 2011. "Proceed at Your Peril: Crowdfunding and the Securities Act of 1933." *Tennessee Law Review* 78: 879.

Leland, H. E., and D. H. Pyle. (1977). Informational Asymmetries, Financial Structure, and Financial Intermediation. *Journal of Finance* 32: 371–387.

Mollick, E. R. 2012. "The Dynamics of Crowdfunding: Determinants of Success and Failure." Available at SSRN: http://ssrn.com/abstract=2088298

Myers, S., and N. Majluf. 1984. "Corporate Financing and Investment Decisions When Firms Have Information That Investors Do Not Have." *Journal of Financial Economics* 13: 187–221.

Nahata, R. 2008. "Venture Capital Reputation and Investment Performance." *Journal of Financial Economics* 90: 127–151.

Nahata, R., S. Hazarika, and K. Tandon. 2012. "Success in Global Venture Capital Investing: Do Institutional and Cultural Differences Matter?" *Journal of Financial and Quantitative Analysis*.

Ritter, J. R. 1987. "The Costs of Going Public." *Journal of Financial Economics* 19: 269–281.

Roe, Mark J. 2003. "Delaware's Competition." *Harvard Law Review* 117: 588–646.

Romano, R. 1985. "Law as a Product: Some Pieces of the Incorporation Puzzle." *Journal of Law, Economics, and Organization* 1: 225–283.

Romano, R. 1987. "The State Competition Debate in Corporate Law." *Cardozo Law Review* 8: 709–757.

Romano, R. 1993. *The Genius of American Corporate Law*. Washington, DC: The AEI Press.

Schwienbacher, A. 2008. "Innovation and Venture Capital Exits." *Economic Journal* 118 (533): 1888–1916.

Schwienbacher, A., and B. Larralde. 2013. "Crowdfunding of Small Entrepreneurial Ventures." In *Oxford Handbook of Entrepreneurial Finance*, edited by D. J. Cumming, 369–391, ch. 12. New York: Oxford University Press.

# Index

Note: Page numbers in *italics* represent tables
Page numbers in **bold** represent figures
Page numbers followed by 'n' refer to notes